Whispers of Wisdom for
Mothers of Preschoolers

365 Daily

Whispers of Wisdom for
Mothers of Preschoolers

A YEAR OF INSPIRATIONAL READINGS

BARBOUR
PUBLISHING

Scripture quotations marked KJV are taken from the King James Version of the Bible.

Scripture quotations marked NIV are taken from the HOLY BIBLE, NEW INTERNATIONAL VERSION®. NIV®. Copyright © 1973, 1978, 1984 by International Bible Society. Used by permission of Zondervan. All rights reserved.

Scripture quotations marked NLT are taken from the *Holy Bible*, New Living Translation, copyright © 1996. Used by permission of Tyndale House Publishers, Inc. Wheaton, Illinois 60189, U.S.A. All rights reserved.

Scripture quotations marked NASB are taken from the New American Standard Bible, © 1960, 1962, 1963, 1968, 1971, 1972, 1973, 1975, 1977, 1995 by The Lockman Foundation. Used by permission.

Scripture quotations marked MSG are from **THE MESSAGE**. Copyright © by Eugene H. Peterson 1993, 1994, 1995, 1996, 2000, 2001, 2002. Used by permission of NavPress Publishing Group.

Scripture quotations marked CEV are from the Contemporary English Version, Copyright © 1991, 1992, 1995 by American Bible Society. Used by permission.

Scripture quotations marked NKJV are taken from the New King James Version®. Copyright © 1982 by Thomas Nelson, Inc. Used by permission. All rights reserved.

Scripture quotations marked ASV are taken from the American Standard Version of the Bible.

Scripture quotations marked AMP are taken from the Amplified® Bible, © 1954, 1958, 1962, 1964, 1965, 1987 by The Lockman Foundation. Used by permission.

Scripture quotations marked NCV are taken from the New Century Version of the Bible, copyright © 1987, 1988, 1991, Word Publishing. Used by permission.

Scripture quotations marked ESV are taken from The Holy Bible, English Standard Version, copyright © 2001 by Crossway Bibles, a division of Good News Publishers. Used by permission. All rights reserved.

Scripture quotations marked NLV are taken from the Holy Bible, New Life Version, Copyright 1969, 1976, 1978, 1983, 1986, Christian Literature International, P.O. Box 777, Canby, OR 97013. Used by permission.

Published by Barbour Publishing, Inc., P.O. Box 719, Uhrichsville, Ohio 44683, www.barbourbooks.com

Our mission is to publish and distribute inspirational products offering exceptional value and biblical encouragement to the masses.

Member of the
Evangelical Christian
Publishers Association

Printed in the United States of America.

Introduction

Nobody has to tell a mother of a preschooler that her job is a tough one. You're already well aware of that.

What you might need to hear, though, are some regular reminders of God's love for you. . .of the vital importance of the job you're doing. . .of the incredible blessings of motherhood in spite of the daily struggles. That's what *365 Daily Whispers of Wisdom for Mothers of Preschoolers* is all about—providing encouragement to help you face your challenges with confidence, hope, even joy.

These 365 devotional readings will turn your thoughts to the unchanging wisdom of the Bible and its heavenly author, who longs to play a major role in your life story—the one He's written especially for you! You'll find insights into the emotions you face, invaluable advice on relationships, inspiration for enhancing spiritual growth, and practical ideas for raising your little ones. You'll be refreshed by the triumphs of other moms and gently challenged at times to make beneficial changes to your own attitudes and actions.

Motherhood is a huge responsibility, and dealing with preschoolers presents its own unique challenges. But with your heavenly Father by your side, you have access to all the wisdom, resources, and strength you need to accomplish everything He's called you to do—to be the best mom you can be. We hope *Daily Whispers of Wisdom* is an encouragement along the way!

The Publishers

Crowned with Goodness

You crown the year with Your goodness,
and Your paths drip with abundance.
Psalm 65:11 NKJV

𝒯he child clung to her mother's hand as they walked up to the door of the day care center. This was a new experience and a new place. The mother understood her child's anxiety, but the unfamiliar had to be faced. Although her daughter was frightened, the mother encouraged her to continue on into the play area.

By the time the mother returned, her daughter was laughing and playing with the other children. She'd made new friends, and she'd had snack time, nap time, and so many fresh adventures to share that she chattered all the way home.

Often we face the New Year with trepidation. The coming months can be full of the unexpected. We don't know what will happen, or if we will be prepared. We want to hope for the best, yet nagging doubts can plague us with what-ifs.

When we are walking the path through the New Year that God has for us, He promises to bring goodness. Will we have hard times? Most likely. Will we suffer disappointment or loss? That, too, could happen. In spite of all the unknowns, we can rejoice knowing our paths will drip with the Lord's abundance. The New Year will be crowned with God's goodness.

Oh, Lord, thank You for Your promises in the coming year.
Help me focus on Your goodness and abundance,
so I'm not concerned with the unknown.
Amen.

Thousands of Millions

And they blessed Rebekah, and said unto her,
Thou art our sister, be thou the mother of thousands of millions,
and let thy seed possess the gate of those which hate them.
Genesis 24:60 KJV

How would you have responded if, prior to your wedding, your family members said to you, "We hope you are blessed with thousands of millions of children"? You likely would have laughed and told them to keep their comments to themselves, and they would have thought it a joke as well. Rebekah's family was sincere, though. In her day, children were considered a blessing from God. The more children a woman had, the more blessed she was. Of course, Rebekah's family didn't expect her to give birth to that many children. They were simply asking God to bless her new family.

Children are God's blessing to you. Whether you have one child or many, you have a unique opportunity to influence the world. As a Christian mother, you can instill your faith in your children while they are still preschoolers. As they grow, they will have the chance to witness to those you might never meet, and the process will continue.

Rebekah only bore two children—nowhere close to "thousands of millions." But one of her sons was Jacob—the father of Christ's bloodline. Rebekah was blessed indeed, and so are you. That's something to keep in mind as you go through your day.

Dear Lord, You have blessed me with beautiful children
and a special opportunity to influence many people.
Help me take this responsibility to heart.

Daily Miracles

Have not I commanded thee? Be strong and of a good courage;
be not afraid, neither be thou dismayed: for the LORD thy God
is with thee whithersoever thou goest.
Joshua 1:9 KJV

God called Joshua, the Israelites' leader, to guide thousands of people into the promised land. Joshua had seen God work for forty years, but he still may have struggled before he and his people crossed the Jordan River. Would the Canaanites attack at the height of the confusion? Even if the Israelites and their livestock made it across, did Joshua really want to face walled cities and giants? They would need daily miracles just to survive! Even though Joshua remembered the Red Sea crossing, he might have ducked under the covers each morning when the alarm went off.

All mothers experience days they would rather not face. Perhaps your morning begins with one little voice bawling for a bottle at 5:00 a.m., waking another who wants her Cheerios *now*. Rivers of toys on the floor, mountains of laundry, plus the responsibility for precious little souls that will live forever—no way can a mother do this without daily miracles.

Fortunately, God did not expect Joshua to accomplish the impossible alone. Nor does He demand this of you. God promises He will supply the daily miracles you need. Even at 5:00 a.m.!

Lord Jesus, I do not know how I will make it through this day.
But I do know who created it. Please help me look to You
for the resources to do Your will.
Amen.

A Mom's Uniform

Therefore we do not lose heart. Though outwardly we are wasting away,
yet inwardly we are being renewed day by day. For our light and momentary
troubles are achieving for us an eternal glory that far outweighs them all.
2 Corinthians 4:16–17 NIV

*W*hen a mother looks into her closet, she may notice that the contents have miraculously rotated. The jeans, sweats, and comfy shirts are now easily reachable in the front, while the untouched business clothes and once-coveted white pants have somehow been relegated to the memorabilia section in back. The dusty trophy of days gone by—those white pants—will most likely not see the light of day for many years, as peanut butter, crayon, and grape juice are now part of the daily repertoire.

Does she retain the same value in the eyes of the world while wearing the "uniform" of a mom? Perhaps not. But what is her worth in the sight of the Lord? Moms need not measure their self-worth on the scale that the world imposes: wealth, wardrobe, and worldly goods. Rather, the true scale used to determine success is measured with eternal glory. While outward appearances may seem to diminish when business attire is traded for play clothes, inward appearances become increasingly glorious as daily sacrifices are made in answer to the call to motherhood.

Lord, thank You for the privilege of being a mom. Help me to remember that
You value this role as one of Your highest callings and greatest challenges.
And help me to see myself as You see me.
Amen.

Whiter Than Snow. . . and Grass Stains

Purify me from my sins, and I will be clean; wash me,
and I will be whiter than snow.
Psalm 51:7 NLT

𝓗ow often have you been sorting dirty laundry only to find that nice white shirt with Kool-Aid streaks, or a pair of pants with grass stains on the knees? They are signs that your child has had some sort of enjoyment, but the stains create hard work for the laundress. After the scrubbing and soaking, most stains can be removed, albeit with much time and effort. But there are those few stains that will never be removed. *If only,* you think, *I could have tried to remove this stain immediately so that it wouldn't have ruined the fabric!*

Just as those stains are more difficult to remove the longer they set, our sins are more difficult to repent of the longer we hold on to them. God has given us the free gift of forgiveness, yet we at times choose to continue in our sinful ways. But God has promised that when we repent, He will remove those sin stains "as far. . .as the east is from the west" (Psalm 103:12 NLT).

God is ready and waiting to remove our sin stains, with perfect, permanent results.

Lord, help me to demonstrate the same urgency in removing the stains
of sin from my life as I do when attempting to remove stains from
my child's clothes. Thank You for Your forgiveness.
Amen.

A Good Day

*And Sarah said, "God has made me laugh,
and all who hear will laugh with me."*
Genesis 21:6 NKJV

$\mathcal{I}$t was a quiet afternoon. Cathy smiled as her active preschooler continued napping. Having an autistic child wasn't something Cathy had planned on. Nor had she planned to have a baby at the age of fifty, but she knew God had planned it that way. Raising a child at her age was difficult; raising one with a handicap was even more difficult. There were times when Cathy wanted to throw her hands up and scream, but not today. Today was a good day. She and her daughter had laughed and played together.

While her little one napped, Cathy took in the colorful artwork—pictures of houses, animals, cars, and people—that decorated her daughter's bedroom floor. She picked up a drawing that resembled a mother and child. Their mouths were open and looked distorted. Cathy wondered what her preschooler had been thinking when she had drawn the picture.

"Do you like it, Mommy?" The sleepy voice came from behind her.

Cathy nodded. Then, feeling little arms circle her waist, she smiled.

"Me, too, Mommy. I like it when we laugh together."

*Lord, help me to see the happy times through the eyes of my child.
I want to experience the joys of motherhood. Thank You for the times when
we can simply love one another and enjoy time together.
Amen.*

Yes, Lord, I'm Listening

Then Eli discerned that the LORD was calling the boy.
And Eli said to Samuel, "Go lie down, and it shall be if He calls you,
that you shall say, 'Speak, LORD, for Your servant is listening.'"
So Samuel went and lay down in his place. Then the LORD came
and stood and called as at other times, "Samuel! Samuel!"
And Samuel said, "Speak, for Your servant is listening."
1 Samuel 3:8–10 NASB

$\mathcal{S}$amuel was just a boy when he woke up and heard someone call his name. Three times he woke Eli up, assuming it had been Eli who called him, and was promptly sent back to bed! After the third time, Eli realized that it was God who was calling Samuel's name. Wisely, he redirected Samuel to listen to God.

As we teach our children to pray, are we teaching them to listen? To recognize God's voice—the small stirrings in our heart that guide us to God's greater path?

God had a plan for Samuel's life. He promises the same for our children, calling each one by name. As we encourage our children to listen for God's quiet voice, we make it easier for them to hear His call over the shouts of the world.

May we all strive to be like Eli, who encouraged Samuel to say yes to God's calling.

Lord, please call my children to You by name
as You called Samuel. And keep calling—as You did with Samuel—
until each of my children has said, "Yes, Lord. I'm listening."

Blessing versus Cursing

From the same mouth come both blessing and cursing.
James 3:10 NASB

*H*ow many times do I have to tell you?"
"Children are to be seen and not heard."
"Oh, Johnny is a good boy. . .when he is sleeping."
"Sit down!"
"Don't chew with your mouth open."
"Sit like a lady."
These sayings will pierce the hearts of young children when they continually hear belittling comments or corrections stemming from anger and frustration. We have heard it takes ten positive comments to refute one negative comment.

God gives us one mouth that we can use to speak blessings or curses over our children. None of us would admit that we intentionally speak curses over our children, but every time we belittle, demean, or speak words of correction out of anger and not love, we are cursing them.

Instead, we can look to what the Lord says to us and about us. For example, we are His children, loved and chosen for the purpose of glorifying Him in all we say and do. We are coheirs with Christ, saved, and blessed. We can correct our children with patience, love, kindness, and God's truth. We can remind our children—and ourselves—of these truths with words of blessing versus cursing.

Lord, please guard my mouth to speak words of blessing
to my children. Help me to hear Your words of blessing
and then speak those blessings to my children.

Looking for Results

*Better is the end of a thing than the beginning thereof:
and the patient in spirit is better than the proud in spirit.*
Ecclesiastes 7:8 KJV

*K*acy carefully guided Cole's pencil over the letters on the paper. As they finished the *e* in his name, Cole grabbed the pencil and began drawing pictures of his favorite animals. Kacy took a deep breath and tried to regain her son's attention, but she was becoming frustrated. Cole had been so excited about learning to write his name. Now, after only about ten minutes, he was completely distracted.

"Come on, Cole," she coaxed. "Let's try again."

Cole turned big, serious brown eyes toward his mother. "You know, Mommy, this is kinda boring."

"But it's important, Cole." Kacy tried to reason with him. She was feeling pressured to teach him because his younger cousin was already writing her name. Cole, however, did not feel the same pressure and only wanted to play outside.

Suddenly, Kacy had an idea. She went to the closet for the box of sidewalk chalk. As she and Cole colored together on the sidewalk, she creatively drew the child's attention back to his writing lesson. Within a short time, Cole's name was childishly scrawled all over the cement.

Lord, at times the process of teaching my children becomes frustrating. Please give me the patience and ingenuity that will reap positive results.

Look Toward the Future

Where there is no vision, the people perish:
but he that keepeth the law, happy is he.
Proverbs 29:18 KJV

*M*ommy, when I grow up, will I be able to drive like Sandy?"

"When I get bigger, who am I going to marry?"

"When I get married, where will I live?"

The five-year-old's questions were never-ending, and almost all of them were about the future.

As the last of nine children, born when her oldest brother was seventeen, she had always been with big kids. From the moment she could talk, her focus, her vision, and her questions were about growing up.

And that is as it should be.

To help give our eager-to-grow-up children a vision for a godly, God-honoring future, the Lord has given us a wonderful tool. It's called the Bible, a life-guide containing lessons about marriage, family, sacrifice, faith, leadership, loss, love, and much more. By sharing stories from this never-ending fount of wisdom and exhibiting a biblical pattern for family life, moms can better prepare their children for the world that awaits them and the responsibilities they may one day take on.

While we don't want our little ones preoccupied with specifics about the future, we can set a firm foundation of faith that will support them today and guide them into tomorrow.

God gives His children a hope for the future.

Let us give our children the same.

Father, help me set a firm foundation in Christ for my children as
they grow up. Let them see me as one of God's faith-filled children,
brimming with hope for my future and theirs. Amen.

Meant to Be Broken?

*If thou shalt hearken diligently unto the voice of the LORD thy God,
to observe and to do all his commandments. . .all these blessings shall
come on thee, and overtake thee.*
Deuteronomy 28:1–2 KJV

We've all heard the phrase "Rules were made to be broken." Our
young children prove this concept all the time. However, their
breaking the rules is sometimes innocent curiosity rather than
intentional disregard for our instruction.

The rules we set in place—like not walking across the street
without an adult, not touching the hot stove, and not eating candy
before dinner—are not meant to make our children miserable.
Instead, they're meant to do the exact opposite: keep our children
safe and happy.

Not surprisingly, God has similar rules and expectations for us
as adults. Although we may not understand why the rules are in place,
we know that God, as a loving Father, means them for our good, to
keep us safe and happy.

As you walk with the Lord today, remember that God is watching
you and leading you in the way you should go. And if, by chance,
you should slip and fall into disobedience—whether intentional or
unintentional—He is waiting to forgive you and help you start over
again, ready to fill your life with blessings as you walk in His will,
His way.

*Lord, thank You for holding me and keeping me safe,
and for blessing my life as I strive to follow You.*

Queen of the Jews

"If you remain completely silent at this time, relief and deliverance will arise for the Jews from another place, but you and your father's house will perish. Yet who knows whether you have come to the kingdom for such a time as this?"
Esther 4:14 NKJV

Esther lived every young girl's dream. After a worldwide beauty contest, the Persian king selected her as his new queen! Esther moved to a palace, wore beautiful clothes, and never washed a dish again.

Her uncle Mordecai's urgent plea upset her fairy-tale existence. Haman, her husband's chief advisor, hated Mordecai and his people and persuaded King Xerxes to allow the Jews' destruction. Mordecai asked Esther to intervene—a dangerous request, as no one approached the king except at his command. If Xerxes awoke in a bad mood, even his queen might be dragged off and executed. Still, in Mordecai's mind, God brought Esther to power for this very purpose. Inspired by her uncle, Esther convinced Xerxes to spare her people and destroy Haman.

You may applaud Esther, but wonder, *What's this got to do with me? I have two toddlers, and I do my own dishes because I haven't won many international beauty contests lately.*

God values your spot in history, just as He charted Esther's course. Who knows what surprising roles your little ones will play in His great plan.

Sovereign Lord, I think too small, with no concept of Your creativity. Give me a glimpse of Your dreams for me and my children. Amen.

In His Steps

For even hereunto were ye called: because Christ also suffered for us,
leaving us an example, that ye should follow his steps.
1 Peter 2:21 KJV

*C*hrist is our example in so many areas, yet for some reason we often feel the need to do things our own way. It's foolishness, really. We know that He understands all that we go through, but we try to make decisions without first turning to Him for direction. We want our children to develop Christlikeness in their lives, but they are watching *us*. They will quickly develop "mom-likeness." So if our desire is that they become more like Jesus, why aren't we willing to be like Him ourselves?

Yes, mothers need to have thick skins to face certain situations, but too often that develops into pride and the do-it-myself mentality. Instead, it should be an I-can-do-it-through-Christ mentality. What a joy to follow in the footsteps that our Savior has left us. What a blessing to realize our children are choosing to walk in those same steps.

You are naturally going to be one of your child's first role models. What kind will you be? There are many options from which to choose, but it is best to be one who looks to Jesus as her own role model.

Thank You, Jesus, for leaving Your footsteps for me to follow.
Help me to never take them for granted.

Whose Life Is It?

*"For even the Son of Man did not come to be served, but to serve,
and to give His life a ransom for many."*
Mark 10:45 NASB

*C*assandra was achievement oriented, goal focused, and strived for
perfection. She continually worked around the clock, rarely taking
time for what was most important in life. Her preschooler would
often ask, "Mommy, are you still working? Can you take a break and
play with me?"

Jesus referred to Himself as the Good Shepherd and to us
as His sheep (John 10:1–18). During Jesus' time on earth, He
was determined to do the Father's will (Mark 14:36), even laying
down His very own life for His sheep (John 10:15). Jesus tells us,
"Whoever desires to save his life will lose it, but whoever loses his
life for My sake will find it" (Matthew 16:25 NKJV).

Just as Christ came to serve, we are called to lay down our life
for the very purpose God intended, a life of service in raising our
preschoolers for His glory. That may require us to give up many of
the activities that bring us joy. Our focus, however, must be on what
is important: serving those God calls us to serve for this season of
motherhood. Career, goals, perfection. . .those things that are not
aligned with God's life must be surrendered at the cross. The benefit?
The abundant life (John 10:10) God has in store for us.

*Good Shepherd, I desire to follow Your Way and lay down
my life for the abundant life of service in motherhood.*

The Great Physician
Is Coming!

After Jesus crossed over by boat, a large crowd met him at the seaside. One of the meeting-place leaders named Jairus came. When he saw Jesus, he fell to his knees, beside himself as he begged, "My dear daughter is at death's door. Come and lay hands on her so she will get well and live." Jesus went with him.
Mark 5:21–24 MSG

*J*airus loved his daughter. She was very sick, close to death, and there was nothing more he could do for her. He had heard about Jesus, maybe even seen His miracles. He knew he wasn't going to return home without Jesus. He was *that* certain of Jesus' power.

Imagine the relief that soared through him when Jesus agreed to come. All would be well! The Great Physician was coming to his home. Jairus had no idea that he was about to witness a miracle to shake the planet: His recently deceased daughter would live again!

When our children are sick, do we seek God in prayer for their healing? Or do we run to the medicine cabinet to find aspirin and throat spray? God wants us to bring everything to Him in prayer. That doesn't mean to exclude modern medicine, but it means to include God in the healing process, too. God cares! Even about stuffy noses and ear infections and broken bones. Jesus cares! Many of His miracles were healing people. And they still are.

Lord Jesus, give me faith like Jairus, who sought You for his daughter's healing. Heal my child, in Your powerful name.

It's Hard Not to Worry, Lord

So do not worry or be anxious about tomorrow, for tomorrow will have worries and anxieties of its own. Sufficient for each day is its own trouble.
Matthew 6:34 AMP

Kay sat beside her little girl's hospital bed. Three-year-old Lacey struggled to breathe. Kay's heart ached with each labored breath. Fear of the coming morning and what the doctors might say gripped her emotions. It wasn't fair! Lacey didn't deserve to be this sick. Horrible thoughts of what could be wrong with her baby plagued Kay's tired mind. She didn't know what she'd do if Lacey weren't in her life.

"How are you two doing?" the nurse asked as she checked the oxygen level on a machine hooked to Lacey's little body.

Kay chewed the inside of her cheek. She didn't bother answering but asked a question instead. "Is she going to be okay?"

"She's doing well. I know it's hard, but why don't you try to get some rest?"

"I can't. What if she stops breathing?" Kay heard the panic in her voice but didn't care if the nurse noticed or not.

"You know. . ." The older nurse paused. "Worrying doesn't help."

"How does a person turn off caring about their child?" Kay snapped back.

"You could try praying."

The reminder hit Kay like an ice-cold bucket of water. Why hadn't she thought of that? Wasn't praying as much a part of her as Lacey? Kay knelt beside the bed and, amid tears of regret that she'd carried the burden alone, she turned her worries over to the Lord. The first ray of hope illuminated her soul, and her heart soared upward.

Heavenly Father, sometimes when I am in trouble and fear has me in its grip, I forget to come to You first. Please, help me to deal with worry the way You would prefer. Amen.

Blowing Off the Blues

A merry heart maketh a cheerful countenance:
but by sorrow of the heart the spirit is broken.
Proverbs 15:13 KJV

*M*others of young children often experience "the blues," not only during the months after childbirth, but periodically throughout the "terrible twos," "trying threes," and "frustrating fours"! Preschoolers possess uncanny instincts for ways to stress their mothers. When little Jeremiah flushes his shoes down the toilet and Kiara decorates living room walls with lipstick just before company arrives, Mom feels like throwing in the towel.

The best antidote for the blues? A break—even a short one. A quick snooze while the kids nap. Or Mom can ask her husband or neighbor to stay with the children while she takes a refreshing walk around the block. If Mom can't get away, a quick let-off-steam phone call to an understanding friend can make all the difference.

A mom can also jump-start her joy. Cartoons or funny Internet forwards often turn her frown right-side up. Watching a silly video with her children or drawing fun pictures together might help heal a morning of aggravation. Best of all, Mom can ask God to help her see the comic side of life. The Lord of Laughter wants to cultivate a sense of humor in her heart that will lift her head, brighten her face, and strengthen her spirit!

Loving Father, how can You parent millions of people 24-7? You must possess
an amazing sense of humor. Please share a few of Your smiles with me today.
Amen.

Want Rest? Invest!

*Correct thy son, and he shall give thee rest;
yea, he shall give delight unto thy soul.*
Proverbs 29:17 KJV

The house was tidy, orderly, and quiet.

Outside, as the breezes blew, the mother of the house relaxed on a lounge chair, visiting with a friend. Inside, her six children were napping or occupied with quiet activities.

"I need this time to rest," the mother explained, "so I can recharge my battery."

And her children let her rest. There were no interruptions, no demands on her time.

How had this happened?

This mother had learned the secret of child rearing. She had lovingly trained her children consistently from their arrival. Her babies' meals, naps, and playtimes were carefully scheduled. And although many of us believe that if we want something done right, we'd better do it ourselves, she gave her older children responsibilities in the form of chores, always on hand to look over their work and give them advice, correction, and encouragement when needed.

Taking the time to consistently train, correct, and encourage our children isn't always easy in the given moment, but such an investment of our time will return peace and joy to the house.

In such peace, a mother can truly rest.

Father, being a mother day in and day out is hard work. Yet I know my children are a good investment of my time and love. Thank You for giving me opportunities to rest in the fruit of this labor. Amen.

Weariness

*Let us not become weary in doing good, for at the
proper time we will reap a harvest if we do not give up.*
Galatians 6:9 NIV

*T*ired. Exhausted. Ready to drop. Mothers of preschoolers know
firsthand the meaning of the word *weary*. Whether we work outside
the home or not, being a preschool mom is physically draining!
Preschoolers are like butterflies, flitting from one location to another.
Simple daily activities such as mealtime, bathing, and bedtime can
turn into major ordeals. Preschoolers can transition from exuberant
laughter to meltdowns in the blink of an eye. It's no wonder some
days we feel like throwing in the towel!

Before we decide to give up, let's consider the spiritual
perspective. God has given us the privilege of planting eternal seeds
of truth in our children's hearts. These truths are communicated
through our actions and by our words. Our children are carefully
listening. They are intently watching. Although at the moment we
are in the labor-intensive stage of planting, one day we will reap a
harvest. Our efforts will make a difference, so do not give up or
quit. On those weary days, cry out to the Lord for help. He will
impart grace and strength. He will equip you for motherhood. What
rejoicing there will be on the day of the harvest!

*Dear Lord, You know how weary motherhood can be.
Give me strength and patience. Help me remember that someday
my efforts will result in a bountiful harvest. Amen.*

First Love

Nevertheless I have this against you, that you have left your first love.
Revelation 2:4 NKJV

*W*hen our children receive a special toy, we get great pleasure by watching the delight on their faces. Everywhere they go, they carry the toy with them. They show it to everyone and tell them all how wonderful it is. The child cries when the present is left somewhere, and is anxious to get it back. They don't want to be parted from their favorite plaything.

Before long, however, the excitement wanes. Interests change. Children find another fascinating item that claims their attention. Soon, the revered toy is left to gather dust in the closet.

When we first became a Christian, our excitement over the gift God had bestowed on us overrode anything else. We had to talk about Jesus. We couldn't wait to tell others about being set free from our sins. Our family and friends could tell something was different about us because we kept Jesus so close, basking in His presence. However, if we weren't careful, everyday cares began to steal our excitement.

We must be careful to keep Jesus as our treasured possession. When life gets hectic or some new interest tugs at our hearts, we have to cling to Jesus, not allowing worldly desires to lead us astray. We should never allow the delight in the gift of salvation to fade from our hearts.

Thank You, Jesus, for Your gift to me.
Help me to always put You first. Amen.

An Eagle's Wings

I remember You upon my bed and meditate on You in the night watches.
For You have been my help, and in the shadow of Your wings will I rejoice.
Psalm 63:6–7 AMP

The eagle is the king of birds. Known for its strength and power, it is stern and wise as it overlooks the goings-on below. Eagles don't start out that way, though. They start out as helpless babies that need to be protected in the shadow of a parent's wing. Baby eagles are just like all babes: They have not a care in the world because they trust in their parents' provision. They trust in it because it's always been there for them the instant that they needed it.

We are like that with our children. We stand over them while they play, making sure that nothing harmful gets near them. We feed them before they feel true hunger; we clothe them before they get cold. We meet their needs long before they even know they have them.

So it is with our heavenly Father. He stands watch over us like a parent eagle, guarding us, lest anything harmful befall us. He spreads His wings, in comfort and security, as we nestle beneath them, unaware of the dangers from which we have been saved.

Thank You, Father, for protecting me and keeping me from harm.
Thank You for meeting all of my needs. Please continue to comfort me
and protect me beneath the shelter of Your mighty wings. Amen.

A Tough Call

Blessed be your discretion and advice, and blessed be you.
1 Samuel 25:33 AMP

The Super Bowl might be an exciting sporting event, but its referee calls throughout the game are nothing compared to a mother's. Some football referees stand on the playing field with the possibility of getting hammered by a three-hundred-pound lineman. However, all of these men, players and referees, would feel way out of their league if ever made to moderate young children's quarrels.

A mother's judgment is nothing short of a miracle. Her abilities to see perspectives and angles, and to hand down appropriate rulings and even punishments, often go unnoticed. An Old Testament account of such a woman was Abigail.

When Abigail went to speak with David, she did so with wisdom and discernment. Instead of allowing David and his army to destroy their people, Abigail made a point to literally meet David halfway. She realized how her husband Nabal's stubborn actions were childish. Nabal took her for granted, but it was his foolish and selfish actions that ultimately led to his demise.

Abigail may not have been a mother yet, but her quick thinking and positive leadership qualities spared not only her life but those of her people.

Lord, please give me good discernment as a mother.

Bring Forth Fruit

But that on the good ground are they, which in an honest and good heart, having heard the word, keep it, and bring forth fruit with patience.
Luke 8:15 KJV

*B*randy's eyes filled with tears, and she swallowed around the lump in her throat. Her five-year-old son, Jayden, had just trusted Christ as Savior, and Brandy was filled with joy. As much as she wanted to have faith, she still struggled at times with a nagging fear that Jayden would reject the Lord. It filled her heart to overflowing to realize that God had answered her prayers.

Some people would say that Jayden was too young to make such a decision, but Brandy knew that wasn't true. Not only had she prayed for the child, she'd taught him the gospel from the time he was born. She'd faithfully taken him to church where he was regularly exposed to God's Word.

Brandy also remembered that Christ had used the example of a child coming to Him. He'd said, "Except ye be converted, and become as little children, ye shall not enter into the kingdom of heaven" (Matthew 18:3 KJV). Jayden had that precious faith of a child. Brandy rejoiced that the seeds planted and cultivated from his birth had been increased.

What joy comes with the salvation of a little one, dear God! Help me faithfully share Your gift with my own children.

The Great Physician

Praise the LORD, O my soul, and forget not all his benefits—
who forgives all your sins and heals all your diseases.
Psalm 103:2–3 NIV

*O*ne of the realities of childhood is that kids will experience health ailments. Common colds, stomach viruses, and countless other illnesses—not to mention injuries—can strike at any time.

As a mom, it is difficult to stand vigil at the bedside of a suffering child. It takes a toll physically, as you console around the clock. It can also be mentally draining, as at 3:00 a.m. you try to recall the last time you administered the fever-reducing medicine.

Many moms offer a silent prayer in these moments of distress, but the next time you're faced with a medical crisis, pray *with* your child. Suggest that he prays, too, asking the Great Physician to restore him to health. And those midnight prayers by her side—go ahead and say them aloud. By your example, she will learn to call on God and trust Him for healing in her body.

Sickness is a reality of life, but we know the One who has created our bodies and has the power to heal them. Remember to call out to Him first, and encourage your children to petition Him who has the power to heal "all your diseases."

Heavenly Father, I pray for my sick child. Please restore him to full health,
and give me the strength I need as I care for him. Amen.

Safe in Christ

For in the day of trouble he will keep me safe in his dwelling;
he will hide me in the shelter of his tabernacle and set me high upon a rock.
Psalm 27:5 NIV

Crack! Boom! "Mommy, I'm scared!" the little girl cried as the
thunder clapped outside her bedroom window. Her mother calmly
replied, "Honey, the thunder and lightning are out there. We are
safe in here." Knowing that an explanation of the physics of static
electricity would not alleviate her daughter's fears, the mother simply
provided a safe haven from the storm.

The storms of life have a way of frightening us also. Perhaps
an upcoming surgery or financial difficulties are looming overhead.
Maybe marital stress or child-rearing issues have cast a dark cloud
over our homes. We may not understand what is happening. It's dark.
It's chaotic. It's ominous. In His wisdom, the Lord tells us all we
need to know: We are safe because He is with us.

Seek shelter from the storm. Run to the Lord's dwelling. He
will keep you safe and grant you peace. He will calm your heart,
reassuring you of His protection. Like thunder and lightning, the
storms we face in life are temporary. The Lord remains. Therefore, we
are eternally safe in His dwelling. Come in out of the storm.

Dear Lord, help me seek shelter from life's storms by coming to You.
Thank You for keeping me safe and secure. Amen.

Café Mom

Then Peter and the other apostles answered and said,
We ought to obey God rather than men.
Acts 5:29 KJV

*C*ome on in! There is coffee brewing, and a delectably sweet bit of something gooey is coming out of the oven. At Café Mom, you'll find rest, peace, comfort, and the answers you need to solve all of life's problems."

Moms often feel like the image of "Café Mom" is what a "good mom" is expected to project. They look around their homes strewn with toys, at the piles of laundry yet to be folded, and the dishes yet to be washed. They fervently hope that no one pops in for a quick visit. They want to hang the CLOSED sign on the door to Café Mom because they just can't serve up those tall orders for yet another day.

But the expectations of other people are not how God determines value. He rates time with our kids, moments of prayer, and times of reading the scripture as far more valuable than finished laundry and a pristine kitchen sink.

Café Mom is a wonderful ideal, and surely it's even a reality sometimes. But Jesus wants us to place His values above the expectations of others. Honor attained from pleasing people is fleeting and empty. His way is much easier, for it is the way to a peaceful heart and a life rich in the blessings of Christ.

Jesus, help me to set aside the expectations that people have of me
and that I have of myself. Help me to only desire Your approval
and to make Your will the only focus in my life. Amen.

*I will look unto the LORD; I will wait for
the God of my salvation: my God will hear me.*
Micah 7:7 KJV

*M*icah, the Old Testament prophet, tried to persuade God's people
to leave their sinful lifestyles and seek Him. Micah's descriptions of
everyday life sound like our television crime shows. Violence ruled
as family members set traps for each other. Judges perverted justice
for their own profit. Micah portrayed a soap-operatic atmosphere in
which neighbors, relatives, and even spouses could not be trusted.

Nobody listened to Micah. He must have experienced down days
when he wanted to give up.

But Micah placed his hope in God. He mourned the
consequences Judah and Israel would reap from their evil actions, but
he knew God loved them and would eventually heal them. Micah also
felt confident that God had sealed his personal salvation and listened
to his prayers.

Micah's world does not only reflect TV fantasies. It looks far too
familiar to many of us who experience family breakdowns or witness
yet another violent neighborhood incident. And when our country,
like his, closes its eyes to God and His laws, we despair for our little
ones' future. But Micah reminds us of God's sovereignty and His
open ear to our prayers. Like Micah, we can bank on God's love and
salvation, even in the midst of an ungodly culture.

*Lord Jesus, instead of raging against others or freezing in fear of the future,
help me to confidently look to You for those I love. Amen.*

Walking with Christ

As you therefore have received Christ Jesus the Lord, so walk in Him.
Colossians 2:6 NKJV

*F*rom the time they can walk on their own, toddlers want their independence. They don't want to stay with their mother or hold her hand. Young children don't understand the dangers in maneuvering through a crowd or crossing a busy street. They just want to go on their own.

When we force them to hold our hand, they will pout or cry. Our child wants to go faster or a different way. They may see something exciting to them and ignore all danger signs. Although we want them to stay close so we can keep them safe, our preschoolers may not listen.

God desires for us to walk close to Him, following His steps. He sees the dangers ahead or the temptations that can lead us astray. He wants to keep us from those pitfalls; He wants to help us maneuver through life with a minimum of stress, yet He never forces us to do so. It is our choice.

Jesus Christ set an example for us. When we are His, we are to walk with Him. We must stay close so that our focus is on Him, not on the worldly enticements that can lead to danger. We must deny self and hold fast to God.

*Thank You, Jesus, for leading the way. Help me to keep
close to Your side and always walk with You. Amen.*

Ready and Waiting

*But sanctify the Lord God in your hearts: and be ready always
to give an answer to every man that asketh you a reason of the
hope that is in you with meekness and fear.*
I Peter 3:15 KJV

$\mathcal{O}$ne of the greatest gifts we can share with others is the hope we
have in Christ. We can do this by being a friend to our neighbors.

One such friend, a mother of preschoolers, demonstrated this
by inviting the neighbor ladies over and even offering to help people
when they were in trouble. Then, when an opportunity arose to share
her faith, the woman didn't hesitate.

Look for opportunities to shine God's light into the lives
of those living without hope. As you meet the moms of your
preschooler's friends and, as your child grows, the mothers of
her fellow classmates, build a firm relationship based on love and
helpfulness. Be a positive example of what it means to follow in
Christ's steps. Then, when you have an opportunity to plant a seed
in another mother's heart, you may be amazed at the harvest God
provides.

When Christ had His earthly ministry, He did talk about sin and
its consequences. However, He approached people with tenderness
and compassion, meeting people's immediate needs and loving them
as friends first.

Lord, help me to be ready to share my faith in a way that will honor You.

A Quiet Response

A soft answer turneth away wrath: but grievous words stir up anger.
Proverbs 15:1 KJV

*B*etty threw a temper tantrum. Her mom, Rose, yelled back in an effort to stop the tantrum, but it only escalated and led to Rose forcefully shoving Betty into her bedroom and then holding the door shut. Inside her bedroom, Betty screamed louder and cried harder, more out of control than before.

In the middle of a crowded store, Karen consoled and instructed her preschooler, who'd had a temper tantrum. In a quiet voice, Karen modeled controlled behavior and spoke soft words of calmness and gentleness to her son. Within seconds, he was silent, listening intently to what his mom was whispering in his ear.

Have you ever witnessed either scenario?

Proverbs 15:1 (KJV) tells us that "A soft answer turneth away wrath: but grievous words stir up anger." Yelling back at our children arouses more anger, commotion, and strife. However, when we patiently respond with soft, gentle, tenderhearted, but firm words of instruction, our children will usually calm down and compose themselves.

Our children desire to be like us, to emulate our every move. When a mom models peaceful behavior, children generally respond in kind, looking forward to the words of affirmation that follow from Mom.

The fact is that children are children, and will, at times, throw temper tantrums. Just remember that that is our golden opportunity to respond calmly yet firmly. The ultimate reward for a quiet response? A peaceful home.

Lord, help me to model calm, controlled, soft responses
to every temper tantrum my preschooler throws.

Inconvenienced

Jeroboam thought to himself, "The kingdom will now likely revert to the house of David. If these people go up to offer sacrifices at the temple of the LORD in Jerusalem, they will again give their allegiance to their lord, Rehoboam king of Judah."
I Kings 12:26–27 NIV

After King Solomon died, the nation of Israel split into two. Jeroboam, leader of the northern kingdom, set up two worship centers. He insisted that the intent was to make worship convenient, so that the Israelites didn't have to travel to the temple in Jerusalem to worship. The truth was that he didn't want the Israelites to travel where they would be reminded of their true spiritual heritage. He made two golden calves for the people to worship. And God—no surprise—declared it sin.

Convenience is not the most important part of worship. And yet it is easy to "settle" on a church because it's down the street and close to our home, because it's a denomination we grew up with, or because a good friend attends. More importantly, we should be looking for a place where the Word of God is being taught. Is this a place where our children will grow up knowing the Bible? Is the ministry embedded in the scriptures?

Convenience isn't a bad thing. But it shouldn't be the first consideration as we choose a church home for our families. This decision is important! Convenience in worship led the Israelites astray—right back into idolatry. They let "good enough" win out over the best.

Lord, guide our family to a church home in which we can honor and worship You.

Motherhood:
An Eternal Legacy

The days of the blameless are known to the LORD,
and their inheritance will endure forever.
Psalm 37:18 NIV

Nothing on earth will last. The handmade quilt from Grandmother Jones, the beautiful painted pictures from Aunt Rosie, the diamond earrings Daddy gave to Mom. . . All will eventually be lost or destroyed because nothing lasts forever. That is, except a godly heritage. Motherhood can be a godly heritage. A mother who has a personal relationship with Jesus can leave her children the most important treasure of life. A mother can model for her children a heritage that will abide forever: a personal relationship with Jesus Christ.

The fruit that is born from a mother's relationship with Jesus is selfless giving to her children and grandchildren; serving her husband, family, and neighbors; faithfully placing the needs of others before her own; modeling generous forgiveness, to name a few. If you want to leave an eternal legacy for your children to remember you by, be a mother who continually articulates the love of God, planting seeds that the Lord will use to draw your children into a flourishing, fruitful relationship with Jesus Christ. This relationship with Christ is the only eternal legacy that a mother can give.

Lord, thank You that the heritage of the blameless abides forever.
Help me to know You better and to leave my children an eternal legacy,
a relationship with You.

I Need Rest!

And the Lord said, My Presence shall go with you, and I will give you rest.
Exodus 33:14 AMP

The baby was finally asleep, and now Jenny gently tucked in her four-year-old daughter.

"Mommy, what are you going to do while I take a nap?"

Jenny kissed her daughter on the forehead. "I'm going to do the lunch dishes, fold Daddy's shirts, and sew a button on one of my blouses."

"Wow, that's a lot."

Jenny sighed. "I know. Now get some rest so you will have lots of energy to play with your sister later."

"Don't mommies need their rest, too?"

This question took Jenny by surprise. She was tired. It would be nice to lie down with the children and just sleep for an hour, but she thought of all the things that needed to be done before her husband came home. "Yes. But. . ."

She stopped midsentence because she knew her precious preschooler would argue that she didn't need to rest either if Mommy didn't need to. Jenny smiled at her little one. When was the last time she'd lain down with her and just rested?

Jenny laughed and returned to the bed. "Scoot over, honey. Mommy's napping with you today."

Thank You, Lord, for being my place of rest. Sometimes life is too busy for me to just lie down, but knowing You are with me makes it much easier to endure the times I feel tired. Remind me, Lord, to get the rest I need so that I can be a good parent to my child. Amen.

Repeated Blessings

"'The LORD bless you and keep you; the LORD make his face shine upon you and be gracious to you; the LORD turn his face toward you and give you peace.'"
Numbers 6:24–26 NIV

*I*n the Old Testament, blessings bestowed from parent to child were taken very seriously. Perhaps that's where the saying "from my mouth to God's ears" first originated. Blessings meant something!

We bless our children whenever we affirm their great value to us and to God, and when we give them a bright picture of their future. One of the ways we can give blessings to our children is to repeat blessings from the Bible. "The Lord has His hand on you," or "May the Lord bless you and keep you."

We can sing blessings to our children, etching a groove in their mind of God's love for them. The song "Jesus Loves Me," as simple as it is, conveys a scriptural truth.

We bless our children when we point out their gifts and abilities: "God gave you such a knack for drawing! I wonder if you'll be an architect."

We bless our children when we prayerfully intercede for them. We are called to be prayer champions for each child, praying faithfully, effectively, and fervently.

Blessings express a child's value, just for being alive. They're not just pats on the back for a job well done. Blessings mean something! And we can't bless our children enough.

Lord, make me a blessing to my family today.
Let my words affirm others of their great value in Your eyes.

Walk in the Light

Come ye, and let us walk in the light of the LORD.
Isaiah 2:5 KJV

$\mathcal{M}$otherhood is a genuine pleasure for the most part, but there are times when it is frightening and confusing. Every good mother wants the best for her child, but there are many factors to consider when deciding what is "best." Once the little one joins the family, every choice the parents make will affect the child either directly or indirectly. There is no doubt that motherhood is a great responsibility.

Many women feel the urge to subscribe to every parenting magazine and purchase a library's worth of child-rearing books to help them in their quest to properly bring up their children. These publications often do contain helpful and encouraging information and suggestions, but they're much more useful if they are used along with God's Word. Only the Bible gives us the wisdom we need to properly raise our kids. Walking in His light gives us confidence and strength to be the mothers God intends us to be. We don't have to spend our time as parents in the dark. God wants us to find this a joyous time of life, and He has the answers.

Light of the World, please clear the fog of confusion and help me to raise my children by the standards in Your Word.

Praise without Pretense

Praise him with the timbrel and dance: praise
him with stringed instruments and organs.
Psalm 150:4 KJV

*I*n her Sunday dress, she was absolutely beautiful.

She danced around the living room, twirling and floating to a happy rhythm that played in her five-year-old head. She started humming to herself, ignoring the taunts of her older siblings to stop her silliness.

But there was no silliness. There was just a deep, natural joy of life. And there was no better way for her to express it than to dance.

At age five, she didn't know she should be proper and quench the urge to dip and twirl. She only knew that she felt like dancing, and she did.

And so she praised the Lord by doing what was natural to do.

Children, like the animals, praise the Lord naturally. The eagle praises its Maker as it soars in the heavens; the fish as it glides through the sea; the bee as it flits from flower to flower gathering nectar.

But as a woman grows and is busy taking care of herself and others, she can forget to praise.

Or if she does praise, she holds back, not wanting to look emotional or silly.

May we learn from the children and let our praises flow without pretense or inhibition.

Out of the mouth of babes You have perfected praise, Lord.
Let my praise be honest and open and pleasing to Your ears. Amen.

Beauty Treatments
and Baggy Sweats

A [girl]. . .had to complete twelve months of beauty treatments prescribed for the
women, six months with oil of myrrh and six with perfumes and cosmetics.
Esther 2:12 NIV

This verse details the beauty treatments required of a girl before
she could go to King Xerxes. Cosmetics and treatments go way back
in history! Not only did she have to look beautiful, she had to go
through a full year of beautification in preparation to be with the king.

As a mom of little ones, some days it's a major accomplishment
to get a shower before 4:00 p.m., let alone complete a beauty
regimen. We tuck loose strands of hair behind an ear while running
about the house in baggy sweatpants and a T-shirt. Sometimes we
forgo pulling ourselves together because we're running a household,
keeping everyone and everything else in order.

Why not take a Saturday morning, let someone else watch the
kids, and go to the mall with a friend to visit a cosmetics counter? Or,
if you need a bigger break, visit a spa. God can use times like these
to give us a renewed energy. We all need a little pick-me-up once in a
while, and although you won't have a yearlong beauty treatment, you'll
most likely be rejuvenated following your morning out.

Lord, I thank You for the ones You have given me to care for.
Please help me to be able to take a little time for myself, to be reenergized.
Amen.

Firm Guidance

Whoso loveth correction loveth knowledge; But he that hateth reproof is brutish.
Proverbs 12:1 ASV

"I can't do it," Sandra said to her husband. "I love Mary. I can't punish her!"

Mary's parents were having a heavy, but necessary, discussion on the living room couch. Their only child was out of control, rude, and even disrespectful. Until tonight, they'd let Mary have her freedom to do what she wanted. If she didn't want to eat all her dinner, she didn't have to. If she didn't want to pick up her toys, she didn't have to. But now their "freestyle" parenting was quickly coming to an end. Mary was beginning to refuse bath time and even going to preschool.

After talking with a friend at church, Jared realized they'd started Mary's foundation wrong. Mary had come to believe that she was in control and, in many ways, she really was. Now it was a matter of convincing Sandra that they needed to pull together as parents.

"We have to be consistent," Jared now told Sandra. "If we really love Mary, we'll set some rules and boundaries before it's too late."

God, as a firm but loving Father, gives us rules and boundaries to help guide us and keep us from harm. By obeying Him, we receive untold blessings and rewards.

In the same manner, we, as loving parents, also need to set rules and boundaries to guide the little ones in our care. When Mom and Dad are on the same team, lovingly, consistently, and firmly guiding their children, their young ones will grow and prosper.

Lord, give me wisdom in raising my children.
Help me to be a firm yet loving mother.

Unbalancing the Scales

"Love the Lord your God with all your heart and with all your soul and with all your mind and with all your strength."
Mark 12:30 NIV

*B*alancing the scales of life—the spiritual versus the earthly—can seem impossible. In our attempt to find balance, we encounter unrest and discouragement. Perhaps it's so difficult for us because it's really not God's desire that the scales be balanced at all. Actually, He calls us to a completely unbalanced life.

In Mark 12:30, the heart represents the things we love, and the soul, our emotions. Loving God with all of our hearts and souls places Him first, above all else. Our strength represents the things into which we put our efforts, our will, and our physical work. Our mind is the sum of our thoughts.

God doesn't want an equal portion of those things after they are divided with the world. He wants and deserves it all. The scales should not be balanced; they should tip as our devotion to God exceeds all else. It is only with that proper balance that He can finally and truly have full reign in our lives. To the believer, that right relationship is the only one that feels natural. Only then, when God is given all of our hearts, souls, strength, and minds, can we feel at peace.

Father, forgive me for trying to balance the scales when, in reality, You should have everything. I give myself over to You fully so that You can reign in my life. Thank You for the peace You bring to my heart. Amen.

Condemnation versus Conviction

Therefore, there is now no condemnation for those who are in Christ Jesus.
Romans 8:1 NIV

*Y*ou are a loser. You can't do anything right. You will never be forgiven. Condemning words pierce our hearts and knock the wind right out of us. They are difficult to overcome. They prevent us from moving forward. Whether shouted in our ear or whispered to our heart, their source is the same. Condemning words originate with Satan. Their purpose is to drive us further away from God by making us feel unloved, unworthy, and hopeless.

Convicting words—you are worthy and precious, you can do all things through Christ, and you are forgiven—on the other hand, have a completely different tone. They originate with the Holy Spirit with the purpose of drawing us closer to God. Although correction and rebuke may be needed, love is always present. Acknowledging our sin is a prerequisite to receiving God's grace and forgiveness. When God's love is experienced in the form of discipline, restoration and freedom are the results.

As believers, we are never condemned because Jesus Christ paid the penalty for sin once and for all when He died on the cross. So, when condemning words stop us in our tracks, we need to stand on truth. Then, move toward the God that always loves, forgives, and yearns for a close relationship with us.

Dear Lord, give me wisdom to discern the difference between condemnation and conviction. May I heed the Holy Spirit and draw closer to You. Amen.

Known By Heart

Study to shew thyself approved unto God, a workman that needeth not to be ashamed, rightly dividing the word of truth.
2 Timothy 2:15 KJV

The mother smiled at her son's obvious delight in the story she was reading. As she finished the final page, he turned back to the beginning and begged her to read the tale over again. She shook her head, marveling that after three times through, he wanted to hear it again.

Later, the mother noted her child sitting by himself, staring at the pages of the book. He began to "read" the story by heart, turning the pages at the right place and pointing to the different pictures as she had done. He'd heard the tale so many times, he had memorized every word.

We should never tire of reading God's Word. Each day we must pray for God to give us a new heart to hear what He has written to us. Our delight in His instructions and encouragement should be childlike awe.

The Bible is God's living Word. The stories, promises, and commandments make us ponder God's will for us. As we hear the Bible over and over, we are filled with a sense of wonder and accomplishment at our ability to remember the scriptures.

Thank you, God, for Your living Word. Help me to memorize the scriptures and keep them in my heart. Amen.

Who Has Gone Before?

In the same way, teach older women to be holy in their behavior, not speaking against others or enslaved to too much wine, but teaching what is good.
Titus 2:3 NCV

*M*entoring is a system of trust in which one woman gleans knowledge and experience through the guidance of another who has gone before. In Titus, Paul charges the aged with living above reproach as an example to younger women. He also calls them to teach and train the younger, less experienced women.

God designed this relationship between women so that each generation would guide the next. Women easily share with each other on a deeply personal level, so they naturally crave the camaraderie and guidance through the tough times that develops through a mentoring relationship.

A mentor must be trustworthy, experienced, and wise. The mentor of a mother with young children, for example, should have walked that road herself, learned many lessons along the way, and have both failures and successes to share. She should also be a loving example of Christ, unafraid to tell the truth.

And, in order to be effectively mentored, a woman must be open and honest with her spiritual mentor. She must have a changeable heart that desires God's will above her own. And she must be willing to lay aside her pride in order to learn from the wisdom of another.

Jesus, please lead me to one whom You have chosen to mentor me.
Help me receive Your wisdom from her. And help me know when You
have called me to be a mentor to someone else in need of guidance. Amen.

Toxic Guilt

But because of his great love for us, God, who is rich in mercy,
made us alive with Christ even when we were dead in transgressions—
it is by grace you have been saved.
Ephesians 2:4–5 NIV

*L*egalism is a misunderstanding of what pleases God, and a catalyst to toxic guilt that erodes faith and weakens the will. God doesn't want our good works or our legalistic rules. "Be in church every time the doors are open, pay your tithes, fast and pray, memorize scripture, have your quiet times," are all good pieces of advice and natural parts of a Christian walk, but will those things win God's favor? No! There is only one thing that earns His favor—our faith in Jesus Christ.

When we hold ourselves to standards that require our actions to be "good enough" to please God, when (not if) we fail, we'll feel guilty. If we fail more often than we succeed, we'll give up in hopeless despair.

It's God's grace, and the Holy Spirit in us, that will bring us to maturity in Christ, not human effort or faithful adherence to a set of procedures. Love is a gift, not a reward for things done in hopes of earning that love. God's gift of love is free and dependent only upon His actions, not on ours. Accept His gift and trust in its unfailing power of grace. True love never fails.

Father, thank You for the free gift of Your love. Help me to accept
it and trust that it is unfailing. Keep me from feelings of inadequacy
and guilt that only weaken my faith. Amen.

What If?

You can go to bed without fear; you will lie down and sleep soundly.
You need not be afraid of sudden disaster or the destruction that
comes upon the wicked, for the LORD is your security.
Proverbs 3:24–26 NLT

*I*n the middle of the night, Sara often wakes with a jolt, her mind racing. Strange thoughts burst unbidden in her mind: Her daughter runs across the street and gets hit by a car. Her son falls off his bicycle and hurts his head. Her kids are swimming in the deep end of a pool, and. . .they can't swim! *What if these things really happen?* she wonders. *What if?*

Such nagging worries are common to all moms. We know how helpless we are, ultimately, to make life turn out well for our little ones. If we could, we would protect them from any harm: scraped knees to chicken pox. Is that so wrong?

Sometimes, our active imaginations can run away from us. Anxieties can hold us captive, preventing us from enjoying our children's risks and accomplishments. That can be all we see—the risks. Not the delight of climbing a tree, only the danger of falling.

Scripture reminds us that there's no place our children can go where they are outside of God's care. Instead of fearing unseen disasters, we should turn our eyes to God, says wise Solomon. God loves our children even more than we do. Remember, our confidence is in the Lord.

Lord, help me to accept the hazards of this life, knowing that
You hold us in Your strong embrace for all eternity.

Greatest Love of All

Greater love hath no man than this, that a man lay down his life for his friends.
John 15:13 KJV

Construction-paper cards, chocolate hearts, and bouquets of flowers are to Valentine's Day what colored eggs, baskets, and bunnies are to Easter. Like Easter, in many ways, Valentine's Day is a celebration of the greatest love of all—the love of a man who laid down his life for his friends.

Valentine's Day was a day decreed to celebrate Saint Valentine, a man who died for love, but it wasn't for romantic love. He died as a martyr for the Christian faith. Like Easter, tradition has overshadowed this precious sacrifice, and the day that was intended to honor it has become a colorful and commercial secular holiday that, in many homes, has nothing to do with the original intent for the celebration.

We should consider the real reasons that we celebrate love today. We should embrace our families, celebrate the blessing of love, and show love to those around us. But, while doing that, we need to remember the greatest possible love, a love so deep that it would enable someone to lay down his life for others. When we say, "Happy Valentine's Day" today, let's remember that we are celebrating the greatest love of all.

Father, thank You for Your great sacrifice of love. Thank You also for those who, in their love for You, have laid down their own lives. Help me to remember that kind of love, and show it to my family, as I celebrate this day. Amen.

Testing Faith

Consider it pure joy. . .whenever you face trials of many kinds,
because you know that the testing of your faith develops perseverance. . . .
So that you may be mature and complete, not lacking anything.
James 1:2–4 NIV

$\mathcal{G}$race sat by the phone anxiously awaiting the call with the results of her preschooler's tests. She feared the worst. . .special needs, autism, learning disabled. The outcome would change life forever.

God's Word tells us that whenever we face trials, we should consider it pure joy! Our natural response is usually not joy but perhaps anger, worry, and anxiety over the potential outcome, or fear about how this may change our lives. However, when we place the trial within God's framework, we can open ourselves up to the truth that this trial can lead to many benefits. For example, as God's Word tells us, the trial will test our faith. Do we truly trust our Sovereign Lord to take care of our preschooler and us even when we dislike the outcome? Will we literally put on God's armor (Ephesians 6:10–18), recount God's faithfulness and wonders of past trials, and walk by faith not by sight (2 Corinthians 5:7)? Perhaps we will even praise God that this trial is to test our faith, develop our endurance, and bring us to maturity in Christ.

Lord, give me a heart of pure joy when I face trials, knowing that
trials are meant to test my faith. Develop my endurance and
bring me to maturity in Christ as I raise my preschooler.

No Time

It is good to give thanks to the LORD, to sing praises to the Most High. It is good to proclaim your unfailing love in the morning, your faithfulness in the evening.
Psalm 92:1–2 NLT

*T*wo mothers waited in line to pay for their groceries. Sharon looked tired and complained about not having enough time in her day. Her four-year-old son tugged at her skirt and whined sleepily. Lisa listened with sympathy. Her child sat quietly in the basket, playing with a stuffed animal, having already had a nap.

"What am I doing wrong?" Sharon asked.

Lisa took a deep breath and answered with a question. "Did you spend time with the Lord this morning?"

Looking ashamed, Sharon admitted she hadn't.

"Spending time with the Lord each morning is what makes my day run more smoothly." Lisa could tell Sharon wasn't completely satisfied with her answer, and she said a little prayer for her as they parted.

A few weeks later, the two women ran into each other again. Lisa noticed that Sharon looked more peaceful and rested. Her child seemed calm and rested, too. "Lisa, thank you so much for reminding me to spend time with the Lord in the mornings. It has changed my life. Not only do I have time to get done what needs to be done, but I have time for the Lord in the evenings as well."

Heavenly Father, it is my desire to grow closer to You. Help me to remember to spend time with You each day—no matter how busy I am. Amen.

There's Power in the Tongue

Death and life are in the power of the tongue;
And they that love it shall eat the fruit thereof.
Proverbs 18:21 ASV

*D*eath and life are in the power of the tongue." Those are some strong words. We can speak life and death into our own lives by the things we say about ourselves. Death comes by way of comments like: "I'm stupid; I'm fat; I'm ugly." Or, we can speak life into our lives with words like: "I'm a child of God; I'm loved; I'm beautiful in the eyes of God."

We can speak life or death into the lives of others. Verbal judgments, gossip, and negative talk all bring doom. But praise, encouragement, and loving speech all bring life. We can deflate someone with just a few words, or we can build them up in confidence with even fewer.

Perhaps most importantly, we have the power, with our tongues, to speak death or life into the lives of our children. Death speech creates discouragement, fear, feelings of inadequacies, etc. But life speech brings hope, confidence, love, trust, and joy. Our children learn about themselves from the words we say to them and about them. As mothers, we have the unique power, in our tongues, to give our children the gift of hope in Christ and confidence in His perfect love for them.

Jesus, Life-giver, help me to control my tongue so that I will always reveal life in my words. Help me never to lash out in anger or bitterness. I want to bring joy and hope to those around me, blessing them with my words. Amen.

Paper Snowflake

For you formed my inward parts; you knitted me together in my mother's womb. I praise you, for I am fearfully and wonderfully made. Wonderful are your works; my soul knows it very well.
Psalm 139:13–14 ESV

Fold a sheet of paper several times until it forms a triangle. With a pair of scissors, cut triangles, circles, notches, and other designs in its edges. Open the paper and see how your cuts have turned it into a unique and beautiful snowflake. We've all made those paper snowflakes before, and now we make them with our own children.

Our children are like that folded piece of paper. Through our parental guidance, we are constantly snipping away at them, trusting that, one day, they will unfold into a completely unique work of art. There is no way to know exactly what the snowflake will look like when the work is complete. We must trust that our efforts at shaping them will be fruitful and create a beautiful result.

Our heavenly Father treats each one of us with that same diligence. He shapes us and snips at our folds by convicting our hearts, teaching us with His Word, and guiding our lives. He shapes us into a unique and beautiful part of His body, one snip at a time.

Jesus, thank You for carefully crafting me into the person You want me to be. Help me to trust that You know what You're doing and that Your work will make me like a beautiful snowflake. Amen.

We Are Family!

*See what kind of love the Father has given to us, that we should
be called children of God; and so we are. The reason why the
world does not know us is that it did not know him.*
I John 3:1 ESV

The grocery store was crowded. The mother had only turned her
back for a second, but one second was apparently enough for her
four-year-old daughter to wander off.

A deep panic set in as her heart pounded in her chest.
Maneuvering her cart past snail-like shoppers, she finally abandoned
the contraption and sprinted for the customer service desk. She
scanned various aisles as she ran.

*Her name is Anna. She is four years old. She has brown hair and green eyes.
She was wearing a blue shirt with a teddy bear on it. She had jeans on. I think she
was wearing her pink gym shoes.*

Turning down one more aisle, the mother reached the service
desk and heard a confident childlike speech. "Her name is Molly, but
I call her Mama. She is wearing a really pretty green shirt and black
pants. She's old—like thirty. Oh, and she's really nice, too."

The lady at the desk laughed when she reunited mother
and daughter and explained that she herself had found the girl
unaccompanied in the cookie aisle. Now allowing her heart to settle,
the mother embraced her daughter—her family. As young as her
daughter was, she knew who her mother was—just as we know God
and God knows us.

Lord, thank You for rescuing me and welcoming me into Your family.

Party Hearty

"Go and celebrate with a feast of rich foods and sweet drinks, and share gifts of food with people who have nothing prepared. This is a sacred day before our Lord. Don't be dejected and sad, for the joy of the LORD is your strength!"
Nehemiah 8:10 NLT

*E*mily studied scriptures on parenting children and prayed for four-year-old Cody and two-year-old Catelyn every day. She loved their sweet prayers and praise songs. Emily's children were growing up to be like Jesus.

One afternoon, both children awoke from their naps, whiny and demanding. Cody hid Catelyn's favorite doll. His sister raised a welt on his forehead with a wooden block. Emily disciplined her children, and by the time her husband, Cam, arrived home, Cody had returned the doll he had shut in the dryer. He and Catelyn were playing together again. Emily and Cam had planned a family night out, but she put her foot down. No way did these kids deserve pizza.

Sometimes as we teach children right and wrong, we forget to include God's grace. During Nehemiah's era, the Israelites committed many sins, but they listened to the reading of God's Law and began to weep in remorse. Some might think God would take pleasure in their sorrow. Instead, He commanded them to celebrate His love and grace with good times for everyone!

Father, we do not comprehend the enormous scope of Your forgiveness or Your gladness when we repent. Please help us enjoy Your grace and make sure our children understand it, too! Amen.

What Should I Do?

Teach me Your way, O Lord. Lead me in a straight path.
Psalm 27:11 NLV

*B*eing the preacher's wife could be a tough job at times.

"You really should think about how you are raising your children."

Francis took a deep breath, counted to ten, and then answered. "What do you mean?"

"Well, I don't think it's right for a preacher's kids to be watching cartoons."

The desire to tell Lois to mind her own business was strong. Francis decided to reason with her instead. "They aren't just watching cartoons. Those videos are Christian-based stories. They are learning about God and how they should behave with other people."

"In my day, we read to our children from the Bible." Lois picked up her purse and headed to the door. She waved good-bye to her grandchildren and then left.

Francis put her mother-in-law's coffee cup into the sink. Was Lois right? Was her method of teaching the children about God wrong? Maybe her children shouldn't be watching cartoons; after all, they were the children of a minister. Francis felt the heaviness of worry descend upon her shoulders.

Knowing worry was not of God, Francis prayed, looking for God's guidance and peace.

Lord, please help me to do Your will and learn not to worry about what others think. I want to be a good example for You, so I'm asking You to show me what is right and wrong. In Jesus' name, amen.

Show Me a Sign!

The angel of the LORD appeared to [Gideon] and said to him,
"The LORD is with you, O valiant warrior."
Judges 6:12 NASB

*G*ideon's appearance on the biblical scene seemed almost comical. The angel of the Lord sought Gideon out, bestowing on him the title "valiant warrior." Gideon was anything *but* a valiant warrior! Immediately, Gideon started objecting. He doubted that the Lord was really with him. He questioned the battle plan that the angel of the Lord spelled out to him. He pointed out that his family was from a very weak tribe. "My clan is the weakest. . .and I am the least in my family" (Judges 6:15 NIV). As if God didn't know!

After three or four objections, it would seem reasonable for the angel of the Lord to move on to a more willing warrior. But no! Patiently, oh so patiently, he dispelled Gideon's concerns. The Lord answered, "I will be with you" (Judges 6:16 NIV).

God was not put off by Gideon's feelings of inadequacy or shallow faith. He would provide what Gideon needed, when he needed it. Even courage! In fact, He encouraged Gideon to "Go in the strength you have" (Judges 6:14 NIV).

Rare is the mother who isn't overwhelmed at times by the task of raising children. This is a long, hard job. But God never intended us to go it alone. He is with us, patiently encouraging us, providing the strength and wisdom we need, just as we need it.

Ever-present Lord, Your Word promises that You are near to everyone who calls out Your name. I'm calling out, Lord, and I thank You for Your loving presence!

A Priceless Parental Resource

Train up a child in the way he should go:
and when he is old, he will not depart from it.
Proverbs 22:6 KJV

*A*s offspring of the fallen Adam, children are themselves fallen. Though they come from the womb, looking sweet and pure, they are born into sin and in need of a Savior.

Children, knowing nothing of the world, don't know the difference between good and evil, nor do they know how to refuse the evil and choose the good.

How will they ever learn? We must teach them.

Timothy, the apostle Paul's son in the faith, was taught the holy scriptures from childhood, giving him "the wisdom to receive the salvation that comes by trusting in Christ Jesus" (2 Timothy 3:15 NLT).

Who taught Timothy the scriptures? Most likely his mother and his grandmother, as Paul writes, "I remember your genuine faith, for you share the faith that first filled your grandmother Lois and your mother, Eunice" (2 Timothy 1:5 NLT).

Teaching children about God, moral absolutes, and accountability is a mother's most important job, especially in today's world. And the amazing thing is that we have an advantage over Eunice and Lois. We have not only the scriptures of Timothy's day, but an entire New Testament! The Bible is a priceless resource for rearing our young and teaching them about life and faith. It should be the first "textbook" your child receives!

Begin training early. Along with biblical lessons, establish and consistently apply boundaries and rules. In doing so, you will be establishing a firm foundation that will support your children throughout their lives.

Like Lois and Eunice, train your children in the way they should go, beginning with today.

Father, help me raise my child in the way You want him to go,
using Your Word to grow his faith.

Get Refreshed

It is a sign between me and the children of Israel for ever: for in six days the LORD made heaven and earth, and on the seventh day he rested, and was refreshed.
Exodus 31:17 KJV

"I just vacuumed that floor," the mother moaned. The carpet was now covered with crumbs from a package of Goldfish Crackers her three-year-old had discovered. She picked up the little boy and carried him to his bed for a nap, fully intending to wash some walls while he slept. It wasn't long before she heard delighted squeals coming from the child's room. She went to investigate only to discover another wall needing washing. It seemed her darling child had earlier squirreled away a purple crayon and was now using his light green walls as a canvas. The mother burst into tears, grabbed the crayon, and stalked out of the room.

Later, she related the events of the day to her husband. "You need a break," he said firmly. "You constantly push at 100 percent, and you never sit down to rest. Tomorrow I'm taking the little guy, and I want you to relax."

It wasn't easy, but she complied. She was amazed at how refreshed she felt.

As moms, so often do we feel we are exempt from the need to rest. We push until we collapse spiritually, physically, and emotionally. We need to take God's example and make time to rest.

O God, I don't know how I have time to rest, but You rested.
If You know it's necessary, how can I refuse? Help me find time to be refreshed.

Jesus Loves Me

"Let the little children come to me, and do not hinder them. . . ."
And he took the children in his arms, put his hands on them and blessed them.
Mark 10:14, 16 NIV

*I*t was music to Nancy's ears to hear her preschooler sing "Jesus Loves Me" and pray with her stuffed animals. Marcella was a sponge, soaking up every bit of truth about Jesus through Christian songs, hymns, and stories.

It is also music to the Lord's ears to hear His beloved children sing, talk about, and talk to Him. Jesus encouraged mothers to bring their children to Him. Picture Jesus with a huge smile and warm embrace, gathering the children up in His arms, praying for them, laughing with them. Jesus loves children. Our preschoolers are innocent and trustworthy. They believe what we tell them. Therefore, let's begin at an early age, telling them about the truth of their Lord. Through their attending Sunday school, reading preschooler Bibles, singing praise songs and hymns, and saying short prayers to the Lord, our children will come to have a foundation that cannot be shaken. They will model for us the simple faith it takes to believe Jesus and know that Jesus loves them.

Lord, help me to teach my children about You. Enable me to
have the childlike ability to trust You and take You at Your Word.

Giving Gladly

Let each man do according as he hath purposed in his heart:
not grudgingly, or of necessity: for God loveth a cheerful giver.
2 Corinthians 9:7 ASV

*T*he mother smiled at her young daughter as the child clutched a dollar in her hand. The girl bounced in excitement as she watched the usher move closer to her pew. When the plate passed, the toddler dropped her dollar in with the rest of the offering then clapped her hands in delight.

Children are so good at expressing heartfelt emotion. When they are excited about something, everyone around them knows. Our influence as mothers can direct our children to look forward to giving to God. This is what God loves.

Often we give from a heart that is not cheerful. We feel obligated to give an amount of money or of time. Jobs crop up in the church. We believe no one else will step forward, so we take on something God hasn't called us to. In those times we begin to grumble instead of serving with a glad heart.

We must carefully consider what God is asking us to do or to give. He'll never ask more than we are capable of. When we follow His directives, and not our own, we will be able to show excitement over our giving. Let's learn to clap in delight at whatever God asks us to do or to give.

Thank You, Lord, for the opportunity to serve You in whatever way You desire.
Amen.

Childish Ways

When I was a child, I talked like a child, I thought like a child, I reasoned like a child. When I became a man, I put childish ways behind me.
1 Corinthians 13:11 NIV

One Sunday morning, a young family was scurrying to get ready for church. Tucking the shirttail into the trousers of her four-year-old son, the mother remarked, "Thomas, you look so sharp! You look like a young man!" She wanted to encourage him to leave his shirt neatly in place. Her son looked at her inquisitively and said, "Mom, I'm not a man. I'm just a kid." He was right! The mother smiled as she immediately pulled out his shirttail!

As mothers, we desire that our children mature properly. Yet sometimes on their journey to adulthood, we do not allow them to be children. We expect them to be grown-up and leave childish ways behind. Adulthood will come soon enough. Do not try to rush the process by putting unrealistic demands on them. Learn to major on the majors and minor on the minors by seeking the Lord's discernment. Ask the question "Does this issue have eternal significance?" If the answer is no, allow your child to talk, think, and reason like a child. As an adult, they will be expected to put those childish ways behind them. Until then, leave the shirttail out!

Dear Lord, I confess that sometimes I want my child to behave as an adult. Give me Your wisdom and discernment. Amen.

A Family Name

Let me live forever in your sanctuary, safe beneath the shelter of your wings!
For you have heard my vows, O God. You have given me an
inheritance reserved for those who fear your name.
Psalm 61:4–5 NLT

*N*ames have meaning. When a mother considers names for her
expected baby, careful thought usually goes into the process. We use
names to get someone's attention, but we also use them to show
family ties. Our names do not define who we are, but for good or for
bad, they do tell who we came from.

In times past, last names held even greater meaning because
they linked distant relatives together. Often, people were referred to
by their first name but also by their father's name, such as so-and-
so, the son of so-and-so. This was certainly true in Shakespeare's
tragedy, *Romeo and Juliet*. The Bible also records ancestral and
descendent names. Christ was known as Jesus, the son of Joseph. In
fact, the book of Matthew even records Christ's ancestral history,
dating back hundreds of years.

Some people are not proud of their last names. They might be
linked back to ungodly people and events or may even be spelled or
pronounced oddly. Fortunately, those who are believers enter into
God's family and are given new names—the sons and daughters of
the Most High God. Put that on your résumé!

Lord, I praise Your name. Thank You for welcoming me into Your family.

My Word!

A word fitly spoken is like apples of gold in pictures of silver.
Proverbs 25:11 KJV

*B*ecause preschoolers do not always speak clearly, we adults sometimes get the mistaken idea that they do not hear or understand what we say. But little ears scan their surroundings like radar, gathering data for future reference. They absorb words we never suspect they have learned.

Rebekah couldn't help grinning when she heard four-year-old Olivia scold her little brother with the same words and tone Rebekah used when she'd hurried her husband to the dinner table the night before: "What are you waiting for—Christmas?" But Rebekah didn't laugh when her daughter suddenly remembered a word she had heard at her cousins' house—and shouted it out at the top of her lungs when their pastor stopped by for a friendly visit!

We cannot protect our little ones from all negative influences. But we parents can give our children the gift of beautiful words every day, verbal pictures that affirm them and guide them toward spiritual truths that will help them know God. It's not easy to stay positive and polite when they make us crazy! Yet with God's help, our daily words become a treasured legacy that will bless our children, their children, and generations beyond.

*Heavenly Father, please let me use only words of value—
priceless gifts more wonderful than silver or gold, which I
can give my children without paying a cent. Amen.*

Things That Go Bump in the Night

God is working in you, giving you the desire and the power to do what pleases him.
Philippians 2:13 NLT

*D*uring Jesus' ministry, He freed a man burdened by demons. He freed a tax collector from his greed. He freed a young girl from an early death, and He freed the world from Satan's grasp.

But can He help free our children? Can He free them from their fears—things that go bump in the night or the panic that sets in when we leave them with a babysitter or at Sunday school? Can He free them from their fixations—pacifiers, blankies, thumb sucking? Can He free them from their natural selfishness—refusing to share toys, demanding their own way? Can He free them from their impulsive behavior—tossing out hurtful words, bonking a playmate on her head, or biting the cat's tail?

Some behaviors are part of normal stages of development. Given time, they'll pass. But some behaviors aren't. They hint at the beginnings of an anxious personality, a tendency to dominate others, or a complaining nature. We need the wisdom to know the difference—when to let it go and when to nip unwise behaviors in the bud.

The Bible says Jesus gives those who love Him a spirit of power, love, and self-discipline. We can pray with confident hope that God is always at work in our children's lives, transforming them into His image, setting them free from proclivities to sin. And giving us wisdom to parent well. We need only to ask Him.

Lord Jesus, where Your spirit is, there is freedom.
Dwell in our family in great power.

Modeling Our
Heavenly Father

*My child, don't reject the Lord's discipline, and don't be upset
when he corrects you. For the Lord corrects those he loves,
just as a father corrects a child in whom he delights.*
Proverbs 3:11–12 NLT

We have heard the saying that the Lord our children come to know is demonstrated in the parent they see in us. In other words, our children come to know what our heavenly Father is like by the type of parent we model.

The Lord Himself even equates His discipline with the discipline of an earthly father.

Disciplining is training and teaching our children godly behavior and shaping their hearts to have attitudes and thoughts consistent with the will of the Lord. The Lord tells us that He disciplines us because He loves us; He delights or finds pleasure in us. Likewise, we should discipline our children because we love them and delight or find pleasure in them. We need not despise, reject, refuse, or grow weary of the Lord's discipline, but rather we should accept that the Lord knows best and His discipline is grounded in love. In full submission to Him, we can achieve our purpose in life of being molded into the image of Jesus. Therefore, in modeling our heavenly Father, we must train and encourage our children to accept the authority God has given us to take care of them in the way we know best, grounded in our love for them.

*Lord, teach me to accept Your discipline because it is grounded in love.
Teach me then to train my children to grow more into the image of Jesus.*

Godly Speech

Watch the way you talk. Let nothing foul or dirty come out of your mouth.
Say only what helps, each word a gift.
Ephesians 4:29 MSG

*W*here in the world did you learn *that* word?" a mother asked,
completely shocked. Without warning, her preschool-age son repeated
the word, now stepping it up by adding it to a sentence.

"Sweetie, that's enough! Did you know that's a bad word? You
need to tell me where you heard it." She watched her son glance down
at his feet, shuffle them side to side, and then make coy eye contact
with her.

"Um, I heard it while playing at the park. Bobby says it. I didn't
know."

The mother sighed as she began to mentally prepare a lecture and
an appropriate punishment. Then she stopped. Sitting down on the
couch and pulling her growing boy up into her lap, she hugged him.

Over the past few months, all she had felt herself doing was
lecturing. *Clean your room. Don't get so dirty outside. Bring your dishes to the sink.*
Her talk may not have been profanity, but it certainly wasn't building
her son up. He needed to learn right from wrong, and good behavior
from bad behavior, but he also needed her to explain the *why* behind her
reasoning. Maybe he wouldn't understand the first time, but she could
certainly do her part and try.

As Jesus constantly explained things to His disciples, we need
to do the same for our children. Although our little ones may not
understand all the words and concepts we use, they will know we are
using God and His Word as our guide. Developing this practice with
them now will serve them a lifetime.

Lord, help me to be a good teacher who shares
Your truths in an understandable way.

Out of the Mouths
of Babes

From the lips of children and infants you have ordained praise.
Psalm 8:2 NIV

$\mathcal{A}$ little girl accompanied her grandmother to the mall's food court after attending Bible study together. As they were eating pizza, the granddaughter noticed a little boy holding a Burger King figurine. She excitedly exclaimed, "Look! Baby Jesus!" The grandmother recalled the children's story that morning: "Wise Men Visit Baby Jesus." At three years old, her granddaughter had gotten it!

Children are like sponges; they take in the contents of their environment. Their minds quickly absorb. Their hearts openly receive. Therefore, every effort should be made to teach them God's truths. A young child can learn to pray and talk to Jesus. They can sing praise songs and recite Bible verses. They can grasp that Jesus loves them.

You may not think they understand. You may believe that spiritual concepts are beyond their comprehension. But that is not true. Many times children are more perceptive than adults. That is one reason why Jesus invited little children to come to Him. He warned adults that they must have faith like a little child, trust wholeheartedly. Let's be quick to teach our children about Jesus. Then His truth will pour forth from their mouths!

Dear Lord, thank You that children can understand and praise You.
May I seek opportunities to instill Your truth in my children. Amen.

Secret Things

The secret things belong unto the LORD our God: but those things which are revealed belong unto us and to our children for ever, that we may do all the words of this law.
Deuteronomy 29:29 KJV

O God, why are You allowing this to happen?"

Have you ever asked that question? As humans, most of us sometimes do. Whether it's a big tragedy or a string of difficulties, we want to know the purpose. There are times, though, that such knowledge is for God alone. His purpose might be simply to strengthen our trust in Him. Perhaps if He revealed the reasons, they still wouldn't make sense to us. They are for God to use for His glory. There are times, too, that if God revealed the bigger picture, we would be so frightened it would do us more harm than good. The important thing to remember is that God will never give us more than we can handle through His grace.

Some things God keeps hidden, but He brings to light those things that will help us be obedient to Him. Our true purpose is to glorify Him and to have close communion with Him. His Word is packed full of everything we need to accomplish this. The proper question is not so much "Why is this happening?" but "How can I approach what is happening in a way that brings glory to You?" That is what will truly make us stronger.

O Holy God, although I don't always understand Your ways, help me to remember that You'll show me what I need to know. Help me live victoriously through You.

But I Feel Guilty

But be ye doers of the word, and not hearers only, deceiving your own selves.
James 1:22 KJV

*A*my strolled to the side door of the church. She hugged her Bible tightly as she advanced into the building. Was this what she really wanted? To join a Bible study group for preschool mothers? When her Sunday school teacher had suggested it, she had thought it would be a perfect excuse to get out of the house for a few hours, even if she did have to hire a babysitter. But with her hectic schedule, did Amy really have time for this? Shouldn't she be home, washing the clothes, loading the dishwasher, and preparing dinner?

The instructor opened with prayer and then asked, "How many of you have time to study your Bible?"

Only a few hands lifted into the air. Amy's wasn't one of them.

"During this Bible study, we're going to learn how to have our own quiet time with God, how to apply what we've learned, and how not to feel guilty for taking extra time out to learn more about God."

Amy listened intently as the instructor told them how important Bible study was. She'd been reading her Bible but hadn't applied what she'd read. As the class went on, Amy realized that she need not feel guilty about putting her chores on hold. It was more important to get ahold of God.

Heavenly Father, I want to spend more time in Your Word and do what it says. Please help me to learn to take time for myself so that I might be more in tune with You. In Jesus' name, amen.

Know God, No Offense

Great peace have they which love thy law: and nothing shall offend them.
Psalm 119:165 KJV

When we are apart from the Lord, we have no peace; anything, however trivial, can upset and offend us. But the more we know and obey God's Word, the more we get to know His heart and plan. When we are secure in the knowledge of the Holy One and His precepts, few things can ruffle our feathers.

Sheltered in God's Word, we do not need to fear the enemy's attacks. In fact, we are told to rejoice when we are insulted and persecuted (Matthew 5:11–12), and to love and pray for our enemies (Matthew 5: 44). When we get hit, we are to turn the other cheek (Matthew 5:39). All of these are unnatural reactions, according to the world, but the correct reaction, according to God. And we will be blessed when we react the way God wants us to!

As our children grow, we need to train them in the Word so they can see how God's Word can be applied to every situation, helping them to respond to others biblically (in the Spirit), not react naturally (in the flesh).

Father, help me to consistently apply Your Word in my family so we will know the peace of Your law. Amen.

Peaceful Slumber

I will lie down and sleep in peace, for you alone,
O LORD, make me dwell in safety.
Psalm 4:8 NIV

*J*oy comes in watching the moments of delight for a child. . .chasing a butterfly, picking flowers for "the best mommy in the world," finger painting, or even being enraptured with a storybook.

While it can melt a mother's heart to see her child engaged in blissful activity, there is a certain joy that fills her when she watches her child sleeping. The peacefulness and innocence is captivating, and there is joy in taking a few moments to watch the little one slumber. All of the activities and busyness of the day are forgotten, and she can take pleasure in her child's quiet rest.

Jesus takes delight in watching His children in moments of happiness. He observes us as we play and laugh with our child throughout the day; however, He must smile as He watches us in our times of resting.

How reassuring to know that even when we're sleeping, He is awake, watching us in our peaceful slumber.

If the cares of the day keep you from falling asleep, meditate on Psalm 4:8 and pray that peaceful sleep will come to you.

Dear heavenly Father, thank You for Your presence, even while I sleep. Please grant me peaceful sleep tonight, as You "make me dwell in safety." Amen.

Eyes of Faith

Day 69

I know that my redeemer liveth, and that he shall stand at the latter day upon the earth. . .whom I shall see for myself, and mine eyes shall behold, and not another.
Job 19:25, 27 KJV

God, what were You thinking?
    God, I can't take it anymore!
    God, are You even there?

Most Christians experience thoughts like these sometime during their spiritual journeys. However, Job's troubles arrived not in threes, but in thousands! In one day, he lost eleven thousand animals—his entire livelihood. Worse yet, Job and his wife lost all ten of their children. Job grew so sick with head-to-toe boils, he wished he had never been born. To top it all off, his friends gave him lots of spiritual advice that made him wish *they* hadn't been born, either!

Unbeknownst to Job, all heaven and hell watched his struggles with bated breath. How Satan must have cringed when, in the midst of Job's pain, he made a statement of faith that still rings down through the ages! And when we, despite lack of earthly evidence, choose to believe God lives and cares, Satan comes face-to-face with this wonderful, awful truth: He is finished. Defeated forever. Soon Christ will come to Earth, and we who have suffered will cheer and throw confetti to welcome Him.

Lord Jesus, I don't understand why life hurts so much. But nothing can take this away from me: I'll soon see You for myself. Thank You for that promise! Amen.

Set Boundaries

What I am saying is that as long as the heir is a child . . .
He is subject to guardians and trustees until the time set by his father.
Galatians 4:1–2 NIV

"Don't touch the stove or you might get burned."

"Don't run into the street without looking."

"Hold scissors carefully, and walk when you carry them."

"Don't play with matches."

Because a mother cares so much, she sets boundaries for her children, not to restrict them but to ensure their safety and guard them from danger. Without rules and restrictions, they may possibly harm themselves or others.

When our toddlers choose to disobey and touch the hot stove, we hurt for them as they feel pain. Still, we must stress the need to follow our instructions. Throughout life, our children will need to understand this valuable lesson.

God gives us rules when we become Christians, not to restrict us, but for our benefit. His desire is for our safety and security. He will not keep us from doing something harmful, but will always point us back to the rule we've broken.

We are given ways to interact with God and with others, and guidelines for behavior on a personal level. Someday, we will come into our inheritance and won't need the boundaries. We will see clearly the reasons God instituted the regulations. Until then, we can rejoice in God's loving guidance.

Thank you, Lord, for Your provision and for our
promised inheritance through Your Son. Amen.

Apathetic Thoughts

His delight is in the law of the LORD, and in His law he meditates
day and night. . . . And whatever he does shall prosper.
Psalm 1:2–3 NKJV

The speaker's topic at the women's one-day conference had been just what Meghan, a mother with a part-time job, needed. She needed to organize and prioritize her life better, but she also knew that the suggested strategies wouldn't solve everything.

The speaker was also a mother who worked part-time outside the home. Meghan appreciated the woman's openness. She spoke about her once roller-coaster emotions and the night when she seriously thought about ending her life. Meghan had sat in the conference stadium seating, brushing stray tears from her eyes. She didn't know what was wrong with her lately. Although Meghan loved her husband and children and didn't even mind the housework, her repetitive, day-after-day life left her feeling apathetic, anxious, and depressed.

When we let the busyness of the days keep us from seeking God, we wind up drifting away from Him and His precepts. Without His presence, our lives and work might feel meaningless and on cruise control. We may find our emotions steering our boat when it is God who should be at the helm. But it doesn't have to be that way. With God's help, we can be free from apathy by learning to delight ourselves in Him.

If you find yourself feeling apathetic, anxious, and depressed, you may want to seek help from a trusted friend or even a counselor or doctor. In the meantime, make a special effort to spend time sitting in the presence of your best Friend, the Counselor, and the Great Physician. Delight yourself in Him, and He will make you prosper!

God, help me to regain control over my emotions.
Let me remember that true joy and hope come only through You.

Faith Farm

Though the cherry trees don't blossom and the strawberries don't ripen, though the apples are worm-eaten and the wheat fields stunted, though the sheep pens are sheepless and the cattle barns empty, I'm singing joyful praise to God.
Habakkuk 3:17–18 MSG

*C*onvinced that God guided them, Katie and Ben left high-paying urban jobs for a farm. The purchase emptied their resources, but with hard work, reduced living expenses, and the help of Ben's brother Jon and his wife, Paige, they'd make it. Katie gladly exchanged suits for jeans, and fed chickens alongside their three-year-old twins. She envisioned shelves of jewel-colored homegrown fruits and vegetables. Ben dreamed of shrinking their loans after harvest.

Instead, the weather turned against them. Farm machinery broke and expenses mounted. Grain prices fell for no apparent reason. Beetles owned Katie's garden. Over coffee with Paige, Katie ranted and raved. How could God get them into a mess like this?

"Tough year." Paige put an arm around her. "But God will work it out."

Paige's optimism got on Katie's nerves. She and Jon were struggling, too, yet her freckled face usually wore a grin. Paige rediscovered God's sunset skies every day. She hummed praise songs as she helped Katie clean the barn. Paige didn't waste time and energy on negative living.

One day Katie decided to follow her example. "Lord, I still believe You brought us here. I guess it's time I trusted You, too."

Father, whether You meet my expectations or not, I know You love me. Help me to rely on You today. Amen.

Better is it that thou shouldest not vow,
than that thou shouldest vow and not pay.
Ecclesiastes 5:5 KJV

*W*hile scripture is clear that no one—man nor woman—can tame his or her own tongue, the Holy Spirit can help us guard our tongues and our speech. He can empower us to season our words so they give grace to the hearers. To exercise a kind tongue. To refrain from idle chatter. To think—and pray—before we speak.

And, most importantly, the Holy Spirit can help us to have integrity in our speech—to mean what we say and say what we mean.

Nowhere is this more important than in our homes with our children.

Children, who can forget our directions in a moment, will remember for weeks, months, and—sometimes—years that we made a promise we did not keep. And there are few things more heartbreaking than the face of a disappointed child.

Prayer is a powerful resource, helping us to obtain "wisdom from above," helping us to choose words that are "first pure, then peaceable, gentle, reasonable, full of mercy and good fruits, unwavering, without hypocrisy" (James 3:17 NASB).

With the help of the Holy Spirit, we have the power to keep little hearts tender by keeping our speech wise and true.

Holy Spirit, tame my tongue! Let my words be true and wise.
Let me say what I mean and mean what I say. Amen.

Poured-Out Blessings

For I will pour water upon him that is thirsty, and floods upon the dry ground: I will pour my spirit upon thy seed, and my blessing upon thine offspring.
Isaiah 44:3 KJV

*W*hat is more refreshing than a cold glass of water after vigorous exercise or hard work? What a pleasure it is to enjoy this natural beverage. Yet how often do we see that simple glass of water as a blessing from God? What about the cool grass beneath our feet or the shade tree under which we relax? When we teach our children to say "bird" or "bunny," do we acknowledge those creatures as delightful gifts from God?

God's blessings surround us. At times we realize they are there, but many of them are overlooked as common, everyday parts of life. We wonder why God isn't at work or doing more for us when in reality He is busy right before our eyes. We're just too distracted to notice. God is with His children. He meets our family's needs daily, and His gifts are wonderful. Let's teach our children to recognize and praise God's goodness. Perhaps as we do this, the scales will be lifted from our own eyes, and we will begin to see God's bounty for what it really is.

Dear God, Your blessings abound, but sometimes my eyes are closed to them. Help me to see Your great gifts that surround me.

Be Real

We all stumble in many ways.
James 3:2 NIV

$\mathcal{L}$et's face it. Let's stop pretending. Let's be real. We are not "super moms." Although we put on a great facade, many days the juggling act quickly turns disastrous. It happens to everyone. You are not alone, so why fake it? Let's admit that we don't have it all together. Motherhood is difficult, exhausting, and overwhelming at times. We need to be real with one another. We need encouragement. How does that happen?

Our identity must be found in Christ alone. It cannot come from our children, husband, friends, or career. When we desire the approval of others, we have to pretend to be something we're not. The Lord knows, accepts, and loves us just as we are: imperfect. When we embrace that truth, we can be ourselves before Him and feel safe in His love. Then we are free to be real with others. Humility and vulnerability become positive character traits rather than something we avoid.

When we dare put aside our "super mom" persona, the response from others is quite remarkable. Sensing a safe environment, they in turn open up to us. We have given them the freedom to be real. Mutual encouragement results when we pass on Christ's acceptance and love. Everyone is blessed when we are real.

Dear Lord, Your love is truly amazing. Help me grasp the unconditional love You have for me so that my relationships with others can be real. Amen.

Photo Editing

For he will be like a refiner's fire or a launderer's soap.
He will sit as a refiner and purifier of silver.
Malachi 3:2–3 NIV

*P*hotographs are taken when someone wants to preserve the memory of certain subjects or events that mean something special. The photographer looks through the camera, zooms in on the subject, and snaps the picture, allowing autofocus to sharpen the image as best it can. Even with a great subject, though, poor lighting, movement, or red eyes can cause a need for photo editing. After applying the right types of editing techniques, the photo will finally convey the image that the photographer was trying to capture.

When a chubby baby has ice cream smeared across her face, Mom takes a picture to preserve the memory of the pleasure of that first ice-cream cone. Others may look at that photo and think it's a disgusting mess, but to Mom it's a reminder of a time when she was able to give her child a new delight, and the photo captures that joy and abandon.

Are we open to editing from God? Do we present ourselves to Him to be cropped, brightened, clarified, and perfected? We are each His treasure, and He lovingly and carefully works to perfect His treasures. He loves to capture the joy and abandon on our faces each time He reveals a new pleasure to us or reveals something new about Himself.

Jesus, thank You for the refining fire of Your Spirit that works to perfect me. Continue to edit me until I am a fully refined reflection of Your image. Amen.

Learned Response

But thanks be to God! He gives us the victory through our Lord Jesus Christ.
I Corinthians 15:57 NIV

From the time they are babies, children can be very demanding. When they're hungry, tired, scared, or just needing comfort, they cry for attention. Babies don't ask politely for you to tend to them. They demand. Because they are unable to verbalize anything, this is the only way they know to get their needs fulfilled.

As our babies turn into toddlers and begin to talk, we want them to say "please" and "thank you." However, these polite ways of communicating aren't natural. We have to encourage them to learn by emphasizing how we speak to them, or by having our little ones repeat the necessary word. Because they desire to please us, our children are willing to learn the proper response.

Christians are to be thankful to God, and we should tell Him how appreciative we are. This is not an ingrained response, it is a learned one. As we mature in our faith, we can choose to become more and more demonstrative through our affection and our attitude. We should desire to please God by thanking Him for all he has done for us and will do for us. This attitude doesn't come overnight; it takes our willingness to learn.

Jesus, thank You for my victory over my old nature.
Help me to remember to thank You in all situations. Amen.

Listen Up!

"But whoever listens to me will live in safety and be at ease,
without fear of harm."
Proverbs 1:33 NIV

*L*isa watched her son, Logan, stop at the edge of the pond. She was far enough away that he couldn't see her but close enough that if he fell in, she'd have time to save him from drowning. Her heart beat faster as he slipped closer to the pond's edge. Once more he stopped. He turned his face toward the house and frowned. Then he again turned to face the water. Lisa could tell Logan debated whether to listen to her warnings about getting too close to the water. She held her breath.

Finally, he moved away from the bank and sat down under a big shady tree. She watched for several minutes as he played in the dirt. While his attention was focused on a bug, she walked to him.

"Hi, pumpkin." She sat down beside him.

He looked up at her with confused eyes. "Mommy, I was going to go swimming in the pond, but I heard a voice tell me not to. Was it you?"

"Not today, but I have asked you not to go the water before. Remember?" She studied his small face.

He poked at the bug with his stick and nodded. "I think it was God telling me."

"It probably was, Logan. Always listen to Him. Okay?"

"Okay, Mommy."

Sometimes I forget to listen for Your voice, Lord, as I make life-altering
decisions. Please remind me to always listen for Your voice,
even in the simple everyday things. Amen.

Don't Cry Over Spilled "Stuff"

Set your affection on things above, not on things on the earth.
Colossians 3:2 KJV

A chubby little cherub looked up at his mommy with horror on his face. He had toddled over to a chair, climbed up onto it, and pulled on a shelf that contained all of Mommy's pretty things. The shelf came tumbling down on top of him. He looked at his mom, not because of pain, but out of fear. His wise mom realized immediately that he was afraid he had disappointed her.

Even though she wanted him to learn safety and obedience, it was more important in that moment that she teach him that her love for him was far greater than any earthly thing she owned. As she reassured him of her love, he began to cry for another reason—he was hurt. He had scrapes and bruises, all marks of disobedience. But his heart was overjoyed because of his mother's genuine love.

We all disobey our Father at times, putting earthly things ahead of the things above. Disobedience always stems from a lack of trust in God's Word and promises. When we fully trust that what He says is true, obedience is natural. But when we do disobey, He is swift to teach us of our wrongdoing, after we are assured of His love.

Heavenly Father, please help me to never put the things of the world ahead of obeying You. Thank You for Your deep love for me and for constantly reassuring me of it. Amen.

Calloused Knees

Three times a day [Daniel] got down on his knees and prayed,
giving thanks to his God, just as he had done before.
Daniel 6:10 NIV

*J*ealous colleagues held a grudge against Daniel. He was a foreigner,
an exile, and yet Daniel was distinguished in the eyes of King Darius
of Persia. Finally, those wily colleagues found a loophole to trap
Daniel. A decree written into law by the Medes and Persians could
not be changed. They advised the king to issue an edict, punishable
by death, if anyone prayed to another god for the next thirty days.

Daniel knew that this document meant that if he prayed, he
would end up being thrown into a den of hungry lions. It was just
thirty days. He could pray silently, upright. Surely, God would
understand.

But Daniel didn't stop praying. Three times a day he bowed
down! He gave thanks to God, in the midst of his dire circumstances,
just as he always did. Daniel held great power in Babylon, and he
answered to the king—the greatest power in Persia. But Daniel knew
the real power was God's.

We need to emulate Daniel's steadfast habit of prayer. Whatever
our circumstances, wherever we are, in whatever position we find
ourselves, we take our thoughts, our concerns, our hopes to the real
source of power in our lives—our Lord. He has the power to shut
the lion's mouth.

Lord, teach me to pray like Daniel. Help me to have an attitude in my heart in
which I kneel before You, all day long, with thanksgiving and hope for my future.

A Desperate Mother's Need

*And my God will meet all your needs according
to his glorious riches in Christ Jesus.*
Philippians 4:19 NIV

*I*n 2 Kings 4:1–7, we read about a mother who was in desperate need because creditors were coming to take her two children from her as payment for debt. The prophet told the mother to borrow many empty vessels from neighbors and then pour her oil, the only resource she had in her home, into each vessel. She was encouraged to sell the oil-filled vessels, pay her debts, and live on the rest. This mother needed money to support her family. God used a more seasoned mentor, in this case Elisha, to provide guidance for her need.

Perhaps you desperately need encouragement or guidance on one of the many issues involved in raising a preschooler—discipline, self-control, obedience, patience, quarrel resolution, sleep, to name a few. Our Lord tells us that He will fully (not just partly) satisfy every need. "And God is able to make all grace abound to you, so that in all things at all times, having all that you need, you will abound in every good work" (2 Corinthians 9:8 NIV). God will not only provide, but He provides in such a gracious manner that we are then inspired to be the vessel that God uses to encourage others. Perhaps after God fully satisfies your need in abundance, you will be the vessel God uses to provide encouragement or guidance to another mother in desperate need.

*Thank You, Lord, for providing for my every need.
Use me to help provide for the needs of other mothers.*

Beholding Beauty

One thing I ask of the LORD, this is what I seek. . .
to gaze upon the beauty of the LORD and to seek him in his temple.
Psalm 27:4 NIV

*T*he mother tried to keep her irritation in check. She had much to do and no time to spend with her demanding toddler. Her chore list was long, and she had to complete her tasks. Instead of playing on his own, her son had been fussy all day.

We all have these days when we have much to accomplish, yet the children want more of our time than usual. Maybe they sense our busyness. Perhaps they are jealous that they can't have more of our time. Sometimes, though, we need to remember to take the time to sit with them, read a book, and enjoy the gift God has given us. Their youth will pass so quickly.

We can let life interfere if we aren't careful, getting so caught up in our job, church, and community that we forget to take time for God or our family. Prayer and Bible study become almost nonexistent. The opportunity to play with our toddlers is put off.

There is no more important job for a mother than to first spend time with God, and then take time with her family. Our chores will always be there when we can get back to them. Let's take the time today to seek the Lord, gaze on His beauty, and enjoy the loveliness of the family He has given us.

Lord, help me to remember to appreciate You every day. Amen.

Well Done, Servant

*"His master replied, 'Well done, good and faithful servant!
You have been faithful with a few things; I will put in you charge
of many things. Come and share your master's happiness!' "*
Matthew 25:21 NIV

*B*eing a mother to small children isn't always easy. Sometimes
mothers feel more like servants than cherished family members.
There are the sleepless nights, the overbooked schedules, and
constant chatter with little people whose sentences never exceed five
words. Although it doesn't always seem like it, this phrase certainly is
true: God never gives mothers more than what is manageable.

In fact, God has entrusted each mother with the number of
unique children she has for a reason. Mothers are the caretakers,
gifted by God to handle even the craziest day. But is it really worth
it? God says it is!

When Christ returns, every person—every mother—will give an
account for her life. She will have a chance to look back and see her
life, including her role as a mother. Did the time, energy, and love she
gave her children come from the responsibility and joy God gave her?

God gifted many women to be mothers. But with that calling
comes an even greater role: To be the King of kings' daughter and a
faithful servant who is promised overflowing happiness.

*Father, thank You for the children You have entrusted to me.
Help me to love and care for them as You care for me.*

Leapfrog

*God put our bodies together in such a way that even the parts that seem
the least important are valuable. He did this to make all parts of the body
work together smoothly, with each part caring about the others.*
I Corinthians 12:24–25 CEV

On all fours, one child patiently and trustingly waits. Running at
full speed, another child runs toward him, plants both hands on the
square of the first child's tense little back, catapults over the top of
his cowering head, and immediately takes the waiting position on all
fours. The cycle repeats itself over and over as the two children travel
forward together.

In the game of leapfrog, there is no hierarchy of pride that
says, "I'm better than that, so I won't do that part." If any one child
refused to take his turn, the game would end.

The body of Christ is designed in exactly the same way. We each
have a role, but we cannot play it alone. Every one of us needs the
support of others along the way if we are to travel forward on the
journey. We all must take our turns at supporting each other and at
receiving support for ourselves. God designed it this way so that we
would be one in purpose, one in Him.

*Father God, You have perfectly and beautifully designed Your body
to function as a unit. You desire that we join together in service to You.
Please forgive me for my pride and grant me the grace I need to
share with others and support them on this journey. Amen.*

Follow the Leader

O LORD, lead me in Your righteousness. . . .
Make Your way straight before me.
Psalm 5:8 NASB

*H*ave you ever observed your youngster playing follow the leader? There are only two roles in the game: leader and follower. Both parts are critical to the success of the game. The followers actually have the easier task, mimicking their playmate at the front of the line. The leader, however, must continually perform new actions and can lead the others astray.

Thankfully, as Christians, we have a Leader whom we can fully trust—one who will never lead us astray and always wants the best for us. Unlike human leaders, He does not take pride in His role as a leader. Remember Jesus washing His disciples' feet? Who wouldn't want to follow a leader like that?

It would seem that following our Leader should be an easy task, but because of our sinful nature, we often run ahead of Him, thinking that we can lead better than He can. Of course, we would never admit that verbally, but when we choose not to trust Him as our Leader, that message is obvious to God, as well as to others around us.

We know what kind of Leader we have; what kind of follower are you?

Lord Jesus, forgive me for the times that I have run ahead of You. I humbly ask for Your help in making me a patient and obedient follower of Yours. Amen.

Thank You, Mommy

*Because that, when they knew God, they glorified him not as God,
neither were thankful; but became vain in their imaginations,
and their foolish heart was darkened.*
Romans 1:21 KJV

*A*nd what do you tell Grandma for your new toy?" the mother
asked her small son.

"Thank you, Grandma."

Saying "thank you" sometimes seems trivial, but it is one of the
most important things a child can learn, because it is the first step in
learning thankfulness.

Thankfulness is fundamental to our relationship with God. A
thankful heart recognizes all that God gives and does in our lives.
In contrast, a proud heart ignores God and takes the credit for life's
accomplishments.

Unthankfulness is at the top of the sin spiral that Paul describes
in Romans 1. As sin waxes worse, pride and disobedience increase.

One way to stay humble and obedient to God is to continually
thank Him. And to instill this gift of thankfulness and obedience in
our children, how about making a habit of thanking God out loud?
And thanking others as well, thus giving our children examples as to
how they should behave. In fact, why not tell them how thankful we
are for them and for what they add to our lives? Not only today, but
every day?

Then, before we know it, our children will be thanking God out
loud and, hopefully, saying, "Thank you, Mommy," as well.

*Father God, thank You for these precious children You have given me.
Thank You for entrusting them to my care. May we all be thankful for
each other and for You, taking nothing and no one for granted. Amen.*

Abba, Father

For ye have not received the spirit of bondage again to fear;
but ye have received the Spirit of adoption, whereby we cry, Abba, Father.
Romans 8:15 KJV

How many times have you taken your child to day care or even Sunday school just to have her cling to your skirt? The fear of being left is almost more than she can bear. You tear yourself away from her, knowing that she'll be fine. With all of your heart you want to go back, gather her in your arms, and take her with you. As she calls out, "Mommy! Mommy!" you bend down to give her one last reassuring hug.

"You'll be fine, sweetheart. Mommy will be back in a while." You know that she's okay and that this will help her gain confidence, but you still long to erase her fears. You think about all that she will face in life and realize she'll encounter situations that are far more frightening than day care. You can help prepare her for these scary times, though. God wants to adopt her into His family. He is capable of alleviating the fears she'll face. It's not to say that He will eliminate the situation, but if her trust is in Him, she will go through fears and trials with confidence. Expose her to Christ's love while she is small. Pray that she will accept His salvation. Set the example of trusting God completely. It will be a great legacy to leave her.

Abba Father, how wonderful to have such a personal closeness to You!
Thank You for comforting me and my children during frightening times.

The Pull of Gravity

*Sitting down, He called the twelve and said to them, "If anyone
wants to be first, he shall be last of all and servant of all."*
Mark 9:35 NASB

*C*hristianity has been described as the upside-down world. Often,
it teaches the opposite of what comes naturally. We strongly dislike,
if not hate, our enemies. God says to love them. We try to sit up
front at special events. God says to take a backseat. On a chilly night,
we snugly wrap up in our warm coats. God says to remember those
without coats and share one of ours.

Jesus said, "The last will be first." Talk about working against
our basic nature! The appeal of self-centeredness in this world is as
strong as the pull of gravity. Just look at a classroom of preschoolers
trying to line up for snacks. Pushing, pulling, elbowing each other in
their fight to be first.

How can we teach our children Jesus' upside-down principles?
Even harder, how do we teach them that there is joy in servanthood?

In the loudest, most dramatic, and most effective way: quiet
modeling.

Ordinary life is where our children learn and practice their
lifelong conduct. They observe our attitudes and behavior every
single day. We can be the first to bring a meal to a sick friend, to pray
for those who offend us, to give away clothing to a homeless shelter.

Each day provides opportunities for moms to demonstrate, up
close and personal, the upside-down world of Christianity.

*Lord, open my eyes today to ways I can practice
Your upside-down, life-giving principles.*

Peace

For he himself is our peace.
Ephesians 2:14 NIV

Toddlers are prone to nightmares. Their active imaginations combined with their limited knowledge can create fear and anxiety. The sound of snoring becomes a roaring lion. Shadows turn into monsters. Suddenly, "Mommy!" echoes through the house. Although we may easily dismiss their fears, from our child's perspective they're legitimate. Calming words may not completely alleviate their anxiety. Yet as we lie down beside them in bed, they feel secure. They sense our protection. Our presence imparts peace.

Because we have limited knowledge and understanding compared to God, we can become frightened and anxious like our toddlers. Although God must marvel at our concerns, He knows we perceive them as real. Our husband's layoff is frightening even though God sees the new job awaiting him. We're anxious about our son's lack of control, yet God sees the mature adult he will become.

We cry out, "Lord, help! Come to me!" We fail to remember that He is always present. As believers, Jesus lives within us by the power of the Holy Spirit. Jesus is called the Prince of Peace. His presence brings peace to our hearts. When fearful thoughts and frightening circumstances overwhelm you, trust that the Lord is right beside you. Let His words comfort your heart. May His presence impart peace.

Dear Lord, Your thoughts and ways are so much higher than mine.
Help me remember that You are always with me so that
Your presence may impart peace. Amen.

Truth and Action

Dear children, let us not love with words or tongue but with actions and in truth. This then is how we know that we belong to the truth, and how we set our hearts at rest in his presence.
1 John 3:18–19 NIV

*C*rystal, a young mother, lived far from her biological family; however, God placed a Christian family within five minutes of her home. This family modeled Christ's love in tangible ways to Crystal and her preschooler—with availability, meals, and babysitting, to name a few. Crystal thanked God for this family.

God tells us that we are to tangibly, in truth and action, reflect God's love to those in need. "If someone has enough money to live well and sees a brother or sister in need but shows no compassion— how can God's love be in that person?" (1 John 3:17 NLT). As we love through meeting the needs of other mothers, they will see Christ in us—they will come to have a clearer depiction of who Christ is. We receive the blessing of knowing we are from the truth and our hearts are assured and comforted. As the Lord's Word tells us, "faith by itself isn't enough. Unless it produces good deeds, it is dead and useless" (James 2:17 NLT). We can model for our preschooler how to live out our faith in Christ through good works. Identify a mother who has a specific need, and in partnership with your preschooler, meet that need. Discuss with your preschooler how the Lord used you to help, in truth and action, reflect His character of love.

Lord, help me to teach my preschooler how to live out faith with good works through truth and action.

Patient Encouragement

"It was I who taught Ephraim to walk, taking them by the arms. . . .
I led them with cords of human kindness, with ties of love;
I lifted the yoke from their neck and bent down to feed them."
Hosea 11:3, 4 NIV

Teaching a young child a new skill takes love, patience, and a very positive attitude. The toddler can become discouraged as he tries to fold his clothes, make his bed, or even learn to use a spoon to feed himself. Each new experience is a chance to encourage our preschooler.

When he makes a mistake, his mother can make the difference in his learning experience. As mothers we can chastise or show anger and impatience, sending a message to the child that he isn't worthy of our love and time. However, when we demonstrate our love by helping him to try again, our toddler will blossom and grow to his full potential. He will learn to trust us and his learned abilities.

When we become Christians, God is the One who teaches us to be like Him. His love encompasses us, and if we feel worthless after making a mistake, that emotion doesn't come from God. He pulls us to Him and holds us close. He uses affection to urge us to try again. His love and patience toward us are beyond expression.

God, thank You for Your example of how I should be with my child.
Thank You for Your tender love and care for me. Amen.

Together Is Better

Two are better than one; because they have a good reward for their labour.
Ecclesiastes 4:9 KJV

*W*hen God made humans, he made them male and female.

The woman was man's helper. Together, they were to be fruitful, to multiply, to fill and subdue the earth, and to have dominion over creation.

In the beginning, two were better than one.

At the beginning of marriage, we operate according to this truth. But then children come. And everything changes.

Although the greatest role shift is that of the woman, the role of the man changes, too. As new fathers, men may feel a greater drive to provide for their family. At the same time, they may be learning how to change diapers and bathe an infant. Talk about pressure!

Meanwhile, as new mothers, we may become consumed with everything we must do for the children.

Because we spend so much time attending to them, we may begin to think we are totally responsible for the little ones and the family, and are "doing it all alone."

But in reality, moms and dads are in it together, partners in this new family they have cocreated. Although Mom may be spending more time with the children, Dad plays an important and necessary role, too. He is the head of the household, and Mom is the manager.

As we love and honor each other in our respective roles, we are teaching our children to do the same.

And as we "at the top work together," our family becomes stronger.

Two are truly better than one.

Father, thank You for my husband. Help us to work together as parents and to love and honor each other as individuals. And, Lord, help him to be the family leader You intend him to be. Amen.

Teach Them to Pray

*Then Jesus told his disciples a parable to show
them that they should always pray and not give up.*
NIV

*O*nce upon a time, a long time ago, a little boy wanted a pet. He would ask God for a puppy, and God would tell him no. Every day he asked for the puppy. Finally, one day, God decided he was old enough and responsible enough to have his own pet. But God made him promise to take care of it. To feed it, bathe it, and most importantly to play with the puppy. The little boy agreed, and God gave him a puppy. The little boy was very happy, and he took good care of his new pet."

Marlo smiled up at his mom. "That was a good story."

"Why do you think the Lord gave the boy a puppy?"

"'Cause God loved him?"

His mother smiled at him. "Oh yes, God loves little boys very much. But did you notice that the boy in the story kept asking?"

Marlo nodded. "Uh-huh."

"I think it was because the boy prayed and asked God over and over. He never gave up, and when he was old enough, God gave him what he asked for."

"I like that."

"Me, too." His mother kissed him and turned off the light.

*Thank You, Lord, for teaching us how to pray and teach through parables.
My children understand lessons so much better when they come in the form
of stories. Please be with me as we learn about You together. Amen.*

The Sting

O death, where is thy sting? O grave, where is thy victory?
1 Corinthians 15:55 KJV

An excited young family was traveling down the road on vacation.
Suddenly, a yellow jacket flew in through a rolled-down car window!
Immediately the children started screaming hysterically. The father
quickly reached up and caught the bee in his fist. After a few seconds
he let it go and exclaimed, "Children, you don't have to worry now.
The bee has stung me. Now it can never sting again."

What a beautiful picture of Jesus' willingness to die on the
cross. He suffered the sting of death on our behalf and rose from
the grave so that we might receive the gift of eternal life. Easter is
the celebration of this new life Christ has given us. Physical death no
longer represents the end, but the beginning. Like Jesus, we, too, will
experience victory over the grave.

We also desire to experience victorious living today. Many
situations can frighten us: a sick child, a job loss, or marital stress.
Yet the Lord does not want us to panic like the children in the car.
He wants us to realize that because He has overcome our greatest
fear—death—He can handle anything that confronts us. That truth
should set our hearts at rest. That truth should bring peace to our
souls. That truth should transform our lives. Remember, there is no
more sting.

Dear Lord, please forgive me when I panic and become frightened.
Help me remember to trust You. Amen.

A Decade Friendship

A friend loves you all the time, and a brother helps in time of trouble.
Proverbs 17:17 NCV

There was something special about their friendship. As high school teens, Melissa and Hannah had made a deal.

"Even if we're married and have children someday, we'll still make time to talk and see each other."

"Deal."

Now, ten years later, Melissa and Hannah were still making good on their promise. Their husbands had graciously agreed to take the children for the day. So they sat in the coffee shop, sipping on their drinks and nibbling on freshly baked scones. They lived more than an hour apart, so seeing each other regularly wasn't exactly convenient. Still, their friendship was a priority.

Melissa loved that even though they might go months without seeing each other, they were able to pick up exactly where they'd left off. Hannah loved that even in the middle of a rather stressful day, she could call Melissa or send an e-mail asking for prayer. That was what their friendship was all about. Even in the midst of life's busyness, they had made a point to know when to rest and receive a recharge.

Honest sharing, chitchat, and even laughter were the keys. Then when their time together would come to a close, they'd savor the last sips of their coffee and pray together. They were eager to return to their families, but not without first planning a date to see each other again.

*Jesus, thank You for "kindred spirit" friends. Even though I enjoy
my girlfriend time, my truest and most immediate friend is You.*

Nameless Dreads

He won't let you stumble, your Guardian God won't fall asleep.
Not on your life! Israel's Guardian will never doze or sleep.
God's your Guardian, right at your side to protect you.
Psalm 121:4–5 MSG

*W*hy do fears pop up in the middle of the night, when there's nothing we can do about them anyway? Nameless dreads, anxieties about the unknown, bundles of what-ifs? Such as. . .

What if my little boy drives his car one day like he drives his Big Wheel now? Reckless and out of control. Or. . .

Will my little girl ever separate from me calmly, or will it always feel as if I'm trying to pry a Velcro-like attachment off my leg when the babysitter arrives? What will happen when she starts school? Will I have to go with her?

Those fears may seem silly, but God takes fearfulness seriously. He doesn't want us to raise our children gripped by what-ifs, frightened by the future, scared of the evening news. "Never will I leave you; never will I forsake you," God told the author of the book of Hebrews (Hebrews 13:5 NIV). Never!

God wants us to fear wisely. When we wake up in the night with a nameless dread, seek His guidance. Ask for discernment. Is this feeling a warning from God? Or is it a faithless fret? If it's the latter, dismiss the fear and replace it with praise for God's presence. Don't fret or worry. Instead of worrying, pray (Philippians 4:6).

Thank You, Lord, that You are always on call to hear my prayers. Teach me to say with confidence: "The Lord is my helper; I will not be afraid."

Identity Crisis

. . .among whom you also are the called of Jesus Christ.
Romans 1:6 NASB

*I*dentity can be an ever-evolving thing. Most women, at one time in their lives, have been a daughter, sister, friend, wife, and, sometimes, all of those things at the same time. When those women have children, they become Mom: cook, housekeeper, babysitter, diaper changer, etc.

Your true personal identity, though, is none of those things. Those are simply descriptions of roles that you fill. You are the called of Jesus Christ. You have been set apart and called by Him into the family of God. You are His Child. That is your true identity. There is nothing any person can do to take that away from you. There are no life circumstances that will alter that identity and no way that any amount of years will cause it to fade.

Begin to see yourself as He sees you. It will make your purpose so much clearer, and your roles will take on a new meaning. There need not be grief as one stage of life moves into the next, nor should there be longing for the next stage or regret over times of the past. You are a child of God. Your true identity will never change.

Jesus, thank You for calling out to me and making me Your own. Help me to realize my true identity in You, and help me to not make my roles more important than that identity to which You have called me. Amen.

True Identity

*God. . .who hath blessed us. . .hath chosen us in him. . .that we should
be holy and without blame. . . . Having predestinated us unto the adoption
of children. . .hath made us accepted in the beloved. In whom we
have redemption. . .the forgiveness of sins.*
Ephesians 1:3–7 KJV

Christie grew up believing lies she was continually told about
who she was. . ."dumb, fat, ugly, and unlovable." She felt worthless.
Christie did not believe God could use someone like her.

What we teach our children about who they are starts at a very
young age. We need to establish a foundation of truth regarding our
children's identity before they hear the lies that TV, advertisements,
radio, and even other children tell them. The very being who
created us in our mother's womb (Psalm 139: 13) establishes this
foundation by clearly articulating who we are. We must teach them
that in Christ, we have been blessed. God Himself chose us before
the foundation of the world to be holy and without blame. That
means we have been "set apart" to be used by God. We have been
consecrated and sanctified for the purposes for which God created us.
We are God's children, adopted into His family, accepted, redeemed,
and forgiven. There is no sin or past failure that God will not forgive
when we ask Him (1 John 1:9). Who else but a loving God would
send His one and only Son to die on the cross for our salvation
(John 3:16).

*My Creator God, thank You that You have told me who I am. Use me for
Your created purposes as I help my children find their true identities in You.*

A Child's View of Heaven

"The beloved of the LORD shall dwell in safety by Him, who shelters him all the day long; and he shall dwell between His shoulders."
Deuteronomy 33:12 NKJV

*W*hen asked what heaven is like, children usually say it is full of singing angels and harps. Sometimes they envision clouds that people sit upon when they aren't using their feathery wings to fly. They rarely say that there will be no hunger, no sadness, no sickness, no pain. They don't realize that heaven, the presence of God, is the absence of those painful things because they haven't experienced them yet. They have rested safe and sound in the shelter of their mother's arms, protected and loved.

Our heavenly Father knows the sadness and pain that we have experienced and witnessed in this fallen world. He longs to comfort us in the shadow of His wings and remind us that in His presence there is fullness of joy and the absence of pain. We may suffer effects of the things of the world, but those effects are temporary. As children of God, we are promised eternal peace and joy in the presence of Christ. When that realization takes hold in our hearts, the pain of today fades quickly away in anticipation of what awaits us.

Father, thank You for being a shield around me that protects me from the effects of the world. In Your presence, I can find true joy and peace. Help me to be a shelter and a haven for my children. Please keep us close to You always. Amen.

MP3 Players

*"It is not what enters into the mouth that defiles the man,
but what proceeds out of the mouth, this defiles the man."*
Matthew 15:11 NASB

MP3 players are a staple of the twenty-first century. They come in all shapes, sizes, and colors. But one thing is standard for them all: What goes in is always what comes out. An MP3 player doesn't manufacture its own sounds or create a new song. It only replays the information that it receives.

Children are like living, breathing MP3 players. They stand ready at every moment to receive new data from Mom. They store the newly collected information in steel memory banks that never fail to recall every detail. They cannot be rebooted, and they can never be filled to capacity.

We must be very careful about the things to which we expose our children. What they hear and see cannot be erased. The information gets processed and stored, and it shapes the way they see things forever. Every moment of every day is a learning experience for them. We must choose carefully what they are learning from our words and actions. What goes into those precious minds will, one day, come out.

*Jesus, please help me to protect the eyes and ears of my children.
Help me to know when they need to be shielded from the world.
Give me Your wisdom as I try to be an example of You to them. Amen.*

Choosing Words Carefully

Be pleasant and hold their interest when you speak the message.
Choose your words carefully.
Colossians 4:6 CEV

Some days, as a result of endless chatter and the many "why?"
questions, exasperation can set in. At times, it's easy for a mom
to tune out the prattle, opting to focus on her task at hand. But
conversation with our youngsters is vital for their educational,
mental, emotional, and spiritual development.

Not only do kids learn by talking, but by listening to the words
spoken around them. The influence of those words can gladden or
grieve young hearts and spirits.

The words moms use can be vital examples of pure, godly speech
for their children. The Bible instructs us to "be pleasant" as we speak
and to "choose [our] words carefully." It is important to think before
releasing our words, because they can never be taken back.

In the everyday routine, as well as during times of godly teaching,
select words that will build up your little one. This practice is not
only for their encouragement, but also for their training in how
God desires that they speak to others. Your words can carry God's
message to their little ears!

Lord Jesus, please control my tongue as I speak today.
Let my words be ones that would please You and build my child up. Amen.

Starting Out Right

*Hallelujah! Blessed man, blessed woman, who fear G*OD*, who cherish
and relish his commandments, their children robust on the earth,
and the homes of the upright—how blessed!*
Psalm 112:2 MSG

$\mathcal{M}$adeline Levine, author of *The Price of Privilege*, spoke to a group
of high school parents about improving parenting skills. In her
counseling practice, she had discovered that the time to try to "fix"
parents or teach them parenting skills isn't when they have teenagers,
but when they first become parents. That is when they are most
pliable and open to change.

Most likely, we initially recognize our limitations when we
become a parent for the first time. As our infant is placed in
our arms, we feel helpless! Stunned, we are in awe of the great
responsibility God has bestowed upon us. Our hearts are at their
softest. This sweet, overwhelming love for our child brings an acute
vulnerability.

God loves a tender, teachable heart! The early years of parenting
create wonderful opportunities to grow and mature in our faith and
in our parenting skills. Read good books. Seek out worthy mentors.
Attend parenting classes at church. As we seek His wisdom to give
us guidance and solve sticky problems, He promises to be right
alongside of us. He gives us hope for a wonderful future.

Because when we are weak, God is strong. What a blessing!

*Lord, Your very presence brings peace to our home and my heart.
We dedicate our home and our lives to You. Give us teachable hearts
so that we may raise our little ones in the light of Your wisdom.*

Recognizing the Cries

I wait patiently for the LORD; he turned to me and heard my cry.
Psalm 40:1 NIV

The conference would be a weeklong event. The thirty-year-old mother sat in her assigned dorm room and eagerly awaited her roommate. It was Dawn's first time out of state and away from home in she didn't know how long. With a preschooler at home and another child just beginning to crawl, the conference wasn't just about a subject she'd personally come to love, but about being away from home for the first time.

When her roommate arrived, Dawn chatted nonstop about all the wonderful things they would get to do together that week. But the next morning when her roommate asked how she had slept, her response was, "I kept waking up, thinking I heard my kids!" Since the mother wasn't accustomed to being away from home, she had no idea that she had trained herself to listen for her children at night. She knew that her husband was taking care of the children and that they were safe, but doors opening and closing and footsteps in the dorm hallway woke her the first night and the second and the third. . .

Like a mother listening for her children, God hears our cries. His heart is constantly tuned to even our deepest hurts and fears. He never takes a break, never sleeps, and never watches from a distance or even the next room. Instead, He turns to us and acknowledges our needs with tender love.

Lord, thank You for being there for me when I need You—day or night.
You always know just what I need.

Good Grocery Store Behavior

*But thou, O LORD, art a shield for me; my glory,
and the lifter up of mine head.*
Psalm 3:3 KJV

*A*ndrea checked her grocery list. She fed three-year-old Clinton and baby Lauren, took Clinton to the potty, then buckled both children into their car seats and drove to the store. Clinton only bumped Andrea's ankles three times as he "helped" push the grocery cart. Lauren cooed at smiling passersby. Andrea could not hide a proud grin. Her beautiful little ones could have graced a magazine cover.

Until Clinton spotted a "big boy" gun in a toy display. When Andrea told him no, he couldn't have that toy, her model child threw a fit. Her efforts to discipline him only made Clint shriek louder. Lauren began a nonstop wail. A man near them whipped his cart around and took off as if insulted. Andrea felt other shoppers' glares as she tried to quiet her children. She wanted to leave, but began grabbing formula, diapers, and other dire necessities instead.

Lord, please help me!

No angels appeared, but peace began to settle over Andrea like a warm blanket. Although her children still fussed, she held her head high as she pushed her cart toward the checkout line. Others may not have realized she was doing the best she could, but Jesus knew.

*Oh, Lord, I'm so glad You welcome all Your children, even when
we're not at our best. When others don't behave well, teach me to
show them the same kindness. Amen.*

Teach the Word

Set your hearts unto all the words which I testify among you this day, which ye shall command your children to observe to do, all the words of this law.
Deuteronomy 32:46 KJV

The preschool age is prime time for learning. How often do you sit back and watch as your child absorbs everything in the world around her? She is curious and excited about the things she is learning. That is why it is so important to begin sharing God's Word with her. She is not too young to be introduced to Bible stories and songs. She is even able to begin memorizing short passages of scripture.

This world has a definite agenda, and it is not based on the Bible. Satan wants to sway as many souls as he can. He begins while your children are very small, but you don't have to let him win. The Word of God is more powerful than anything Satan can hurl at you. God will bless you as you faithfully pray for your child and teach her scriptural truths.

It's more than a head knowledge, though. God not only expects you to teach your child what the Bible says, He also expects you and your child to live by it. Make a daily effort to set a godly example and to biblically train your child.

Wise God, help me to use Your Word to prepare my child for Satan's inevitable attacks. We want to learn and live by Your truths.

Mindful Prayer

"I pray for them. I am not praying for the world,
but for those you have given me, for they are yours."
John 17:9 NIV

The mother sat at the table, looking up a number to call a friend. When she picked up her fussy toddler, the child quit crying and began to turn the pages of the phone book. The young girl ran her finger down the page. She stopped, bowed her head, and began mumbling, interspersing Jesus' name. Once again she ran her finger down the list of names, stopping on a different one, and speaking a prayer only God could understand.

When we look at the plight of the world, we are often overwhelmed with all the needs. There aren't enough hours in the day to pray for everyone. Even Jesus did not pray for all the world, but for those God had given to Him.

God gives each of us people to pray for at different times. Sometimes we hear of needs when someone requests prayer. Other times we begin to think of a person we know, whom we haven't thought of in a while. Their name is on our mind, giving us an opportunity to bring that person before God even when we don't know their need. We may not see the blessings or protection our prayers can bring to those God has given us, but we can trust that we are doing God's will.

Jesus, thank You for Your example as I pray for
those Your Holy Spirit brings to mind. Amen.

A Joyful Harvest

They that sow in tears shall reap in joy.
Psalm 126:5 KJV

*T*he home is a greenhouse; the mother, a gardener.

Like a good gardener, a mother prepares the home soil with encouragement, compassion, and good home cooking so that each of her plants will grow strong and true.

She nourishes their bodies, souls, and spirits, always considering the needs of each tender seedling. One may need extra love; another, extra patience; another, laughter.

She guards her plants jealously, praying always for their protection from dangerous friendships, poor choices, and other weeds that threaten to choke life from them.

Yet despite her faithfulness, she cannot control their growth. Some flourish with little effort, while others need more attention. As she labors, she often becomes weary and worn. She sweats and cries over them, praying always that the Master Gardener will water them with wisdom and truth.

Often when He does intervene, the mother-gardener is tried. Her vines may be pruned or her seedlings transplanted. Sometimes He'll allow weeds to grow, and it's all she can do to keep her hands away, to stay out of the marvelous work that He is doing.

But she trusts the hand of the Master Gardener.

And waits for a joyful harvest.

You have given me tender plants to nurture, Father. Sometimes the gardening is difficult because Satan wants to destroy what You have planted. Often I find myself watering the crops with tears. Remind me that You will always return that investment with a joyful harvest. Amen.

A Simpler Life

"Whoever becomes simple and elemental again,
like this child, will rank high in God's kingdom."
Matthew 18:4 MSG

*L*ouise looked out the window to where her child, Marty, amused himself under a tall oak tree. He played quietly with his toys. They weren't high-tech toys, just simple cars and trucks. Marty had created roads in the dirt and set up rocks to represent houses and stores. He placed clumps of grass beside the roads to symbolize trees. He smiled at some secret thought, and Louise found herself wishing that her life were as carefree as a child's.

She thought of the pile of dishes that needed to be done and the loads of laundry waiting to be washed and folded. Then, while Marty slept, she'd go to the hospital to work a twelve-hour shift. When had her life become so busy? All Louise knew was that her baby was now a preschooler, and she wanted to enjoy precious time with him.

Have you been feeling the stress of a superbusy life? Go to the Lord and ask Him to reveal to you what is essential. He will show you how to live at a slower pace, and He will invite you to give your cares to Him.

Dear heavenly Father, please reveal to me some things that I can
remove from my to-do list. I want a simpler life in You. Amen.

Excessive Materialism

Keep your lives free from the love of money and be content with what you have,
because God has said, "Never will I leave you; never will I forsake you."
Hebrews 13:5 NIV

*R*ebecca's heart's desire was to stay at home with her children. Her husband and she did not know how they could make ends meet if she quit her job. After reviewing needs and wants, developing a budget, and spending much time on their knees in prayer, the Lord asked them to "walk by faith, not by sight" (2 Corinthians 5:7 NASB).

Jesus tells us that the greatest commandment is to love God with all our heart, soul, and mind (Matthew 22:37). We cannot serve two masters, God and money (Matthew 6:24). "For the love of money is a root of all sorts of evil, and some by longing for it have wandered away from the faith and pierced themselves with many griefs" (1 Timothy 6:10 NASB). These passages certainly do not mean that all women should become stay-at-home moms; however, they do encourage us to ensure that our family's financial decisions are founded on God's principles. Our culture calls us to satisfy our materialistic desires with more and more things, often creating a tension that blurs the distinction between luxuries and needs. God calls us to be freed up from materialism, to be satisfied with what we have, and to remember that He is our Jehovah-Jireh, our Provider.

Lord, help me to not be wooed into a pursuit of excessive
materialism over Your will for my family and me.

Today's Focus

"Who of you by worrying can add a single hour to his life?"
Matthew 6:27 NIV

Two young mothers were next-door neighbors. Stephanie had a rambunctious three-year-old boy, and Jenn had a two-year-old. Stephanie would often warn Jenn of what she could expect from her child, Justin, at the next developmental stage. "Just wait until Justin turns three!" Stephanie would lament. Jenn began to dread the future. Yet as time passed, she began to realize that reality was not as ominous as she had feared. Needless anxiety had been robbing her of time, energy, and enjoyment.

Worrying about the future is counterproductive. Fretting does not affect future events. Anxiety does not alter tomorrow. However, worry and anxiety rob us of joy today. If our mind is absorbed with fear of the future, we are unable to enjoy the present moment. Living an abundant life today is impossible if we are focused on the unknowns of tomorrow. Worry prevents us from acknowledging God's blessings.

Rather than fearing tomorrow, have faith in the Lord today. Focus on Him and the blessings He has bestowed. Trust that He will take care of tomorrow and all that comes with it. Faith displaces fear and worry. The Lord has our future in His hands. Let's leave the future with Him so that we can live today to its fullest.

Dear Lord, forgive me for my tendency to worry and dread about what tomorrow might hold. Help me to trust You wholeheartedly. Impart peace to my heart. Amen.

In His Time

Then Jesus told them plainly, "Lazarus is dead! I am glad that I wasn't there, because now you will have a chance to put your faith in me. Let's go to him."
John 11:14–15 CEV

$\mathcal{M}$artha, Mary, and their brother, Lazarus, were close, personal friends of Jesus. When Lazarus fell ill, they sent for Jesus, believing that He could heal their brother. But Jesus was too late! When He finally arrived, Lazarus had already been dead for four days, and Martha was upset. She knew that if He had been there, her brother would have lived.

Jesus said, "I am the resurrection and the life. He who believes in Me, though he may die, he shall live. And whoever lives and believes in Me shall never die. Do you believe this?" (John 11:25–26 NKJV). Martha didn't quite understand, so Jesus said, "Lazarus, come forth!" (John 11:43 NKJV), and her brother came out of the tomb. Martha had been seeking a physical healing because, in her limited understanding, she just wanted Lazarus alive. But Jesus wanted a resurrection.

Sometimes we limit God by expecting Him to work according to our timetables and expectations, which are always based on our limited understanding. Thankfully, God will not be put under our time constraints or held to our schedules. Therefore, there will be times when our circumstances don't make sense. Even then, we need to trust Him and thank Him for having bigger and better plans than we could ever conceive.

Jesus, thank You for knowing my needs so intimately that You work things on Your schedule, not mine. Help me to remember that and accept it without grumbling. Amen.

Child of Grace

The LORD thy God in the midst of thee is mighty; he will save, he will rejoice
over thee with joy; he will rest in his love, he will joy over thee with singing.
Zephaniah 3:17 KJV

Kendra hauled Thom to a time-out corner, clasping him in an iron grip while he howled and kicked. Kendra looked at the clock. Not yet 9:00 a.m. Days like these made her wish she had remained single.

A gorgeous baby with big blue eyes and a sideways smile, little Thom changed overnight after his second birthday. He methodically destroyed the house. His biting habit made it impossible for Kendra to take him to playgroups or the church nursery.

This morning, Thom tried to flush Bob the cat down the toilet. Soppy and cold, Kendra and Thom now sat in the time-out corner until he finally quieted. Kendra wiped his runny nose—and Thom's rage erupted all over again.

Lord, can I give him away?

At the thought, her arms tightened around him. Though his diaper erupted with unspeakable odors and he buried his nasty nose in her neck, Kendra knew she would never, ever give Thom up. Instead, she held him close and sang to him.

In the Old Testament, God's chosen people seemed anything but a holy nation. They threw endless tantrums and disgraced His name. Yet He remained faithful and even rejoiced over them.

Lord Jesus, I often come to You like an obstinate, dirty, smelly two-year-old,
yet You hold me on Your lap. Thank You for loving me. Amen.

Joy in God's Word

*Thy words were found, and I did eat them; and thy word
was unto me the joy and rejoicing of mine heart:
for I am called by thy name, O LORD God of hosts.*
Jeremiah 15:16 KJV

Children have amazing ears. You might think that you can sneak a
forbidden snack without their knowledge, but you will soon learn the
truth. No matter where the children are in the house, if you open the
cupboard for a piece of candy or a few chips, they will come running.
They have begun to realize that those treats bring a few moments
of savory pleasure. You must share or risk becoming the "mean
mommy."

Have your children discovered even more joy in the delightful
words of the Bible? While you might wish to horde that last brownie,
you ought to always share God's Word with your little ones. It
should be a special time filled with praise for God and love for one
another.

When you are excited about a truth you find in scripture, your
children will pick up on that. They will begin to understand that
God's Word is the sweetest pleasure they will ever enjoy. Maybe as
you share a snack of cookies and milk, you can learn a verse together.
What a wonderful way to share God's Word with your little ones!

*Father, Your Word is delightful.
Help my children and me to savor it together.*

Blind Trust

And thine ears shall hear a word behind thee, saying,
This is the way, walk ye in it.
Isaiah 30:21 ASV

*T*oddlers have a mind of their own. They can have every intention of going in the direction their mother tells them, but the instant they see something interesting, all other intentions are lost in the desire to investigate. Preschoolers are impulsive and love to see new and interesting things that catch their eye, even if that puts them in danger.

Our children want to know for sure that the path we're taking them on is the right one to follow. When they can't see for sure, they have to learn to trust us. This takes a multitude of patience on the mother's part. We have to be willing to repeat our directions and hope that our children will learn to listen.

God is always with us, giving us directions on which path to follow. The lure of the world can entice us to take an excursion along a route that is different than the one God has for us. When this happens, we can be in danger, physically and spiritually. We must train our ear to hear God's voice. He doesn't shout directions. When we are still and quiet, listening for Him, we will hear the way He has for us. We no longer have to fret about anything, but can rest in His decisions.

Thank You, Lord, for caring about every step I take.
Please help me to hear You. Amen.

*He who began a good work in you will carry
it on to completion until the day of Christ Jesus.*
Philippians 1:6 NIV

*J*enny didn't feel she had adequate Bible knowledge to be able to teach her preschooler the Bible. There were even times in raising her preschooler that she had questions about what to do. She desired people with whom she could discuss her child-rearing ideas and learn what worked for other mothers.

God promises that He will complete the work of growing us spiritually. When we accepted the Lord Jesus as our personal Savior (John 3:16), the Holy Spirit began to live in us. That Holy Spirit empowers us to understand what God is teaching us as He matures us spiritually (John 14:26). Our Christian walk is a process of growing into the image of Christ. As imperfect individuals in a fallen world, it is no wonder that sometimes we feel inadequate in our Bible knowledge and our ability to apply it.

There is no course in being the perfect mother, so it is no wonder we sometimes feel inadequate in raising our preschoolers. But God provides solutions through the body of Christ. We can join a Bible study for moms, take a parenting class, and read Christian books on raising preschoolers—all will assist us in growing spiritually and as mothers. Rest assured, God will complete the good work that He has begun in us.

*Lord, lead me to the Christ-centered resources You provide in growing me
spiritually and as a mother to raise my child for Your glory.*

Blessed Are You

*Blessed are ye, when men shall revile you, and persecute you,
and shall say all manner of evil against you falsely, for my sake.*
Matthew 5:11 KJV

*A*ll who will live godly in Christ Jesus will be persecuted.
All.

That includes the dear mother who has chosen to work while
raising her children, the one who has decided to be a full-time stay-
at-home mom, and all the moms in between.

Although some people will disagree with the choices we make,
that's okay. God has a plan for our lives. All He asks is that we love
Him and our children, raising them up in His Word. When we do, we
will be rewarded for our faithfulness. Our husbands and children will
rise up and call us "blessed"!

Take heart as you follow God's leading. He will turn the negative
words of the world into a positive blessing in your life.

Keep to the task, following God above all else. Ask Him to help
you make vital decisions that affect you and your family. Speak the
truth about motherhood in love. And in the end, you will shine as a
light in a dark world.

*Father, sometimes the world makes me doubt Your perfect plan for me.
Help me to be faithful to my calling, knowing that I am, and will be, blessed.
No matter what my situation, bless my work and my family. Amen.*

Authenticity:
The Fruit of a Changed Heart

Pure gold put in the fire comes out of it proved pure; genuine faith put through this suffering comes out proved genuine. When Jesus wraps this all up, it's your faith, not your gold, that God will have on display as evidence of his victory.
I Peter 1:7 MSG

The dictionary defines authenticity as having a verifiable origination. It also claims that authenticity is never copied or counterfeit. A heart truly changed by God will be verifiable. Its conduct will never contradict its words, and it will clearly reveal who authored its change.

When a woman has genuine faith in God, she will absolutely trust what He says and will irrevocably and undeniably surrender her life to Him. When actions call faith into question, that faith must be examined for its depth. When weakened resolve leads to poor choices and sinful mistakes, repentance, renewed focus, and prayer will always strengthen and rebuild that diminished faith.

We can tell whether or not our authenticity reveals that the Lord is our God by what our acquaintances say about us. When we are truly living as servants and children of God, there is no question of the origination and author of our faith. We are living evidences of His victory and His grace, and others will testify to that.

*Father, let me be a living testimony of the faith You have authored within me.
I want Your light to shine so brightly from me that there could
be no question of its origin. Amen.*

Overflowing Joy

[The Lord God says] And the redeemed of the Lord shall return and come with singing to Zion; everlasting joy shall be upon their heads. They shall obtain joy and gladness, and sorrow and sighing shall flee away.
Isaiah 51:11 AMP

*K*ristina knew the midautumn walk would do her son and her some good. The week had been extremely hard, especially on five-year-old Brian. Kristina's father had died of cancer three days earlier. As a single mother, Kristina found the loss exceptionally difficult. Her father had been the boy's best friend.

The two stepped outside into cool air and crunching leaves underfoot. Brian was less talkative than usual, so Kristina practiced her father's eulogy silently. She would give it tomorrow. The man was a believer, so she had reassurance that her father had no pain and was in Jesus' arms. Still, her sorrow was enough to make her find the nearest park bench and sit.

Kristina brushed a runaway tear from her cheek as Brian attempted to put a short arm around her shoulder. Kristina glanced at her son and saw that he was staring intensely at a tree.

"What are you looking at?" she asked.

Brian offered her a half smile.

How much can a five-year-old really understand about death? Kristina wondered.

"I think that tree is clapping, Mommy. It's clapping for Grandpa because he is forever happy. I think we should be excited, too."

Kristina looked at the tree and noticed how the sweeping wind caused the leaves to dance. She chuckled, now having the perfect ending for her father's eulogy.

Father, thank You for preparing my eternal home and for helping me find joy amid sorrow.

Playing House

By this we may know that we are in him: whoever says he abides
in him ought to walk in the same way in which he walked.
1 John 2:5–6 ESV

Children love to play house, but they often argue over who gets to play the much-coveted role of Mom. Once they decide whose turn it is, they begin to act out home life as they have interpreted it. A lot can be learned by the way a child acts when pretending to be Mom. We can watch and, from their actions, we can discover what they have learned from ours.

As moms, and as Christians, we are called to be models of Jesus Christ. This is true for our worldly relationships and our relationships at home. It's easy to become complacent and comfortable, taking out our frustrations on those who are closest to us—our family members—because they love us and will forgive our shortcomings. But Jesus wants us to treat them with behavior that shows them how important they are to us, not dump our anger and disappointments on them by snapping at them or being crabby.

Instead of giving our families whatever is leftover after the rest of the world gets the best of us, let's resolve to make them our number one priority, giving them the best we have to offer.

Jesus, I want to live my life as an example of how You lived Yours.
Help me to treat my family in the same way You would treat them.
Let me be an extension of You. Amen.

The Geese in Our Gaggle

A friend loves at all times.
Proverbs 17:17 NIV

There are a number of reasons that geese fly in a *V* formation. The formation conserves energy. The geese face less wind resistance, receiving a boost from those flying in front. The farther back a goose is in formation, the less energy it needs in the flight.

An additional benefit to the *V* formation is that it is easy to keep track of every bird in the group. Fighter pilots often use this formation for the same reason. When a goose tires or drops out, another one or two fly down with it, keeping it company until it is ready to resume the flight. The geese are keeping a close eye on the gaggle.

A gaggle, to us nonfeathered types, might be compared to a group of friends. We need each other. We need encouragement, advice, attention, even laughter. We need to take care of all of the geese in our gaggle.

In the book of Acts, Barnabas was known as an encourager to his friends. He was the first to extend trust to the much-feared Saul after his conversion. The apostles were skeptical of Saul, but Barnabas persisted, describing Saul's dramatic encounter with Christ on the road to Damascus. Barnabas brought Saul into the gaggle, opening the door of ministry to the most effective evangelist on Earth.

Who knows the impact we might have on others, by bringing them into the gaggle?

Jesus, Friend of all who look to You in need,
help me to care for others as You would.

Thankful for God's Wisdom

I thank thee, and praise thee, O thou God of my fathers, who hast given me wisdom and might, and hast made known unto me now what we desired of thee.
Daniel 2:23 KJV

*A*ngela and Valerie were enjoying a visit over a cup of coffee. As they reminisced about their college days, their children shared a playdate nearby.

"You know, Val, it's amazing the new perspective a person has on life once she has children," Angela commented. "When I was in college, it seemed like I was the only one affected by my decisions. Back then I thought I had some tough decisions to make, but now every choice impacts the lives of my husband and son."

Valerie laughed, thinking of some of the crazy adventures they had shared. "I doubt very much that all of our earlier actions affected only us," she said. "But seriously, I know what you mean. Suddenly life requires more responsibility. I want only the best for Adeline, but I don't always know what that is. God's wisdom has never failed me, though. Some decisions aren't easy, because what He wants is sometimes different than what my family and friends want, but He shows me what's right."

Angela nodded. She knew just what Valerie meant.

Thank You, God, for giving me the strength and wisdom to do what's right even when I face adversity.

Jesus Loves Me

"For God so loved the world that he gave his one and only Son,
that whoever believes in him shall not perish but have eternal life."
John 3:16 NIV

*J*esus loves me, this I know, for the Bible tells me so. Little ones to Him belong. They are weak, but He is strong."

We've probably sung that song dozens of times with our little ones, but have we considered its message? It actually teaches four huge doctrinal truths. First, we see that Jesus loves us. He loves us so much that he gave His own life as a sacrifice (1 John 3:16). Next, the song assures us that the Bible is worthy of being believed, for its words are true. We can be confident of this because "scripture is God-breathed" (2 Timothy 3:16 NIV).

Third, this song reminds us that even the little children belong to Him. The Bible tells us that our faith is to be like that of a child, and we are to come to Him as little children (Mark 10:15).

Finally, we are reminded of one of the greatest promises of hope for the believer, that His strength is made perfect when we are weakest. We could not live an effective Christian life in our own strength (2 Corinthians 12:9).

Allow your faith to become like that of a child, and seek Him in the simple things. Let even the words of a simple children's song bathe your soul in comforting truth.

Jesus, thank You for making Your lessons simple enough that a child can understand them. Help me to be more childlike in my faith. Amen.

Blessed Rest

Then God. . .rested from all His work.
Genesis 2:3 NASB

The schedule of a mommy is so full, typically without a moment to spare. The day begins with getting your child dressed and fed and doesn't slow down until you wearily drop into the closest chair—or your bed—after getting them tucked in. It's then that you realize that not only have you not taken any time for yourself that day, you find that you can't remember the last time that you had "me time."

It may not be realistic to visit the spa once a week, but think of something that you enjoy that could bring some refreshment to your wearied body—then do it! Take a few moments to read. . .even if it's just one article from your favorite magazine. Or relax for a few minutes while you listen to your favorite music. Just those few brief moments can be revitalizing!

This isn't time meant to compile your list of things to do tomorrow. This is time set aside just for you. And don't allow guilt to creep in: Remember, God has set the example of rest after work. . .and if He did it, it must be a practice that has merit!

Dear God, remind me to take the time to rest, just as You did,
so that I can be the mommy You want me to be. Amen.

Reflecting God

For the message of the cross is foolishness to those who are perishing,
but to us who are being saved it is the power of God.
1 Corinthians 1:18 NKJV

As the mother pushed the cart through the huge warehouse store, searching for the items she needed, her young daughter sat in the basket. Becoming bored, the child began to sing. The mother could tell she was singing songs she'd learned in Sunday school, although the words wouldn't be clear to anyone else.

The reaction of the people they passed was varied. Some smiled at the enthusiastic songs, while many gave a glance and passed on. One man scowled and grumbled at the mother to make her daughter stop singing. After a moment of doubt, the mother realized she couldn't dampen her child's delight in God.

When we are enamored with God, we shouldn't hide the joy we have in our relationship with Him. God wants us to bubble over with enthusiasm for Him. Our exuberance reflects the character of God to a darkened world around us. Even in times of trouble, we should be filled with a peace and quiet joy that makes the world wonder what we have that is different.

Some people will understand our joy; others will only give a passing glance. There will even be a few who will grumble at our ability to find delight in the midst of adversity. We must reflect God, no matter the outlook of those around us.

Lord, help me to be joyful in my relationship with You. Amen.

Just in Case

[Job's] sons used to take turns hosting parties in their homes, always inviting their three sisters to join them in their merrymaking. When the parties were over, Job would get up early in the morning and sacrifice a burnt offering for each of his children, thinking, "Maybe one of them sinned by defying God inwardly." Job made a habit of this sacrificial atonement, just in case they'd sinned.
Job 1:4–5 MSG

Job was a man considered blameless and upright, fearing God and shunning evil. Scripture introduces us to Job by informing us that he was the greatest man among all the people of the East. And in the next verse, we learn what kind of a father Job was: concerned, attentive, realistic, and a prayerful interceder for his children.

Scripture doesn't really say whether Job's children were party animals, spoiled rich kids, or sinners. It only tells us about Job's prayer life. Just in case his children sinned, just in case they insulted God, Job prayed. He woke up early, offered burnt offerings, and prayed.

What a lesson from Job! What a teacher he was. Do we pray for our children with such dedication? Are we willing to be inconvenienced, like Job was, to be woken early to pray for their day? Or to lift up their areas of potential sin to the Lord, asking God for guidance and forgiveness? Are we open to seeing the truth about our children?

Just in case his children needed prayer, Job prayed. Just in case. And so should we.

Lord God, open our eyes to the need for prayer for our children.

Memorizing Scripture

Your word I have treasured in my heart, that I may not sin against You.
Psalm 119:11 NASB

"Then Manoah entreated the LORD and said, 'O Lord, please let the man of God whom You have sent come to us again that he may teach us what to do for the boy who is to be born'" (Judges 13:8 NASB).

Have you often thought or prayed words similar to Manoah: "O Lord, I pray, teach me what I am to do concerning raising my children"? Just as Manoah and his wife received direction in how to raise Samson (Judges 13:4–5; 13–14), we, too, receive direction from the Lord in how to raise our children.

As we seek God's way for raising our children, we find God's Word gives us the instructions we need. The Bible is the blueprint that outlines how to live according to God's plan. However, we are encouraged not only to read God's Word for the path of rearing our children, but also to memorize scripture. The Lord tells us to treasure, hide, or store His Word in our hearts. As we store God's Word in our hearts, the Holy Spirit uses it to convict us of thoughts or actions that are contrary to God's ways and are, hence, sin. Memorize the scriptures that God is using to instruct you, and teach God's Word to your children.

Lord, assist my family and me in memorizing Your Word so we can learn to live in Your Way.

March!

As the body without the spirit is dead, so faith without deeds is dead.
James 2:26 NIV

*Y*oung children love to march! Perhaps that is why they are captivated by the story of Joshua marching around the walls of Jericho. Joshua obeyed God's specific orders. For six days, Joshua and his men marched around Jericho. On the seventh day they marched around seven times with priests blowing trumpets. When a long blast sounded, the people gave a loud shout and the walls of Jericho tumbled to the ground.

What if Joshua had responded by saying, "God, that sounds like a silly plan. How will trumpets and shouts bring down fortified walls?" Joshua was required to step out in faith and believe God. He had to trust that God could miraculously tumble Jericho's walls. Joshua demonstrated his trust by marching—by obedience.

What walls or obstacles are staring you in the face? Pray. Ask the Lord to bring the walls down. Then listen. The Lord will give you marching orders. He will call you to step out in faith and believe that He can intervene. It might not be the way you would have chosen, but He will come to your rescue. Like Joshua we are asked to demonstrate our faith through actions. Our response is obedience. God responds by bringing down the walls. Let's do our part so He can do His!

Dear Lord, nothing is impossible with You! Help me step out in faith and obedience so that I can experience Your power at work in my life. Amen.

Please Don't Lie

I have no greater joy than to hear that my children are walking in the truth.
3 John 1:4 NIV

$\mathcal{S}$helly listened as her two toddlers argued over the doll. She heard the unmistakable sound of ripping fabric before she could reach the girls.

"All right you two, what happened?"

The twins looked up angelically. And each pointed a finger at the other. "She did it," they announced in unison.

"So you both tore the arms off this doll?" Shelly knew the answer but felt this would be a good time to talk to the girls about telling the truth and not arguing so much.

They looked at each other and then nodded.

"Why did you do this?" Shelly asked, picking up the toy.

"I wanted it."

"I wanted it, too. It's mine."

Shelly took each child by the hand and moved to sit on the bed with one of them on each side of her. She wrapped her arms around them and said, "Thank you for telling the truth, but if you didn't argue all the time, you wouldn't tear up your things. Please try to be nicer to each other. Okay?"

The girls nodded and hugged her. "We'll try, Mommy."

As mothers, we try to walk in the truth—but sometimes we give in to the temptation to place blame on someone else. What a comfort to know that we can rely on our heavenly Father to give us the guidance and strength we need to draw us back to Him.

Father, teach me to walk in truth. My heart is filled with joy when my child tells me the truth, and it is saddened when she lies. I want to bring joy to Your heart just as my child does mine. Amen.

Know Boundaries

*As thou knowest not what is the way of the spirit, nor how the
bones do grow in the womb of her that is with child: even so
thou knowest not the works of God who maketh all.*
Ecclesiastes 11:5 KJV

*L*iving in the Information Age, we assume we can know it all. We
type a line on our computers, hit ENTER, and wait impatiently for a
hundred Internet answers to appear on our monitors.

Yet when a woman is expecting a child, an age-old sense of
wonder fills her days. The life within her grows, moves, even hiccups.
She cherishes the first picture of her baby, the ultrasound that tells
her whether to buy pink or blue. Her husband marvels at the tiny,
strong feet that deliver a good, swift kick in the middle of the night!
While both may investigate the medical details of their child's birth,
nothing prepares them for the miracle of ten perfect baby fingers and
ten marvelous baby toes. And nothing compares with the delight of
watching a baby learn to walk, talk, and think.

Just as we cannot comprehend God's originality and skill in
designing our children, we will not understand His creative Spirit
and all He does. But as we hold our little ones in our arms, we can
worship their Maker and the Lord of all life.

*Holy Spirit, my mind is too small to even begin to grasp Your amazing artistry.
Still, I praise You with all that is in me. Amen.*

Remembering the Lord

I will remember the deeds of the LORD; yes, I will remember your miracles of long ago. I will meditate on all your works and consider all your mighty deeds.
Psalm 77:11–12 NIV

*W*hen God created our minds, He did an amazing thing. Not only are we able to think and live in the present, but we have the ability to look back on the past. Even with today's digital photos and family videos, nothing is as complex as our memories.

As we look back on our lives, we are able to see accomplishments and maybe even a few mistakes. We may have attained certain goals. Or perhaps our plans haven't gone exactly the way we'd envisioned. Whichever the case, our bodies cannot go back to the past, but our thoughts can. Our memories open windows and opportunities for us to "change the future" based on how we deal with our past.

In the scripture above, the psalmist writes about remembering what God has done. He has done great things for us personally, but also for humankind and believers throughout the centuries. If we belong to God's family, then the miracles God performed and the works He continues to do were and are for us. Our personal stories have no DELETE button; but with God, even the worst memories can have a purpose we can turn around and use for Him.

*Lord, I praise You for everything You have done in my life.
May I continue to move forward while being mindful of the past.*

The Source of Real Strength

My soul melteth for heaviness: strengthen thou me according unto thy word.
Psalm 119:28 KJV

*B*eing a mother is like being a marine—it's the toughest job you'll ever love. But unlike marines, who must find strength within themselves, a Christian mother has the source of real strength—the Word of God.

Yet while we mothers have a ready arsenal of strength to help in time of need, when the going gets tough, our time in the Word is often the first thing that goes.

Instead of running to the Father and the Word in a crisis, we turn to others for comfort and are hurt when they fail us. Instead of crying out to the Lord for help, we try to pull ourselves out of pits we have dug until we are exhausted.

Spurred on by the same mentality that affects our preschoolers, we stomp our feet and say, "I can do it by myself!" But we know we cannot.

Fortunately, our patient Father loves us too much to allow us to stay in this sorry state too long. He will lovingly orchestrate circumstances to bring us back to Himself and to His Word.

And there we will find wisdom and comfort and strength.

O God, my strength, thank You for Your Word. Even though I hold the window to Your heart and mind, at times I do not open it often enough. When I begin neglecting Your Word, lovingly pull me back to it, for it is the true source of strength. Amen.

Twenty-One Days
to a Habit

Your word I have treasured in my heart, that I may not sin against You.
Psalm 119:11 NASB

Setting lofty goals is often a great way to drive change. Sometimes, though, the simple, daily disciplines seem almost impossible to maintain and more difficult to implement than those lofty goals. Reading the Bible is a great example of this. Most Christians would agree that it's a vital tool for growth and that it's something that God desires for us to do. However, most Christians have also said that they are just too busy to take the time to read it.

To create a habit, it's sometimes necessary to force the action for a short time, until it becomes natural. Experts agree that it takes twenty-one days to form a habit. This means that doing something twenty-one times helps to make it a part of a routine.

First, decide specifically what it is you need to do. Then schedule the time to do it. Make sure that you allow at least twenty-one days, and protect the time you set aside for accomplishing your goal. If you happen to miss a day, you should start over with a new set of twenty-one days.

Once you have completed those days with forced determination, you will likely realize that it got easier as time went on. The daily discipline that you were trying to develop will now be a natural part of your day.

Jesus, show me what habits I need to instill in order to live a life more pleasing to You. Give me the strength and determination to make them a reality. Amen.

Don't Run with Scissors

The proverbs of Solomon the son of David, king of Israel;
to know wisdom and instruction; to perceive the words of understanding.
Proverbs 1:1–2 KJV

$\mathcal{D}$on't run with scissors, don't play with fire, and don't throw a ball in the house. Those are all pieces of motherly wisdom that have been handed down through the generations. The book of Proverbs is referred to as the book of wisdom because Solomon was endowed with both spiritual and practical wisdom from God. Wisdom is being able to discern the things that produce good results and also understanding what causes negative results. But wisdom is just the first step.

We notice, in Proverbs 1:2, that wisdom is linked with instruction. If we ask God to give us His wisdom, we will receive not only His wisdom, but He will also give us the ability to discern His will. Once we know His will, it is up to us to follow it. We can pray for wisdom, and we can search the scriptures for knowledge, but without action, our knowledge means nothing. Even Satan knows the Word of God! It's not the knowledge that's key, it's the application of that knowledge. So, if we are to truly be wise, we should not only know but act upon the will of God.

Jesus, please give me a new dose of Your wisdom so that I can know and understand Your will. Then give me the strength to carry it out through my actions. Amen.

Showers of Blessings

*"I will cause showers to come down in their season;
there shall be showers of blessing."*
Ezekiel 34:26 NKJV

*N*o" is a word every preschooler hears often. As our children grow and explore their new world, we tire of using the negative. We are called to come up with creative ways to use positive encouragement. Still, there are times mothers and children are exhausted by the use and hearing of the word no. If we aren't careful, the child can lose sight of any uplifting guidance we give them.

As new Christians, we had to learn a new lifestyle—one that was pleasing to God. Our old self lived with a different set of habits that needed to be broken and a mindset that needed to be transformed. This new way of living can seem awkward as we try to adjust. We may feel God has more negatives than positives for us, or that the noes outweigh the multitude of benefits.

As we develop as Christians, we come to understand the showers of blessings God bestows on us. He loves us more than we can imagine, and His love is always refreshing when we focus on Him. His blessings demonstrate the abundance of love He has for us. The more mature we become, the more we see God's encouragement for us.

*Thank You for caring so much for me, Lord. Help me stay close to You,
to learn Your ways, and to enjoy Your benefits. Amen.*

Forever Safe

"I give them eternal life, and they shall never perish;
no one can snatch them out of my hand."
John 10:28 NIV

A precocious three-year-old slowly approached the cage of a sleeping lion at the zoo. Suddenly, the old lion opened its mouth and let out a deafening roar! The frightened toddler turned and ran frantically in the opposite direction. Although the bars had rendered the lion powerless, the little girl felt that her life was in grave danger.

Have you ever felt like that terrified toddler? Unfortunately, Satan has a way of frightening us. He plants "what-if" thoughts in our mind that evoke fear. He speaks condemning words to our heart. Undermining God's work in our lives is his goal. Yet we must realize that all Satan can do is frighten us. He has no power over us. He cannot harm us. He cannot pluck us from God's hand.

The toddler reacted out of fear, not realizing that she was safe. The lion was contained behind bars. We must grasp spiritual truth. Although Satan may scare us, we are eternally safe because Jesus has defeated Satan. Jesus imparts that same victory to believers. Satan can only roar. He cannot destroy us. The bars of Jesus contain him. Greater is He that is in us than he that is in the world. Christ has rendered Satan powerless in our lives. Let's not be frightened, but feel safe and secure in our Father's hand.

Dear Lord, thank You for reminding me that You have defeated Satan
and given me victory. Help me remember that I am safe in Your hand. Amen.

David:
Optimist and Realist

*There be many that say, Who will shew us any good? L*ORD,
lift thou up the light of thy countenance upon us. Thou hast put gladness
in my heart, more than in the time that their corn and their wine increased.
Psalm 4:6–7 KJV

*O*ptimists are becoming an endangered species. Newspaper headlines report dangers and disasters that keep us awake at night. Experts predict future problems that cause us to hold our children close and wish our families lived during a safer era.

David, the author of Psalm 4, experienced dangerous times, too. God considered him a man after His own heart and eventually made him king. But David faced many enemies, including several in his own family who tried to dethrone him. He continually called on God throughout his life to protect him. At times, even godly friends or advisors must have viewed David's situation as hopeless. Assessing the circumstances, David probably agreed with them. He might have been a poet, but David was also a realist. He had spent too many years running from his murderous father-in-law, Saul, to trust in an exalted view of human nature! But David also was an optimist. He asked God to shine His light on him, knowing He gives gladness that goes beyond comfort and safety.

Father God, thank You that I can be both optimistic and realistic
during these crazy times. I praise You, Light of My Life,
and pray that I reflect Your warmth. Amen.

Thank-You Note
from Jesus

"And the King will answer them, 'Truly, I say to you,
as you did it to one of the least of these my brothers, you did it to me.' "
Matthew 25:40 ESV

*E*very mother of a preschooler will agree that caring for little children can be completely draining and exhausting. And, usually, it's a thankless task, with no end in sight. The pile of laundry never grows smaller, the toys never stay in the toy box, the dishwasher seems to be on an endless cycle, and there is always a game to be played or a book to be read. There are play groups, preschool classes, swimming lessons, and, oh, we mustn't forget doctor's appointments and church activities. All of those things are managed by Mom, with nary a thank you.

Matthew 25:40 is a thank-you note from Jesus. He says thank you for the noses you wipe on His behalf; thank you for the tears that you dry when offering His comfort; and thank you for the hugs that you give as an extension of His love. Whatever is done, in the name of Jesus Christ, for the weak ones whom He has placed in your charge, it is done for Him.

Thank You, Jesus, for the reminder that I serve You as I carry out my tasks as a mother. I offer my day and my time of service unto You. Be glorified in all that I do, and please continue to use me to share Your love. Amen.

HELP!

But Jesus beheld them, and said unto them, With men this is impossible;
but with God all things are possible.
Matthew 19:26 KJV

She was here just a few minutes ago," Josie cried to the store manager.

The man patted her hand. "Don't worry. I'm sure we'll find her."

Josie twisted her hands in her lap. Megan had been standing beside her one moment and gone the next. Josie listened to the manager talk to security on the phone; she couldn't just sit in his office and wait. She headed back into the store.

Her heart pounded as she searched.

"Lord, I can't find her. What am I going to do? Please protect my baby," Josie prayed as she looked under clothes racks for her precious daughter. The three-year-old had never wandered off before. Tears ran down Josie's cheeks as she looked.

The search continued for thirty minutes, and then the store manager told Josie that the local police had been called. Megan was nowhere in the store.

Panic threatened to choke Josie. She closed her eyes and prayed. The urge to go to the bedding department pulled her in that direction. As she entered, she called her daughter's name.

A quiet little voice answered, "Mommy?"

Josie watched as her daughter crawled out from under a pile of fluffy pillows. She ran to her little girl, hugged her close, and praised God above for finding her baby.

Thank You, Lord, for the safety of my child. I would like to
think that I am in control of every situation, but I know I am not.
I'm glad You are always with me and my child. Amen.

Teach by Example

Moreover as for me, God forbid that I should sin against the LORD
in ceasing to pray for you: but I will teach you the good and the right way.
1 Samuel 12:23 KJV

$\mathcal{N}$ow I lay me down to sleep. . . ." How precious and promising it
is to hear a young child who is learning to pray. It is precious because
the sweetness of that child's heart overflows as he communicates with
the heavenly Father. It is promising because it indicates that there is
someone in that child's life who loves him enough to teach him the
importance of prayer.

Our little ones need us to pray for them. Not only should they
know they are included in our conversation with God, but they
should also be able to observe this. Although we need our private
time with the Lord, our preschoolers need to be invited to share in
special prayer times as well.

When we fail to pray, we are sinning against God. All sin,
regardless of what it is, is an abomination in His eyes. We must
choose to do right for our children both in interceding to God on
their behalf and in setting a good example of what a proper prayer
life should be. There are so many things our little ones need to learn.
Let's make their spiritual training a priority.

Heavenly Father, help my children as they are at the beginning of life's journey.
Let them learn the joy of prayer even now.

What's in a Name?

Among these were some from Judah: Daniel, Hananiah, Mishael and Azariah.
The chief official gave them new names: to Daniel, the name Belteshazzar; to
Hananiah, Shadrach; to Mishael, Meshach; and to Azariah, Abednego.
Daniel 1:6–7 NIV

Daniel and his three friends were only fourteen or fifteen years old
when Nebuchadnezzar of Babylon laid siege to Jerusalem and took
the boys into bondage. These young teenagers were now in Babylon
for the rest of their lives. Separated from their families, their culture,
and their God.

Back up fourteen years. These intelligent, capable boys had been
born in Jerusalem, to families of nobility, during the reign of Josiah.
There was a great revival period in Judah during Josiah's reign. The
names of these four Hebrew boys have roots in their God. We don't
know anything more about their families.

Nebuchadnezzar had a strategic plan to educate these boys and
press them into service. They were given new names to represent
new gods—a symbolic act of forcing them to forsake their God and
heritage.

But in private, the boys called each other by their Hebrew names
(Daniel 2:17). Another symbolic act. These boys were holding on. . .
to their God, to their moms. They couldn't e-mail, they couldn't call
home, but they were not letting go of what they had been taught as
children.

What's in a name? What's in those early years of childhood? An
enduring foundation to last a lifetime!

How thankful I am, O Lord, that You are grounding my
children spiritually during their early years of childhood.

Activity Overload

"Dear woman, why do you involve me?" Jesus replied,
"My time has not yet come."
John 2:4 NIV

Sarah closed her car door and walked toward the other moms in the elementary school parking lot. They still had fifteen minutes before their kids would be done for the day, but Sarah didn't mind. Approaching the five women, she was greeted by smiles as the conversation continued. Becky was speaking, holding her PalmPilot in her hands.

"We're so busy," Becky stated. "Jim and I really want the kids to be well-rounded." She began poking at the PalmPilot screen. "There is the homework and school activities, of course, but the kids are also involved in community sports, dance, and music lessons. Our oldest is taking up wrestling, and our youngest girl is going to start ice-skating lessons."

Sarah understood the looks the other moms were giving each other. They all knew that Becky and her husband pushed their kids hard. They wanted their gifted children to excel at everything, but at what cost to the children's need for a childhood and sanity? Life would get busy enough on its own.

Jesus' mother, Mary, did a similar thing to Jesus at a wedding. She knew that her Son was the Messiah and that He had God's power. In a way, she was pushing Him to reveal His glory before His time had come. Jesus recognized this and lovingly let His mother know she needed to step back and allow Him to be who He was at that time.

Lord, help me to guide my children through
their days without being controlling.

Can't Stop Praying

Pray without ceasing.
I Thessalonians 5:17 KJV

*P*aul must have been addressing men when he wrote "Pray without ceasing."

Women—mothers in particular—need no reminder to pray. As soon as the first baby is laid in her arms, the prayers begin. And they never end:

"He's crying, Lord. What should I do?"

"Father, I'm tired. Don't let me drop her if I fall asleep."

"I don't know who's telling the truth here. Lord, please give me wisdom."

"Father, he's had so many disappointments this year. Let Him see Your hand in all of this. Humble him, and make him useful to You."

"Lord, make him a good husband."

While mothers rarely cease praying, we don't always see ourselves as "prayer warriors" because we don't have the luxury of spending hours before the Lord. Often we don't have a regular "quiet time," or we are frustrated because our devotions are often interrupted by our little ones.

There's no need to despair. God knows all about our children, our needs, and His glory. When He sends a divine interruption in the form of a child, we must use that opportunity to instruct our little one in prayer.

There is nothing more sublime than teaching a child to commune with the Father.

And nothing more powerful than to train the next generation to pray without ceasing.

Father, how often I've become frustrated when my children have interrupted my quiet times. I've been wrong in this, Lord. Help me see that sharing You with my children is more fruitful than keeping You all to myself. Amen.

Comfort in Prayer

If we are distressed, it is for your comfort and salvation;
if we are comforted, it is for your comfort.
2 Corinthians 1:6 NIV

*A*ll toddlers go through different phases as they grow. There are times when they may test the boundaries set for them, which, in turn, will test a mother's patience. Some stages are so difficult we wonder if they will ever pass. The mother can feel isolated, particularly if none of her friends have had children go through the same experience.

In this situation, the best resort is prayer. God understands all we are going through. His "children" often go through periods where they don't listen to His leading. He is the parent with the most patience and the most trying children. He will listen, and He will help you through this time of aloneness.

When one stage passes to the next, we can breathe a sigh of relief. The relief may not last long, but that particular stage is over. Then we can file away in our memory how we felt. God allows us to be distressed so that we can encourage others in similar situations. When another mother confides in us, we can pray with her and assure her that God is there to see her through.

Lord, thank You for seeing me through. Help me to be there for
other mothers and to encourage them with Your love. Amen.

Teach Me about You

That I may know him, and the power of his resurrection,
and the fellowship of his sufferings, being made conformable unto his death.
Philippians 3:10 KJV

Jessica opened her Bible and began to read where she'd left off the day before. The sound of bare feet running down the hallway reached her ears long before her three-year-old daughter rounded the corner.

"Whatcha doing?"

Jessica pulled her onto her lap. "Reading my Bible."

"Why?"

"Because I want to learn more about God." She closed the book, knowing the twenty questions had just begun.

"Why?"

Jessica stood and carried her daughter back to the bedroom. "Because, I want to know all about Him. I want to understand why He died for our sins, and there are a lot of things that I don't understand, so I like to read my Bible." She tucked her daughter back into her bed.

"I want to learn, too. Mommy, read me a story, pleeease."

Jessica picked up the children's Bible that had been sitting beside the bed and opened it up. "I'll read you one story, and then you have to take your nap." Satisfied with her daughter's agreeable nod, Jessica read her the story of David and Goliath. The little girl fell asleep long before the story was complete.

Father God, sometimes life is busy and I forget the importance of
reading the Bible to my children. Thank You, Lord, for reminding me
to teach them to read Your Word daily, too. I love You very much. Amen.

A Peaceful Home

"Blessed are the peacemakers, for they will be called sons of God."
Matthew 5:9 NIV

*A*re you a child of God? Do you strive to live life like Jesus? Do you have a peaceful home? Are you modeling Christ, "the Prince of Peace" (Isaiah 9:6 NIV), to your preschooler?

In the Sermon on the Mount, Jesus provided the "beatitudes," or the Christ-centered way of being blessed. Jesus provided the mind and heart perspective and the avenue to be blessed, fortunate, or happy. We will be blessed by being called God's children when we are peacemakers.

What does it mean to be a peacemaker when we have a preschooler in the home? First, it means we have a steadfast mind, as we trust Him (Isaiah 26:3); we "set [our] minds on things above" Colossians 3:2 NIV); we "fix our eyes on Jesus" (Hebrews 12:2 NIV). Second, we invite Jesus to schedule our day. Through the Lord's leading, we provide a structure that is most suitable to a peaceful home. For example, scheduled morning devotionals, mealtimes as a family, nap and rest times, playtimes. There is routine and predictability about the day for each member of the family. Finally, through Mom modeling a right relationship with the Lord, the result will be inner peace, quiet resting places, and a peaceful home (Isaiah 32:17–18).

Lord, please help me to fix my eyes on You and model in mind, heart, and behavior the Prince of Peace.

A Shaky Blend of Faith and Unbelief

Jesus said, "If? There are no 'ifs' among believers. Anything can happen."
Mark 9:23 MSG

A desperate father brought his demon-possessed boy to Jesus. As the father described the boy's condition, his broken heart was almost palpable. His request seemed almost defeated, as if he didn't really think Jesus could heal his son but he was at the end of his options. "If you can do anything, take pity on us and help us" (Mark 9:22 NIV).

Jesus seemed to bristle at that request. He knew this was a spiritual battle, of God over the forces of evil in the son, of faith breaking through darkness in the father. He responded by pushing the boy's father to the issue at heart. Jesus said, "If? There are no 'ifs' among believers. Anything can happen" (Mark 9:23 MSG).

Out of the father's mouth came revealing words: "Then I believe. Help me with my doubts!" (Mark 9:24 MSG). It was almost as if the man were drowning and clutching at Jesus for rescue. And Jesus did not fail him! He rebuked the evil spirit, commanding it to leave the boy and never enter him again.

The father turned to Jesus in desperate need, offering a shaky blend of faith and unbelief. We can all understand his despair! Nothing hits us harder than when our kids are in trouble. Jesus responded to that shaky mixture. He saw the light breaking through the darkness, the hand reaching out to Him for rescue. And He grabbed it!

Lord, You don't want me to have faith in my faith,
but faith in a great God. Thank You that I can come to You and say,
"Lord, I believe! Help my unbelief!"

Fellowship

Let us not give up meeting together, as some are in the habit of doing, but let us encourage one another—and all the more as you see the Day approaching.
Hebrews 10:25 NIV

*O*ne Sunday morning a newlywed couple awoke to the sound of rain pelting their bedroom window. The wife was tempted to pull the covers over her head and skip church. As a child, her mother had occasionally used the rain as an excuse to sleep in. The husband had just the opposite inclination. His family always went to church on rainy Sundays because playing golf was not an option. Laughing about their different perspectives, they decided that their family would attend church come rain or shine!

Christians need one another. Just as a burning pile of coal radiates heat and light, so fellowship with other believers fans our spiritual flames. We are encouraged, built up, and spurred on. Together we radiate God's love to a world needing the Light of Truth.

If a piece of coal is removed from the pile and set aside by itself, it quickly turns cold and burns out. Do not give in to temptation to skip church. Do not think you can live the Christian life by yourself. God has made the church body for you, and you for the church body. We need each other. Purpose to fellowship, come rain or shine!

Dear Lord, help me realize the importance of Christian fellowship. I need other believers and they need me. May I be committed to fellowship. Amen.

Patient Love

Charity suffereth long, and is kind.
1 Corinthians 13:4 KJV

*T*he two young mothers sat together, enjoying a rare bit of quiet time. As they talked, they shared the many joys and woes of motherhood.

"I feel like such a failure as a mother," the one lamented. "No matter what I say or do, I just can't seem to get through to my daughter. After so long, I either break down and cry, or I just start yelling. I know it's wrong, but I just can't seem to help it."

"Don't feel like you're alone," her friend replied. "We all go through it from time to time. Just keep loving that precious little girl. Your prayer and patience *will* pay off. Just be sure to give your struggles to Jesus every day—even several times a day."

It was encouragement that both friends needed. They realized there would still be tests of wills. Children need to know what their limits are. At times those lessons are more difficult for the mother than they are for the child. But persistent and patient love pays great dividends. With God's help, the battle that at first looked like a lost cause will become one of the most precious victories ever won.

Dear heavenly Father, I know that I must often frustrate You,
but You're still lovingly molding me into Christlikeness.
Help me also to show loving patience as I raise my child.

Loving Your
Children's Daddy

*Each of the younger women must be sensible and kind,
as well as a good homemaker, who puts her own husband first.*
Titus 2:5 CEV

As the days come and go, suddenly the realization can hit that with all of the busyness of life and taking care of your precious little ones, there has been no time set aside for their father. It can be assumed that he will understand that there just hasn't been enough time in the schedule to get away. However, he does have the need to spend "alone time" with you, too.

Understandably, your schedule is not as open as it was back when you were dating. But most likely you can both find some time to set aside to go out together. If you have a difficult time finding a babysitter, how about planning your date for a Saturday lunch, when babysitters are in less demand? Or how about finding another couple that you could swap "date nights" with: You watch their kids when they go out, and they in turn watch your kids for your special time away? Your kids will benefit from seeing you set aside time for their daddy and putting him "first," as the verse above states. And he will appreciate your placing importance in improving your relationship.

*Jesus, please help me to remember the importance of spending
time with my children's father, both for the growth of our
relationship and for the example to the children. Amen.*

A Single Mom

*"I will be found by you," declares the LORD, "and will bring you
back from captivity. I will gather you from all the nations and places
where I have banished you," declares the LORD, "and will bring you
back to the place from which I carried you into exile."*
Jeremiah 29:14 NIV

*L*auren saw the way others in her hometown looked at her. The other
moms who waited outside her daughter's preschool acted kind to her
face, but they often whispered behind her back. Lauren knew why,
too. She was a single mother. What the other mothers didn't realize
was why Lauren was a single mother.

It was true that she had been promiscuous during high school,
and some of the mothers knew that. But since committing her life to
Christ during college, Lauren hadn't been with a guy—except for the
night that she was raped. That rape had led to her pregnancy and her
eventual decision to keep the baby, the girl who was now bounding
out the school doors toward Lauren.

"Hi, Mommy!" she exclaimed. "I learned about polar bears in
school today!"

Lauren braced herself for the hug. As they walked hand in hand
to the school parking lot, Lauren wished others might know that
the girl she was in high school was not the woman she was today.
Her story was about forgiveness and redemption, but mostly about
God's faithfulness. Lauren and her family knew the truth about
her pregnancy. And Lauren was glad. At the end of the day, it was
ultimately God, and only God, she answered to.

God, thank You for accepting me as I am.

It's a Wonderful Life

You prepare a table before me in the presence of my enemies.
Psalm 23:5 NIV

There is a scene in the movie *It's a Wonderful Life* in which George is hastily pacing through the house, heavily burdened with stress. His young son is behind him, tugging on his coattail, saying, "Excuse me! Excuse me!" George Bailey ignores him for what seems like forever, and the boy continues tugging and saying, "Excuse me! Excuse me!"

Finally, Dad turns to the boy and, in exasperation, he asks, "Excuse you for what?"

The boy innocently replies, "I burped."

Mary, the boy's mother, quietly excuses the boy and sends him off.

It's a sweet, innocent family scene, but it's also a reminder that amid the chaos of life, with all of the stress and pressures it brings, there is still innocence and, with children in the house, you are always someone's source of comfort and joy.

Psalm 23:5 says that God prepares a table for us, even in the very presence of our enemies. That means He doesn't tell us to run from trouble or hide from it, but rather, He tells us to throw a party right in the middle of it! That's how little effect the trials of the world actually need to have on us. What freedom there is in that promise!

Thank You, Father, for preparing that table for me right in the middle of all of my struggles. Help me to keep my focus on You so that I can hear my children when they are calling for my attention. Help me to never let the noisy clamor of the world drown out the call of my family. Amen.

Perseverance

We also rejoice in our sufferings, because we know that suffering produces
perseverance; perseverance, character; and character, hope.
Romans 5:3–4 NIV

*N*ot again! It seemed more than any parents should have to bear.
Their four-year-old daughter was facing her third open-heart surgery.
At two days old, she had experienced the first, and another at nine
months. Everyone had prayed that this third operation would not be
necessary. It seemed the Lord had other plans.

How do we persevere through trials that seem unbearable?
Where do we turn for help when we cannot understand God's ways?
Our only hope is to turn toward God and not away from Him.
Trusting the Lord in the midst of suffering is an act of obedience. It
is refusing to go down the path riddled with despair, hopelessness,
and anxiety. Instead, it is choosing to lean upon the Lord's strength,
faithfulness, and power. We rejoice because He enables us to stand
in circumstances that otherwise would have swallowed us whole. He
imparts inner peace in difficulties that scream despair. His presence
carries us during times we would have surely fallen down. When we
persevere, Christ's character is revealed in and through us. Hope is
realized. Let's persevere in our sufferings in order to obtain the hope
that God has promised.

Dear Lord, You know how difficult suffering can be. Help me turn
to You and persevere. Build my character and give me hope. Amen.

Comfort Zone

*Whosoever will come after me, let him deny himself,
and take up his cross, and follow me.*
Mark 8:34 KJV

New experiences can be frightening for a young child. Perhaps it's the first day of nursery school, a new babysitter, or simply a situation not encountered before. Often the toddler will want to hide behind his or her mother, unsure how to act.

When we encourage our children to do something despite their misgivings, they often enjoy the experience more than they could ever have imagined. As their horizons expand, preschoolers will want to do more and try new things. They will be more willing to step outside their normal activities.

Jesus asks us to witness for Him in a multitude of ways. For some, this means to go into the mission field in a foreign country. For others, they are to reach out to those they come in contact with in everyday situations.

Often, the thought of doing this makes us uncomfortable. We don't want to step outside our comfort zone. We fear rejection or ridicule. Yet we must remember this is what Jesus asked us to do. We don't have to know the whole Bible. We simply tell people what Jesus has done for us and how much He loves them. When we follow His directive, we will be blessed beyond measure.

*Thank You, Jesus, for Your encouragement.
Help me to take that step of faith and reach out to others. Amen.*

Love of My Life

My beloved spake, and said unto me,
Rise up, my love, my fair one, and come away.
Song of Solomon 2:10 KJV

*B*ut Michael's so little!" Stacy could not bring herself to leave their son, even for a special anniversary weekend away. "And he was sick last week!"

"The doctor said he's fine!" Brad insisted. "He's two years old now. Besides, your mother and dad will take good care of him."

Stacy sighed. What if the fever returned? Michael wouldn't understand why she wasn't there to hold him. What if he needed tubes in his ears? What if—

"We never spend time together." Brad's voice caught her heart.

For the first time during their argument, Stacy looked into his eyes. "Does this trip mean that much to you?"

Brad turned away and said nothing for a moment. Then he muttered, "When Michael's around, it seems like you don't even know I'm there."

Stacy turned hot with indignation. *I have two babies instead of one!* But his bowed head and sagging shoulders told her something she'd forgotten amid the craziness of nursing, nap schedules, and diapers: Brad missed her! He wanted to spend time with her. Stacy took a deep breath and touched his cheek. "I'll call Mom and tell her we're going."

Jesus, I want to be the best mom I can. But thanks for bringing my husband and me together for a lifetime that starts not in twenty years but today. Amen.

A Christ-Centered Home

"Choose for yourselves this day whom you will serve. . . .
But as for me and my household, we will serve the LORD."
Joshua 24:15 NIV

*H*annah Maria grew up in a Christ-centered home. She reflects back fondly on parents who modeled daily how to seek the Lord for wisdom regarding both small and big decisions. As a child, she felt encouraged by morning devotions and specific prayers for her. Now, as a mother of a preschooler, Hannah Maria desires to develop her own Christ-centered home.

What is a Christ-centered home?

One that deliberately chooses to serve the Lord. The foundation of a Christ-centered home is believing parents (Romans 10:9-10). By daily walking with Christ, parents model for their children how to have a personal relationship with Jesus. With God at the center of the family, all decisions are filtered through seeking God's face (Deuteronomy 4:29; 2 Chronicles 15:4). The parents are growing in their relationship with the Lord through individual quiet time and Bible study. The Bible is used for guidance and instruction in living and raising the children. Time fostering a relationship with Christ among the children is cultivated in family devotions, prayer time, memorizing and using scripture to address life's challenges, and being actively involved in a growing church. The benefit is "no greater joy than to hear that my children are walking in the truth" (3 John 1:4 NIV).

Lord, enable me to develop a Christ-centered home for my preschooler.
I praise You for the joy that will come as my preschooler walks in truth.

Gone in a Moment

So teach us to number our days, that we may apply our hearts unto wisdom.
Psalm 90:12 KJV

*I*t's a boy!" the doctor said as he pulled her firstborn from her womb.

A boy, she thought. Her father's first grandson.

As she lay on the operating table while the cesarean section was completed, she thought of her baby boy. What would he be like in a year? In ten? In twenty?

She shuddered. She couldn't imagine him in twenty years; it was too far away.

Once home with her newborn, life became busy. Diapers. Feedings. Hugs. Kisses. Pictures. Housework. Appointments. Life with her boy was just so constant.

Before she knew it, there was another boy. And then a girl. Then there was homeschooling. And more children.

Each day the first one grew, but in the constant activity, she didn't always notice. In her mind, there would always be time for one more lesson, one more chat, one more hug, one more laugh. If she missed time with him one day, there would always be another.

Then one day, he was twenty.

And he was gone. Off to college and beyond.

Where had the time gone? It had flown—carrying her son to manhood without stopping for a breath.

Time stops for no woman, but a little wisdom can slow it down.

Dear Lord, although time is a difficult taskmaster, You created it to put order in my life. Let me order my days wisely so in my haste I will not forget You or the children you have entrusted to me. Amen.

Anything but That!

*He said, "Take now your son, your only son, whom you love, Isaac,
and go to the land of Moriah, and offer him there as a burnt offering
on one of the mountains of which I will tell you."*
Genesis 22:2 NASB

*W*hat God asked Abraham to do was absolutely shocking. Sacrifice
his promised son, whom his wife Sarah was amazingly able to have
after her youth.

The story tells us that just as Abraham was about to sacrifice
Isaac, an angel of the Lord called down from heaven and told
Abraham not to lay a hand on his son. Even today, many people
wonder why God asked Abraham to sacrifice Isaac and then changed
His mind at the last minute.

Abraham had a faith and trust in God that defies today's need
for information. We want to know *who, what, where, when, how,* and
especially *why.* Abraham undoubtedly wanted to know, too. Still, he
never questioned God. If God told him to do something, Abraham
did it.

God was actually testing Abraham. And while God delights in
knowing who and what we love more than Him, it's also true that
God was trying to teach and grow Abraham. Because of this test,
Abraham realized again that Isaac did not belong to him, but to God.

Like Abraham, we have been entrusted by God to love and care
for our children.

*Lord, I want to love You more than anyone else! I give myself
and my children over to You because You are the true Father.*

Growing Up

And you have been given fullness in Christ,
who is the head over every power and authority.
Colossians 2:10 NIV

Jimmy worked alongside his mother in the garden. She pushed the hair from her sweaty forehead and watched him scrub a squash she'd picked earlier. She really didn't need him to wash the vegetable, but it kept him occupied while she weeded the garden. As he cleaned, Jimmy asked lots of questions.

"How do veshibles grow?"

She smiled at his pronunciation. "God sends rain and sunshine to make them grow."

Jimmy twisted the vegetable around to get a better grip on the neck of the yellow squash. "Does God make them grow big, too?"

"Yes, He does."

"Am I a veshible in God's garden? I'm growing up, too."

She laughed. "Well, you aren't a vegetable, but you are one of God's children."

"And I'm growing up?"

A sigh slipped from her lips. "Yes, you are."

"Daddy says we are blessed to have this garden. Is that right?"

She thought of all the food that she'd put away for the winter. It was tiring work, but it was also a blessing. Her husband worked in construction, and sometimes the weather limited his working hours. During those times, the home-canned goods would feed them when there was no money for groceries. "Yes, we are very blessed, Jimmy."

Thank You, Lord, for filling my life with love and supplying all our needs.
Sometimes I forget that You are the One who takes care of us.
Thank You for providing for my family. Amen.

God's Mouth

*"As the rain and the snow come down from heaven, and do not return
to it without watering the earth and making it bud and flourish, so that
it yields seed for the sower and bread for the eater, so is my word that goes
out from my mouth: It will not return to me empty, but will accomplish
what I desire and achieve the purpose for which I sent it."*
Isaiah 55:10–11 NIV

$\mathcal{D}$oes God have a mouth? Pink lips? White teeth? He probably
doesn't have a mouth as we would imagine it, but He does have a
great desire for us to draw close to Him and experience His love.
To do that, we need to be able to picture Him in human terms. To
communicate with us, He must speak a language that, like rain and
snow, originates in heaven but can descend to our level. A language
that our earthbound minds can embrace.

Author Peggy Parker wrote, "The Bible is not humans using
human language to grasp God, for we never can grasp God. The Bible
is God using human language to grasp us, to give Himself to us, at
least as much of Himself as we are capable of taking in."

In scripture, God takes His thoughts and feelings and reduces
them—down, down, down—to our understanding. Personifying
Himself as a human was His way of helping us feel close to Him. He
taught us how to introduce big topics—such as God's appearance—
to our children.

Does God have a mouth? In a way, yes. It's called the Word.

*Lord, You are so much more than words can describe.
We exalt You! May we bring You glory today.*

Lying Down

He maketh me to lie down in green pastures:
he leadeth me beside the still waters.
Psalm 23:2 KJV

$\mathcal{D}$o you ever wonder why your child fights you when it's nap time? You try desperately to get him into his bed for some much-needed midday rest. As you struggle, you think, *Why is this child refusing this wonderful opportunity? No one would have to tell me twice to take a nap.*

Why is it then that our Shepherd has to make us lie down in green pastures? It might be true that we would like to rest a few moments here or there, but there are just so many things to be accomplished. When our children finally do nap peacefully, we use that time to cram in as much as we can because there are too many distractions otherwise.

Pushing hard isn't always in our best interest, though. Consider this: God rested; Jesus rested, and He commanded His disciples to rest, too. Why is it that we mothers feel we are exempt from this need? For our sakes and our family's sake we must take a break so that we are refreshed in many ways. If we ignore this need, Christ might need to "make" us take that rest. Why not allow yourself this much-needed pleasure today?

Dear Shepherd, You've shown me that I do need rest to function properly.
Help me to find time and not be stubborn about it.

Guarding Our Children's Hearts

Above all else, guard your heart, for it is the wellspring of life.
Proverbs 4:23 NIV

The moms went around their small group and discussed their purpose as a mother. One mom said, "My purpose is to teach my children the ways of the Lord." Another said, "My purpose is to raise my children to have a personal relationship with Jesus." Another said, "My purpose as a mother is to teach my children how to get sidetracked from God's will for their entire lives." Okay, while we may not intentionally select this last purpose, how often do our *actions* choose it?

The Lord tells us that, above all else, we need to guard our hearts because from them flows the wellspring of life. Our preschoolers do not know how to guard their hearts. Therefore, the responsibility resides with us as their mothers to guard their hearts until they are mature enough to do it for themselves. How do we guard their hearts? We need to be diligent in not allowing anything of the "world" to permeate their lives. That means we guard with vigilance what our children are exposed to in regard to TV, Internet, friends, books, and magazines. It also means we focus on what we do want our children to be exposed to, such as the Bible, church, Sunday school, or other children raised with the same Christ-centered purpose we have.

Lord, direct me to guard my children's hearts from all that is contrary to a Christ-centered purpose, and guide me to expose my children's hearts to all that is in line with Your purpose.

Faith Demonstrated

Since they could not get him to Jesus because of the crowd,
they made an opening in the roof above Jesus and, after digging through it,
lowered the mat the paralyzed man was lying on.
Mark 2:4 NIV

The men were desperate and undeterred! Their friend was paralyzed, and Jesus was preaching at a house in Capernaum. When the crowded room would not accommodate the paralytic's stretcher, they hoisted him to the roof. After digging a hole, they lowered him inside the house through the opening. Jesus was moved by their faith and healed their paralyzed friend.

These men believed that Jesus was the answer to their friend's need. Their faith moved them to labor intensively on their friend's behalf. Jesus commended their faith.

What are we willing to sacrifice to bring our friends before Jesus? To what extent are we willing to be inconvenienced?

Like the paralytic's friends, we, too, must believe that Jesus is the answer. Our faith will then compel us to lay our friends before the Lord in prayer. This will require sacrifice and hard work. Are we willing to do whatever it takes to have them receive help? Are we desperate and undeterred? Let's put our faith into action by diligently placing our family and friends before the Lord in prayer. The Lord will faithfully answer.

Dear Lord, may I demonstrate my faith in You by diligently praying for others.
Give me strength and determination to persevere. Amen.

Me? Homeschool?

For I know the thoughts that I think toward you, saith the LORD,
thoughts of peace, and not of evil, to give you an expected end.
Jeremiah 29:11 KJV

*M*ary sighed. This was the third time in a month that the principal of the Little Tykes Preschool had called her in. She wondered what her twins had done to warrant the summons this time.

"Thank you for coming in, Mrs. Pope." The elder woman walked around her massive desk.

Mary sat up straighter in her chair. "You're welcome."

"I expect that you know why we've asked you here?"

"What have the twins done now?" Mary asked, feeling herself slip down into the cushions of the chair as the principal began reading off her list of grievances against the children.

Later, as she drove the children home, Mary prayed. She wanted what was best for the twins but felt that public schools were not the answer. The thought that she could homeschool them entered her thoughts. Would she be able to do the job right and teach the children what they needed to succeed in life? She felt the Lord's urging and knew deep in her heart that she could.

Heavenly Father, thank You for the promise that assures me that You have
my and my children's best interests at heart, and that You will never bring
us to harm. Please be with me, Lord, as I strive to make the right decisions
where my children are concerned and continue to allow Your peace to
reside in me. In Jesus' name, amen.

Making Cookies with God

For we are His workmanship, created in Christ Jesus for good works,
which God prepared beforehand that we should walk in them.
Ephesians 2:10 NKJV

"I want to help!" Preschoolers are notorious for turning a simple job, like making cookies, into a dreaded chore and an unbelievable mess. Inevitably, with the help of a preschooler, there will be flour sprinkled on everything, eggshells in the batter, extra dishes to wash, and a chocolate-covered face to scrub upon completion of the task.

Of course, the task would be accomplished so much faster and more neatly if Mom just waited and did it by herself during her preschooler's nap time. But then her child would miss out on the experience of working toward an accomplishment, along with the joy of working with Mommy. When the cookies are finished, the preschooler takes full credit—"Look what I made!"—and Mom sighs in exhaustion and smiles as they enjoy the fruits of their labor.

So it is with our heavenly Father. He could accomplish His will with much greater effectiveness and efficiency without our help. Yet He chooses to use us to help Him carry out His plans. It is for our benefit that He lets us get our hands dirty in the cookie batter of life. He simply smiles when we feel like we have done well, and He waits until we aren't looking to pick out the eggshells.

Father, help me to be as patient and understanding with my child as You are with
me. Please use me today so that I can take joy in serving You. Amen.

Refreshment

Therefore my heart is glad, and my glory rejoiceth:
my flesh also shall rest in hope.
Psalm 16:9 KJV

*D*o you ever feel like you're being pulled in a dozen different ways? Before your eyes open in the morning, one of the children is crying or calling for you. Someone in your family asks you a favor. The church wants you to help with a program. A friend needs someone to talk to. By the end of the day the kids still need help getting ready for the night, and your husband wants you to spend time with him.

When you finally crawl into bed, you are exhausted. In the midst of caring for little ones and doing what you can for others, you've had no time for God. Guilt rears up, because you know spending time with God is the most important part of every day.

God never makes demands on us. He invites us to come to Him. He is always there waiting for us. God understands the necessities of our daily lives. He knows the needs of our children, families, and friends.

When we fall into bed at the end of the day, we have the opportunity to take a few moments of spiritual refreshment with God, before getting the much-needed physical sleep. We can relax into His rest, knowing there will come a day when we'll have more time with Him.

O God, make my heart glad because You are patient and understanding.
I can be renewed in my hope of You. Amen.

Michelangelo's David

For we are His workmanship, created in Christ Jesus for good works,
which God prepared beforehand so that we would walk in them.
Ephesians 2:10 NASB

The block of marble that Michelangelo eventually chiseled into the well-known sculpture of David had been neglected for twenty-five years. The sculpture had been commissioned to one artist, then another, until it was finally abandoned. It sat for a quarter of a century in the yard of a cathedral workshop, as rain and wind pummeled it down to a smaller size than it had originally been.

Still, the giant hunk of marble was valuable, and authorities were determined to find another artist who could turn it into a finished work of art. Twenty-six-year-old Michelangelo earned the commission. He looked at that abandoned, neglected block of marble, and he saw young David at his prime, right before the battle against Goliath.

What does God see when He looks at us? Although we may be focused on our flaws and sins and areas of neglect, God sees a work in progress. He considers us to be a masterpiece in the making, being shaped and molded and transformed into His image.

Do we perceive our children the same way God sees us? Just like us, they are emerging out of that marble block into the person God intended. They are His masterpieces in the making!

Thank You, Lord, that I can be confident that the work You have
begun in my life, and also in my children's lives, You will finish.

My God Knows

Your Father knoweth what things ye have need of, before ye ask him.
Matthew 6:8 KJV

*H*ow are you when it comes to asking for help? It's true that all mothers have different personalities, but in general we want to be self-sufficient. We don't like to admit it when we are completely worn out, when we can't figure something out, or when we barely have time to pick up our children's toys or make a decent meal. We want to appear competent, so we just keep quiet.

We might burn ourselves out, fooling those around us, but we can't fool God. He knows what our needs are before we even share them with Him. He wants to help us, but we have to want His help. There is no point in pride. We do ourselves and our families a huge disservice by trying to cover up what God already plainly sees. Why not willingly give your needs and concerns to Your heavenly Father, who loves you and wants so much to help you? It will relieve a tremendous amount of pressure and bring much joy to your home. Swallow your pride. It's a foe that almost always defeats, but God will give you the victory.

*Father, I'm sorry I've tried to hide my concerns from You.
I place them in Your hands today, knowing You'll care for me.*

Will They Ever Grow Up?

And the child Samuel grew on, and was in favour
both with the LORD, and also with men.
1 Samuel 2:26 KJV

We spend our days cleaning up spilled milk, being interrupted when providing instruction, and breaking up fights over toys. Some days we wonder, *Will they ever grow up?*

Oh yes, they will grow up.

They will get bigger, stronger, more coordinated. They will learn to talk and, eventually, to converse.

And they will learn to think for themselves.

We really can't stop them from growing.

But we can help them in their journey to maturity by consistently providing limits or boundaries in their lives and being patient when they make mistakes.

If we want our children to be like Samuel, growing in favor with God and men, we need to be as patient with our little ones as God is with us.

We need to speak to them firmly but gently, encouraging them as they grow and steering them in the right direction.

Kids will be kids, so we shouldn't be surprised when they act like kids.

They will all too soon grow up, and we'll be wishing they were little again.

In the meantime, be patient.

After all, there's no use crying over spilled milk.

Father, thank You for being patient with me;
help me be patient with my little ones. Amen.

Your Body, God's Temple

You surely know that your body is a temple where the Holy Spirit lives.
The Spirit is in you and is a gift from God.
1 Corinthians 6:19 CEV

*M*any moms, when viewing themselves in the mirror, can quickly count up multiple changes they would like to make. Maybe the hairstyle is out of date, or a few pounds should be shed, or those laugh lines aren't really so funny. It's amazing how quickly the imperfections can be spotted and criticized.

It is essential to keep our bodies healthy for our own well-being as well as for the sake of our children, but that should not be where we invest all of our time and effort. God desires that we keep our hearts and minds in shape, too, maintaining a pure place for His Spirit to dwell. After inviting Christ to live in your heart, your body becomes His home, "a temple where the Holy Spirit lives." God does not require that our bodies be ones of perfection; however, out of a heart of love for Him, we should choose to maintain His temple to the best of our ability.

Just as we take time to spruce up our home before a guest arrives, take some time today to "clean up" the Holy Spirit's temple.

Father, help me to accept myself today as a woman created by You for the purpose of housing Your Holy Spirit. Thank You for this amazingly precious gift. Amen.

Our Merciful Father

Through the tender mercy of our God, with which
the Dayspring from on high has visited us. . .
Luke 1:78 NKJV

The women's ministry conference topic dealt with fears. The speaker began by telling a recent story about her son.

"My son and I attended a carnival at his elementary school. My son had always been afraid of the dark, but he was determined that we would crawl through a winding, pitch-black maze." The speaker laughed, describing the contraption setup. "I'm surprised I fit through the tunnels, but even before we got down on our hands and knees to begin, my son made me promise something. He said, 'Mommy, we can do this. But only if you hold my hand the whole way.' So, I did."

The audience enjoyed the speaker's facial expressions as she mimicked their pitch-black journey into the wilderness. "Then," the speaker continued, "my son, who was ahead of me in the tunnel but still holding my hand, stopped and let out a piercing scream. Not knowing what to do, I had to scream at the top of my lungs to get him to calm down. As soon as I did, he stopped."

The audience was wide-eyed, waiting for the speaker to resolve her story. "I spoke in a soft tone and asked him what was wrong. When he responded, he did so with giggles and continued moving forward in the tunnel. 'I'm sorry, Mommy,' he said, 'for a second, I forgot I was safe and holding your hand.'"

Lord, thank You for holding me through hard and dark times in my life.

How Far?

For as the heaven is high above the earth, so great is his mercy
toward them that fear him. As far as the east is from the west,
so far hath he removed our transgressions from us.
Psalm 103:11–12 KJV

After days of clouds and rain, we mothers breathe a sigh of relief
and take our kids to the park. Most of us do not think about the
source of our bright, lovely weather—the sun, our closest star,
located ninety-three million miles from Earth.

"That's nice," we say absentmindedly. Babies in swings need
gentle pushes and lots of conversation. Preschoolers on jungle gyms
need constant supervision.

Facts and figures about the stars may fascinate astronomers and
astronauts, but we must focus attention on our little balls of fire that
zoom past us like miniature meteors. Who has time to ponder how
far the east is from the west? What was the psalmist talking about
when he wrote in such poetic, cosmic language long ago?

Just this: Jesus went out of His way—much farther than ninety-
three million miles—to sacrifice His holy life for us. His love is
so high it can never be measured. And God has hurled our sins an
infinite distance away. He will never look at them again.

Lord Jesus, I cannot comprehend the vastness of Your love and mercy.
But thank You for the poets of the psalms, who help me
understand You a little better. Amen.

No Place for Envy

Let us not be desirous of vain glory, provoking one another, envying one another.
Galatians 5:26 KJV

*Y*ou want to be a good mother. Maybe you even promised God that if He would give you a child, you would be "the perfect parent." Now you find yourself in a grocery store checkout line. Your sweet little angel is showing a rather wild side as he crawls over the cart, pulls gum and magazines from the rack, and screams when you deny his request for a treat. Your personal desire is to creep out of the store in embarrassment and never return.

As you finish paying for your purchases, you catch a glimpse of the children in the next aisle. They are sitting or standing quietly in their proper places, and you begin to think, *Why me? Why is my child so difficult and that woman's kids so perfect?* Instead of being thrilled with the little one God blessed you with, you compare him to others. You resent the "perfect" mom because her "perfect" kids are making you look bad, and because she's having an easy time while you are deeply involved in a battle of wills.

Take a deep breath. Remember that all kids are different, and so are moms. You have strengths that other moms only dream about. Your little one was designed by God especially for you. Teach him well, and love him always.

Dear God, sometimes I'm jealous of other moms' abilities.
Forgive me, and help me to be a mother who honors You.

Future Saints

I will pour out my spirit upon all flesh;
and your sons and your daughters shall prophesy.
Joel 2:28 KJV

*W*hat a hot afternoon! Sarah felt extra glad she and Rob had bought a wading pool for the twins' birthday. It created a nice, cool break before the kids' naps. Three-year-old Callie and Carter played happily with their new water toys. Sarah settled into her lawn chair at water's edge.

For exactly twenty seconds.

She didn't know why the afternoon exploded into disaster, but Sarah found herself separating her screeching children. She tried to calm them, but they nearly yanked her arms off as they fought like little tiger cubs. Sarah even tried to pray, as the expert suggested in her latest book on Christian parenting, but she feared the twins would kill each other before the amen. Sarah dragged them inside and stuck them in their rooms while she mopped up water and tried to get her head together.

It never failed. Whenever Sarah attempted to grow spiritually, her kids always turned into nasty little heathens. *Lord, what will they be like when they're sixteen?* She shuddered. But Sarah decided to keep trying.

Fourteen years from that day, Callie and Carter were singing in a Christian band on a beach. Several other teens came to hear the music, and they helped lead a girl and guy to Christ.

Father, in the daily war to survive, help me never underestimate
what You do by Your Spirit in my children's lives.
Thank You for making me part of the miracle. Amen.

Tough Love

Let everything you do be done in love (true love to
God and man as inspired by God's love for us).
1 Corinthians 16:14 AMP

$\mathcal{P}$aula pulled her preschooler's bedroom door shut behind her. His sobs pierced her heart. Why did he have to be so stubborn? It would be so easy to go back into the bedroom, pull him into her arms, and simply love on him. But she knew that if she did, he wouldn't learn the lesson she was trying to teach him.

She walked to her bedroom, knelt beside the bed, and prayed. Tears streamed down her face as she visited with the Lord about her little boy's refusal to obey the simple rules she'd put into place. Her heart swelled with love for the child. As she sat quietly, Paula realized her actions were correct and true.

Tough love had to be administered now while her baby was still young. Paula knew she wanted her preschooler to grow up to be a godly man. She stood to her feet and tiptoed to his room. He'd cried himself to sleep. Paula kissed his forehead and heard his soft whisper, "I love you, Mommy."

"I love you, too, pumpkin," she whispered back, thankful she hadn't caved earlier but had taken her feelings to the Lord.

Father God, thank You for giving me the strength to love my child
in all that I do concerning him. I want to be the parent You want me to be.
I know that I need You to help me when I have to use tough love and
then stand my ground. I love You, Lord. Amen.

One Thing

*One thing I have desired of the L*ORD*, that will I seek: that I may dwell in the house of the L*ORD *all the days of my life, to behold the beauty of the L*ORD*, and to inquire in His temple.*
Psalm 27:4 NKJV

One thing. People spend the majority of their time on the urgent things, not necessarily on the important things. It takes wisdom to know the difference. Consider Mary and Martha. Jesus said, "Martha, Martha. . .you are worried and upset about many things, but only *one thing* is needed. Mary has chosen what is better, and it will not be taken away from her" (Luke 10:41–42 NIV, emphasis added). Martha allowed the urgent things that arose in her day to crowd out the one important thing: time with her Savior.

As moms, we could all make a list of the urgent things that need to get done each day. And they are truly urgent things; people count on us. But knowing that they need us to be the best that we can be, and knowing that we can only achieve that through a right relationship with God, we need to set aside the urgent things in order to make time for the *one thing* first. That *one thing*—time with our Father—is the most important thing in our day.

Father, please help me to identify the things in my life that seem urgent to me but only serve to crowd out the one thing that You desire from me. Help me to dedicate more time to simply being with You. Amen.

The Right Hand

*Whither shall I go from thy Spirit? Or whither shall
I flee from thy presence? . . . Thy right hand shall hold me.*
Psalm 139:7, 10 ASV

We've all experienced the sinking feeling when we lose track of our children. Maybe we're checking out in the store, and they wander off. Perhaps they were playing in the yard and disappeared. In fact, mothers would testify that nothing moves as fast as a toddler. They can be out of sight in an instant. We feel relief only when they are once more in our arms.

As mothers, we have a connection to our children. When we lose sight of them, we begin to panic, until we take the concern to God. Even then we know nothing will be the same until we hold our child's hand in ours once again. The relief we feel as we touch our newly found son or daughter is inexpressible. We don't want to ever be separated again.

There are times when we feel far from God. We don't enjoy the closeness we once experienced in His presence. We can trust that God never loses sight of us. He always knows right where we are. There is no need to fear or panic. All we need to do is reach out and know that He is holding us with His right hand. We are always in His care. Because we are His, we have no need to worry about being apart.

*Praise You, Lord, that I can be secure in the knowledge
that You are there for me always. Amen.*

A Peaceful Life

*"Peace I leave with you; my peace I give you. I do not give to you as
the world gives. Do not let your hearts be troubled and do not be afraid."*
John 14:27 NIV

What gives you peace? A conflict-free life? No stress or worries?
Obedient children?

We know that in this life, there will be conflict, stress, worries,
and disobedient children. There is no way we can avoid the sinful
nature of this world. However, in the challenges of raising children,
Jesus has left us with—and desires to continually give us—peace.
The stipulation is that the type of peace the world gives—the
temporal, brief, counterfeit peace—is not God's eternal peace. When
we believe in our hearts and confess with our lips that Jesus is Lord,
we are saved (Romans 10:9-10). We automatically are in a peaceful
relationship with the Lord. As believers we have Jesus' spirit (John
15:5), the Holy Spirit (John 14:26), the Prince of Peace (Isaiah
9:6) indwelling us. With the eternal security of being at peace
with the Lord and peace indwelling us, we are then free to "not be
anxious about anything, but in everything, by prayer and petition,
with thanksgiving, present [our] requests to God. And the peace of
God, which transcends all understanding, will guard [our] hearts and
[our] minds in Christ Jesus" (Philippians 4:6–7 NIV).

*Lord, I praise You that my heart does not need to be troubled or
afraid in raising my preschooler. Your peace that surpasses all
understanding is given to me so I can live a peaceful life.*

Stuff

"Do not store up for yourselves treasures on earth, where moth and
rust destroy, and where thieves break in and steal. But store up for
yourselves treasures in heaven, where moth and rust do not destroy,
and where thieves do not break in and steal."
Matthew 6:19–20 NIV

The bumper sticker on the red Porsche read THE ONE WHO DIES
WITH THE MOST TOYS WINS. Our culture is obsessed with the
accumulation of "stuff." Second homes are commonplace. Clothes are
bulging from dresser drawers. Storage facilities on every street corner
are overflowing with unusable earthly treasures.

Jesus reminds us that everything we see is temporary. None of
our earthly possessions will enter heaven's gates. Everything will be
left behind. Then why do we spend so much time, money, and energy
obtaining temporary treasures? Jesus encourages us to concentrate on
eternal treasures instead. Spending time studying God's Word and
growing closer to Him is a wise investment. Pouring our lives into
people reaps lasting benefits. Using material blessings to spiritually
impact others is commended.

Rather than storing up "stuff," let's pass it on so that others
may be blessed. Clean out a closet. Empty a drawer. Give to those less
fortunate. Then focus on things that will last forever and never lose
their value. When we store up heavenly treasures, we will be blessed in
this life and the life to come.

Dear Lord, help me focus on heavenly rather than earthly treasures.
Open my eyes to see life from Your perspective. Amen.

But the Lord said to Ananias, "Go! This man is my chosen instrument to carry my name before the Gentiles and their kings and before the people of Israel. I will show him how much he must suffer for my name."
Acts 9:15–16 NIV

Sarah knew the woman had been crying. She noticed the wet circles under the woman's eyes and the way she held her head low until she was seated in the church pew. Sarah had seen her a few times before, but she had never made it to the back of the church to say hello before the woman left at the service's end.

Sarah told herself that she would say hello after the service. But even before the opening songs were over, Sarah's thoughts were somewhere else. Then the sermon began. The pastor told the story about Ananias and Paul. Fortunately, Ananias's questions and own schedule weren't enough to keep him from meeting Paul. Ananias's obedience impacted Paul, and Paul's life continues to reach people today.

Deeply moved by the message, at the end of the service Sarah immediately rose from her seat and walked to the back of the church. It took a few seconds to weave her way between the people. As she approached the woman, she wondered why she had been crying. Sarah knew that everyone has a story, but many are ignored or overlooked. What was this woman's story?

"Hello, I'm Sarah."

The woman smiled, not making eye contact. "I'm Alyssa."

Sarah noticed Alyssa's protruding abdomen. Maybe this was why God wanted her to meet Alyssa.

Lord, open my eyes to see people who are in need.

Under Construction

Be cheerful no matter what; pray all the time; thank God no matter what happens. This is the way God wants you who belong to Christ Jesus to live.
1 Thessalonians 5:16–18 MSG

$\mathcal{S}$urely, when God said to give thanks for everything, He didn't mean the time when the baby had the stomach flu and shared the virus with the entire family. He couldn't have been thinking of when we had to scrub an unidentifiable stickiness off the new carpet. Or when the dog chewed up the TV remote.

This parenting gig is a long and exasperating process at times. Often, it seems as if so much of what we do is routine, mundane, or just plain hard.

But God didn't qualify His biblical admonishment of giving thanks in all things. He really meant all things! Every circumstance in our life—annoying, frustrating, even ordinary moments.

God notices those moments! He cares about them. He promises to never leave or forsake us, even in the middle of the night when the baby has a dirty diaper. Or while we're scraping off a half-eaten Pop-Tart from the car seat.

Giving thanks reminds us that what really matters is what's going on inside of us. God is at work, fixing, renewing, and cleaning up our mess. Our patience is growing, our kindness is stretching, and our love is being made perfect. At all times, we're in process and under construction.

Lord, thank You for continuing to do Your good work in me and in my children. Make me more mindful of giving thanks at all times.

Happy Are Those Who Endure

Behold, we count them happy which endure. Ye have heard of the patience of Job, and have seen the end of the Lord; that the Lord is very pitiful, and of tender mercy.
James 5:11 KJV

*A*lone with her baby in a newborn intensive care unit, the tired mother kept vigil. Hour after hour she stayed by her baby's side, watching monitors, wrestling with tubing and cables as she tried to nurse, lifting her heart and soul up to God, and asking Him to see her through this crisis.

In the quiet moments, she watched the other parents in the nursery as they labored over their infants, most of whom had been born prematurely. They, too, kept long hours with their tiny miracle babies. Each weight check came with anxiety; each ounce gained brought hope.

During her stay, the mother watched several families come and go.

With each discharge, there was great joy on the ward, the parents and staff rejoicing when a baby was big enough to leave. They all shared the success, because they had all known the struggle.

Happy were those who endured.

Father, in an hour of crisis, I readily seek Your mercy and find the strength to endure. But in the daily routine of motherhood, I sometimes forget that You are there to sustain me, to give me hope and peace. Bless me with patient endurance. Thank You for being with me through thick and thin. Amen.

Resting and Waiting

*Rest in the LORD, and wait patiently for him: fret not thyself
because of him who prospereth in his way, because of the
man who bringeth wicked devices to pass.*
Psalm 37:7 KJV

There was a tug at the blanket. "Mama, it's light outside, and I'm
hungry," three-year-old Megan stated firmly. Erin groaned as she
looked at the clock. 7:30. How could that be?

Another sleepless night filled with nothing but worry and fearsome dreams,
Erin thought dejectedly. How much blacker could the circles under
her eyes become? It seemed like her life was completely consumed by
fear. *What if I don't raise Megan right? What if she gets mixed up with the wrong
crowd? If something happens to me, what will become of her?* The more Erin
worried, the more sleep she lost. The more sleep she lost, the more
she worried. It was a horrible cycle that she couldn't break.

Finally, she talked to her pastor's wife. "Erin, there are many
things beyond our control, but they aren't beyond God's control,"
the wise lady reminded her. "You need to let Him manage your fears."

As Erin prayed, her burden began to lift. That night, her rest was
sweet. Her life was beginning to turn around.

*Dear God, many times I am fearful, and rest evades me.
I now cast my cares on You, for You will see me through.*

I will greatly rejoice in the LORD, my soul will be joyful in my God;
for he hath clothed me with the garments of salvation,
he hath covered me with the robe of righteousness.
Isaiah 61:10 KJV

*H*ave you ever watched your child and been struck by the depth of love you have for him? This is a love so intense it is almost a physical ache. At that moment you may want nothing other than to spend more time with your toddler, watching and getting to know him as he grows.

Each developmental age of a child is different, full of surprises, trials, and delights. We can stand in wonder as we watch our offspring learn new skills or discover the world around them. We thrill over first hugs or kisses, never getting enough and thankful for each one bestowed. Even the independent do-it-myself stages can charm us as our child grows.

When we stop to contemplate the gifts God has given us— salvation, love, grace, mercy, etc.—we are filled with incredible wonder. The God who created everything loves us enough to want to have a personal, intimate relationship with us. We can rejoice, knowing that God will always delight in us as much as we delight in Him. He, too, is thankful for each expression of love we extend to Him.

Thank You, God, for Your indescribable gift through Your Son,
Jesus Christ, and for the depth of Your love for me. Amen.

Ups and Downs

Why are you downcast, O my soul? Why so disturbed within me?
Put your hope in God, for I will yet praise him, my Savior and my God.
Psalm 42:11 NIV

*I*n the book of Samuel, King David led the ark of the covenant to Jerusalem. "David and the whole house of Israel were celebrating with all their might before the LORD, with songs and with harps, lyres, tambourines, sistrums and cymbals" (2 Samuel 6:5 NIV). Such joy! Such confidence in God! Such harmony among the Israelites!

But skip forward to Psalm 42. David isn't singing or dancing or rejoicing anymore. In this lament, he has to remind himself to hope in God. David's words sound wooden, forced. As if he is barely hanging on to his faith.

Aren't we just like David? Our journey of faith has ups and downs, great days and frustrating days. There are days when praising God is such a natural response. Some days we seem to soar. Joy bubbles up like a child's giggle.

Then there are days when God feels distant. Problems overwhelm us and prayer feels a futile exercise, as if our pleas stop at the ceiling. There is no harmony in our homes, and we have little joy. Even worse, our confidence in God feels shaky.

Still, David reminds us to praise God. . .despite our doubts. Despite our discouragement. Despite the stack of problems that face us. For He is our Savior and our God!

Lord, thank You for David's reminder to hope in You.
I trust that You hear my prayers and are working in my life,
prompting me to sing and dance and have joy once again.

Hope for Healing

*"I will heal their waywardness and love them freely,
for my anger has turned away from them."*
Hosea 14:4 NIV

*F*amily picnics, baseball games, ice-cream cones, fireworks—there's nothing like the Fourth of July! We give our children flags to wave at parades as we celebrate our country's birth.

Sometimes, however, we watch the national news on television and wonder what the future will hold for our little ones. What a mess! Corruption, immorality, outright hostility to Christianity. We hold our precious children close, wishing we could raise them in a country whose citizens respect God and His laws.

Hosea, God's prophet to Israel, tried to warn his nation of impending disaster because of its sin. In chapter after chapter of the book that bears his name, Hosea pleaded with his people to change their minds and turn back to God. Even when the children of Israel persisted in idolatry, sexual sin, dishonesty, and hypocrisy, God longed for them to repent and envisioned what it would be like when they returned to Him. He was all about healing, not hating.

God asks us, like Hosea, to take a stand for righteousness in our country and teach our children to do the same. With the prayers of God's people and His help, our nation can experience spiritual awakening and be blessed with His healing and love.

*Lord Jesus, sometimes I live in my own little world and forget
to pray for my country's leaders. Please remind me every
day that You are big enough to heal nations. Amen.*

Source of Strength

I love you, O LORD, my strength.
Psalm 18:1 NIV

*C*ynthia conversed with the Lord, asking, "How am I going to get through this day? I am exhausted from mothering my preschooler, being pregnant with another baby, trying to meet deadlines for work, helping with church projects, doing laundry, cleaning, and the list goes on! Heavenly Father, help me! Give me strength!" Do you ever sound like this?

The Lord promises to help and strengthen us, to uphold us with His "victorious right hand" (Isaiah 41:10 NLT). God's Word tells us repeatedly He is our source of strength (1 Chronicles 29:12; Psalm 68:35; Colossians 1:11). Sometimes in our weary and exhausted state, God calls us to wait on Him, promising that those who wait will renew their strength (Isaiah 40:29–31). As we rely on God's supernatural strength, He does provide mothers with practical tips on how to survive life: prayer, walking in close union with the Lord (John 15:5), trusting and allowing the Lord to prioritize our commitments, saying no to what is not God's will, taking naps when our preschoolers nap or have quiet playtime in their rooms, going to bed thirty minutes earlier at night, staying organized, and making meals over the weekend that will provide leftovers for several nights. As an exhausted mother of a preschooler, take hope. The Lord, our source of strength, will empower us to accomplish all things in His will (Philippians 4:13).

Lord, I thank You for being my source of strength and hope. I praise You that I can raise my preschooler and complete the work You have for me in Your power.

Speak, Lord!

So Eli told Samuel, "Go and lie down, and if he calls you,
say, 'Speak, Lord, for your servant is listening.' "
1 Samuel 3:9 NIV

*A*fter many years and much prayer, Hannah gave birth to Samuel. And after being dedicated to the Lord, he served Eli, the priest in the temple. One night the Lord spoke to Samuel, but the young boy assumed it was Eli's voice. Following the second attempt, Eli realized that the Lord was trying to speak to Samuel. So Eli instructed Samuel to lie down and when he heard the voice again, respond by saying, "Speak, Lord, for your servant is listening."

God may not speak audibly to us today, but He does speak. He speaks clearly through His Word. Nature declares His praise. Other people communicate God's truth. Circumstances can confirm His will. Are we listening?

Today's women are bombarded by voices that emphasize having perfect children, Martha Stewart homes, and youthful bodies. We strain to hear God's voice whispering truth amid the clamor. What is the solution? We must purposefully choose to quiet our hearts. As we spend time reading the Bible and praying, we become attuned to His voice. The more we listen and obey, the more He speaks. Any relationship grows over time through communication. Listen. The Lord is speaking. Can you hear Him?

Dear Lord, may I be like Samuel and desire to hear You speak.
Help me set aside quiet time each day to spend with You.
Give me ears to hear and a heart to follow. Amen.

Helping Other Moms

Offer hospitality to one another without grumbling.
I Peter 4:9 NIV

*H*urricane Katrina hit, and Courtney knew life would never be the same for her family. Her home was one of the least damaged in the community where she lived. Devastation surrounded them. She wanted to help those around her but didn't know how. Courtney took food to her neighbors and warm blankets to the shelter where many families were staying because their homes had been destroyed.

She didn't know what else to do. But the answer came from her four-year-old daughter, Misty. Misty asked her mother why she couldn't still play with her friends from preschool.

Courtney didn't know how to explain to her child that a hurricane had come and torn up their lives and the lives of their friends. She searched Misty's face. "Can't we just ask them to come to our house to play?" Misty asked.

Why hadn't she thought of that? Courtney realized that if she took the preschool-age children into her home during the day, it would help their mothers. She and Misty walked hand in hand through the neighborhood. Soon they had ten children going home with them to play.

Lord, please open my eyes so that I can see how to help others.
I know that because of You I have a deep love in my heart for those around me.
Show me how to be a blessing to them. Amen.

Speak to Me

*In the beginning was the Word, and the Word was with God,
and the Word was God.*
John 1:1 KJV

A baby's first words are monumental for any parent. Slowly and over time, the baby's brain is developed enough to not only recognize and interpret words and phrases, but to create understanding and use words in the correct context. Words carry great power. They have the ability to build up and teach, but they also have the capacity to hurt and destroy.

When a baby says his first word, parents are confident that their child is not only fascinating, but incredibly intelligent. Phone calls are made to distant relatives and congratulatory words are offered. But as time passes, people aren't satisfied with mere words; they want sentences.

Some parents jokingly admit that they would be content going back to a time when their chatterbox toddler or especially stubborn middle school student had no speaking ability whatsoever. With the ability to speak comes the opportunity to not only agree or disagree, but say such impacting yet diverse phrases as "I love you" or "I hate you." Words are powerful!

When the apostle John wrote about Jesus, he referred to Him as "the Word." Another way to understand "the Word" is to recognize that Jesus is the Truth. If something is true, it means that it is unchanging. John wanted readers to understand that Jesus stays the same, no matter what.

As our children grow and change, we can be reminded that their growing knowledge should always be based on "the Word"—God's Truth.

Lord, help me to teach my children about Your constant love and truth.

Rest Assured

It is vain for you to rise up early, to sit up late,
to eat the bread of sorrows: for so he giveth his beloved sleep.
Psalm 127:2 KJV

A mother spends individual time with each of her little ones, reading books and teaching them their ABCs. They learn Bible verses every day. Mom takes them outside for hours of fun and exercise. She folds and puts away every stitch of laundry and makes bread from scratch. Her house sparkles. Her church and community know her as a ready volunteer. Plus, she works outside her home forty hours a week.

Did I mention she has not slept since the year 2000?

A mother who makes such impossible demands on herself is sure to self-destruct. New babies, sick children, and extra projects inevitably disturb a mother's schedule. But months, even years, of sleep deprivation do not promote good stewardship of the wonderful body God created. Physical, mental, and emotional problems eventually result, damaging a woman's marriage and family, as well as herself. Husbands and children need someone who has recharged her batteries and stands ready to handle the day's challenges with enthusiasm, energy, and a sense of humor.

So take a nap when the children nap! Don't demand perfection in things that don't matter, because God doesn't.

Jesus, when You grew weary, You rested so You could care
for people who needed You. Please help me let go of unrealistic
expectations so I can get much-needed rest. Amen.

Your Special Dwelling Place

*"In My Father's house are many dwelling places; if it were not so,
I would have told you; for I go to prepare a place for you."*
John 14:2 NASB

*M*oms spend much of their time maintaining their home: cooking,
cleaning, laundering, organizing. . .the list is endless. Because sin
entered into the world, work came along as a consequence. Even now
you may be multitasking. . .wondering what to make for dinner and
if you should go grab that pack of chicken from the freezer so it has
time to thaw.

But take a moment to rest in the promise Jesus gave in John
14:2. He informs us that there is a place waiting for us that will
require nothing on our part. Jesus tells us that in His Father's house,
there are plenty of rooms for everyone—no one has to fight over who
gets the "top bunk"—and there will be a place tailor-made for you.
Just imagine Him talking with God, saying, "Father, [insert your own
name here] will be joining us soon. I'd like to make a special room
just for her."

What a joy to know that He has found time to prepare a place
for *you*. . .one that you will never have to worry about painting,
decorating, or cleaning!

*Jesus, please give me the strength to maintain my earthly home,
but also help me to remember the special home that You
have prepared for me, waiting in heaven. Amen.*

Way of Escape

No temptation has seized you except what is common to man. And God is faithful; he will not let you be tempted beyond what you can bear. But when you are tempted, he will also provide a way out so that you can stand up under it.
1 Corinthians 10:13 NIV

*H*ow would we function without an answering machine? Everyone has one. Although they have become standard telephone equipment, initially many people were hesitant to use them. That awkwardness has subsided. Messages can be left instead of having to repeatedly call until the person returns home. We can listen to recorded messages and even replay them over and over if necessary.

Pushing the PLAY button on our answering machines is one thing. But have you ever replayed a negative conversation in your mind? It's like hitting the PLAY button over and over again, obsessing over what was said. The more we replay the unpleasant interaction, the more our emotions spiral downward. Discouragement, anger, resentment, and pain await us at the bottom of the pit.

We don't have to head down that path. Instead, God has provided a way of escape. It's called forgiveness. Instead of pushing PLAY, hit DELETE. Forgive the person. Refuse to replay the hurt. God does not want us to dwell on painful words. He desires to bring healing and restoration. Forgiveness has been provided as an antidote for bitterness. Take the way of escape that God has provided.

Dear Lord, help me avoid replaying hurtful conversations in my mind. May I forgive others and receive Your healing. Amen.

Season of Discontent?

But as for me, my feet were almost gone; my steps had well nigh slipped.
For I was envious at the foolish, when I saw the prosperity of the wicked.
Psalm 73:2–3 KJV

Children have a way of changing a woman's life.

When she goes from "wife" to "wife and mother," she may also go from office to house; from briefcase to diaper bag; from power lunches to late-night feedings.

Those who go from two incomes without children to one income with children may find it difficult to make ends meet. Even those who have chosen homemaking as their first ministry may be surprised by the stress a new little person puts on an already tight budget. And those who have chosen to continue working may wonder how they will ever get everything done as time becomes an increasingly precious and fleeting commodity.

In any case, it is a prime time for temptation. As money for things gets diverted to children, things are repaired, not replaced. When a child is sick, a vacation day is used to stay home and nurse him. As we look at others around us who seem more financially blessed and seem to have hours of time on their hands to rest, relax, and vacation, we can become jealous. They have so much, and we have. . .kids. The spring of motherhood can easily become the season of our discontent.

Like the psalmist, we must look ahead. The end of the unsaved is eternal separation from the Father. They will not enjoy their prosperity beyond this life. But we have the hope of taking our children with us to heaven.

Nothing invested in a child is wasted; it yields eternal rewards.

Father, I may not have the world's wealth and hours of leisure time on
my hands, but You have given me a greater heritage through my children.
Thank You for these blessings that will yield eternal fruit. Amen.

Running for Comfort

Be merciful unto me, O God, be merciful unto me; for my soul
taketh refuge in thee: Yea, in the shadow of thy wings will I take refuge,
until these calamities be overpast.
Psalm 57:1 ASV

The mother jerked awake at the sound of tiny feet pattering across the floor. Lifting the covers, she pulled her trembling child into the bed with her. She cuddled him close, his small hands fisted in her nightgown. She could almost picture his fear from whatever had awakened him.

Each night when her child woke from a bad dream, the mother held him close, comforting him with soothing words and touches. He would cling to her until the frightening presence of his dream faded, and he relaxed into sleep, content in his mother's arms. In this safe embrace he found peace once again.

Often, events in our lives can be upsetting, sometimes terrifying. We tremble in fear, our peace and contentment far away. The struggle can become unbearable if we try to be brave and solve the problem or handle everything on our own.

Our only hope is to run through the dark to God, lifting our hands to Him. He is always there to pull us close. With words of comfort, God lets us know He will care for us. We don't need to fear anything. He will always soothe us and give us peace.

Thank You, Lord, that I can run to You for comfort when life gets scary. Amen.

Scattered Seed

"Please test your servants for ten days: Give us nothing but vegetables to eat and water to drink. Then compare our appearance with that of the young men who eat the royal food, and treat your servants in accordance with what you see."
Daniel 1:12–13 NIV

After ten trial days in King Nebuchadnezzar's court, Daniel and his friends looked healthier and better nourished than the captives from Jerusalem who had eaten the king's food. So Daniel was granted permission to carry on with his nutrition plan.

The word used for those vegetables was an Aramaic word for scattered seed. Daniel ate anything that had been planted by seed: vegetables, fruits, and grains. It was a balanced, healthy diet.

It was also kosher. Daniel was holding on to the belief system he had been raised with back in Jerusalem. So did his three trusted friends, known as Shadrach, Meshach, and Abednego.

What about the other Hebrew captives? What were they thinking as they watched Daniel and his friends eat a different diet? And how did they feel when they saw Daniel and the others bow their heads before a meal?

Daniel wasn't just eating scattered seed, he was acting like scattered seed! We can be Daniel-like to others, too. Each time we pray before a meal, whether we are at home, on vacation, at a restaurant, or entertaining guests, we are acting as scattered seeds. Three times a day, as we offer grace for our food, we remind our families to honor God.

Lord, teach us to pray like Daniel, who always knew the real power was Yours.

God-Focused Priorities

*Delight thyself also in the LORD: and he shall give thee the desires
of thine heart. Commit thy way unto the LORD; trust also in him;
and he shall bring it to pass.*
Psalm 37:4–5 KJV

With what or whom do you delight or take pleasure? Good movies, shopping, conversation with girlfriends? How do these activities shape your priorities?

Christina recalls taking great pleasure in a retreat she attended where she was able to spend precious time with the Lord. This time of solitude and prayer enabled her to reprioritize her life.

The Lord tells us to delight or take pleasure in Him. But how do we delight in Him? We spend time getting to know the Lord more intimately through daily quiet time, reading and studying the Bible, continual prayer, and corporate worship. However, how often have you thought, *I am way too busy to be engaged in these spiritual disciplines—I have a preschooler!*

It is precisely because we are so busy that it is imperative to spend time with the Lord. Spiritual disciplines enable us to align our priorities with His will. As we know the Lord more intimately, our desires become one with His.

Gracious Lord, I surrender my priorities to You and ask that You would align them with Your priorities, Your best for my family and me.

Faultless, Not a Failure

Now unto him that is able to keep you from falling, and to present you faultless before the presence of his glory with exceeding joy, to the only wise God our Saviour, be glory and majesty, dominion and power, both now and ever. Amen.
Jude 1:24–25 KJV

Alex did her best as a parent, but she struggled when Mandy and Matt pushed her past her limits. Her husband, Kevin, often criticized Alex's discipline methods. They came from such different backgrounds—Kevin from a solid Christian home, she raised by her grandmother because her parents did drugs.

Because of her troubled family, Alex often felt inferior. She even felt ashamed to confess her shortcomings to the Lord, until she read in the Bible how Jesus is able to present all Christians to His Father, not as failures, but as faultless! He would present her—her, Alex!—not with an apology, but with great joy.

As Alex absorbed this truth, she grew less defensive and asked Kevin for his parenting insights. They still sometimes disagreed, but they learned to discuss their differences and pray together for Mandy and Matt. The kids seemed to sense their growing solidarity, and tensions at home began to relax.

Now, instead of dreading the day she would see Jesus, Alex looked forward to standing by His side and feeling His smile of approval.

Lord Jesus, when my sins and mistakes overwhelm me, help me remember Your hand keeps me from falling, and Your love will guide me to heaven. Amen.

Keep It Simple, Be Consistent

*"But let your statement be 'Yes, yes' or 'No, no';
anything beyond these is of evil."*
Matthew 5:37 NASB

*C*hrist's teaching on communication is good advice for mothers of toddlers.

Our Lord's clear say-what-you-mean-and-mean-what-you-say approach is the best to use when teaching and training small children. Instant obedience is more easily achieved when requests are clear, short, and specific.

For example, before age two, a child can be expected to follow a specific one-step direction. Instead of saying, "Pick up your toys and put them away," we can say, "Put your truck in the toy box." This clear direction eliminates choice and makes it easier for the child to obey. Either the truck is in the toy box or it isn't. There's no gray area, no room for debate.

Simple directives also make it easier for mothers to remain consistent. If you are given to many words, misunderstandings may arise, you forgetting exactly what you said or the child not fully understanding the direction.

Making our "yes" a true yes and our "no" a true no will make our lives simpler.

Anything more may mean trouble for little ones and busy mothers.

Oh Father, Your directions are so clear and so wise. Help me to be a wise communicator. Remind me to talk less, to say what I mean, and to mean what I say. Help me to be consistent with my training and directions so my children learn obedience and godliness. Amen.

And he said unto them, Why are ye so fearful? how is it that ye have no faith?
Mark 4:40 KJV

The crash of thunder wakened Dena with a start. As her thoughts became oriented, she rolled over and looked at the doorway, expecting at any moment to see three-year-old Jackson standing there. When he arrived, she held out her arms, inviting him into the safety of her bed.

"Mama, I don't like the thunder," Jackson whimpered.

"I know," Dena replied. "It's loud and scary, but remember how I told you that Jesus is with us even during noisy storms? He's even in control of the storms, so we can trust Him to take care of us."

Jackson believed what Dena said, but he still preferred to have his mother's comforting arms around him. As Dena cuddled her son, she thought about the inevitable storms in life. She didn't fear thunder, but there were situations in which her faith was sorely tested. She knew God allows trials for a reason and that He is in charge, but those trials still weren't easy to face. She, too, desired that the loving arms of her Father be wrapped around her.

Loving Father, when I am faced with wild storms, help me not to cower in fear.
Instead, let me grow stronger in faith.

The Perfume of Sacrifice

Live a life filled with love, following the example of Christ. He loved us and offered himself as a sacrifice for us, a pleasing aroma to God.
Ephesians 5:2 NLT

Today, perfume is an exciting, feminine luxury. It is often sweet or flowery, and it can be delicate or very strong. It can be either a pleasant scent worn daily or an intoxicating and glamorous accessory to evening wear.

In biblical times, perfume was a sign of great wealth. It was given as a gift at the birth of Christ and then, later, it was sacrificially used to anoint Him before His death. We are told in Ephesians 5 that true love is following the example of Christ and loving others sacrificially. That sacrifice of love is like a perfume, a pleasing aroma to God.

Every day in the life of a mom is a living sacrifice—a sacrifice of self. Once a woman becomes a mom, she lives her life, even the mundane duties of each day, for someone else, and her needs become secondary. Moms sometimes feel personally lost in the shuffle, like they are suddenly unimportant. The truth is, though, that God takes great pleasure in the sweet scent that wafts before His throne, which can only come from the type of love that incites great sacrifice.

Your sacrificial love is like perfume, pleasing the senses of God.

Heavenly Father, thank You for placing great value on what I do as a mom. Help me to remember that my daily sacrifices are precious to You, as precious as the sweetest perfume. Amen.

Childlike Praise

He has given me a new song to sing, a hymn of praise to our God. Many will
see what he has done and be amazed. They will put their trust in the LORD.
Psalm 40:3 NLT

*W*hen a baby says his or her first word, most mothers react as
though the newspapers and evening news should be contacted.
The little life once carried inside the mother is now not only vocal
through cries, but also through words. These words will eventually be
strung together to form sentences and even songs.

Children rarely have knowledge as to whether their singing is on-
key or off-key. Their songs—especially when they don't know anyone
is observing—reflect a lightheartedness that adults lose and forget
about all too quickly. One day children will reach an age when their
singing no longer reflects the carefree innocence of childhood. They
are either told they have mediocre musical talent, that they could
make big money on the next nationwide televised event, or that their
singing should probably be reserved only for church.

But the Bible says that God created us to praise Him. He gives
us new songs for different circumstances and seasons. Whether
musically inclined or not, we can bless God's heart by singing
loudly—with our children.

Lord, I thank You for filling my heart with praise.
Today I will sing with the carefree voice of a child—Your child.

Small Group, Babylon-Style

*Then Daniel returned to his house and explained the matter to his friends
Hananiah, Mishael and Azariah. He urged them to plead for mercy from the
God of heaven concerning this mystery, so that he and his friends might not be
executed with the rest of the wise men of Babylon.*
Daniel 2:17–18 NIV

Nebuchadnezzar, the ruler of Babylon, had a troubling dream.
Known for his explosive temper, he ordered the execution of all wise
men when a few couldn't interpret his dream. That order included
Daniel!

So what did Daniel do? Disappear over the plains of Babylon? Of
course not! That wasn't Daniel's style.

Daniel went back to his friends—we know them as Shadrach,
Meschach, and Abednego—and asked them to pray that God would
reveal this mystery, in order to save their lives and the lives of other
innocent men.

In modern-day language, Daniel sought out prayer support from
his small group. Trusted friends who would drop everything to pray,
and would continue to pray until the answer came. And it did come!
The crisis was averted in a God-glorifying way.

God knew that Daniel would need those prayerful friends. He
understands our need for friendships, too. Everyone needs a friend,
a safe place to unload. Especially mothers of young children. It can
be a lonely, isolating, twenty-four-hours-a-day job. We can ask the
Lord to guide us to the right friends. Maybe even to be that friend to
another.

*Lord, thank You for providing friendships to me.
Help me to use them to glorify You.*

Sincerity

Love must be sincere.
Romans 12:9 NIV

In an attempt to disguise her anger, a young mother addressed her child in a singsong tone of voice. Her child responded by saying, "Mom, I can tell you are mad, so you don't have to pretend you're not." Children are not easily fooled. They can spot a fake. Even the tone of our voice cannot mask our emotions. Children are quite perceptive, seeing right through to the heart.

Love must also come from the heart. It must be sincere—genuine. People can tell the difference. We may be wearing a smile. We may be saying the proper words. We may be doing the right things. Yet, if our heart does not match our outward demeanor, others quickly detect the inconsistency.

There is a solution. First, we can receive God's love. Then we can allow the Lord to change our heart by making it more like His. He is the potter; we are the clay. When we choose to be pliable, He molds and shapes our heart. This is not an overnight process. Yet gradually our words and actions will flow from the heart. Our sincerity will be evident to all. Even our smile will be naturally radiant. When we emphasize the heart, everything else falls into place.

Dear Lord, change my heart and make it like Yours.
Then my love will be sincere, and my words will bring glory to You. Amen.

Don't Be Afraid

*Let us therefore come boldly unto the throne of grace,
that we may obtain mercy, and find grace to help in time of need.*
Hebrews 4:16 KJV

"Mommy, I broke your pretty jar." Tears filled Kasie's eyes as she told her mother what she'd done.

Laura had a feeling she knew which flower vase Kasie spoke of. She knew that Kasie's confession had been a long time coming. "What jar, sweetie?"

"That one by your chair in the living room." A lone tear slipped over Kasie's chubby cheek.

"The one that Jordan was blamed for breaking?"

Kasie nodded. Guilt and shame reflected on her small face.

Kasie had allowed her baby brother to take the blame. Since he couldn't talk very well yet, it had seemed like the perfect way to stay out of trouble for the four-year-old.

"I'm sorry I lied." She covered her eyes, and a wail escaped her lips.

Laura gathered her up and hugged her close. "When Jordan wakes up from his nap, you have to tell him that you're sorry. Okay?"

"Okay, Mommy." Kasie hugged her mother close. "You aren't mad at me?"

Laura returned her hug. "No, darlin'. I know it took a lot of courage for you to tell the truth."

*Lord, thank You for being a loving and merciful God.
I'm so thankful I can come to You and know that I have nothing
to fear because You will be there to help me. When my child comes to
me with truth in her heart, remind me to be loving like You. Amen.*

Distractions from Our True Calling

"Everyone who is called by My name,
And whom I have created for My glory. . ."
Isaiah 43:7 NASB

*A*ngela was in over her head. She asserted that God came first, family second, and work and extracurricular activities last. However, when she evaluated how she spent her day, there was little if any time spent communicating with the Lord, and she didn't have much energy and enthusiasm for her family.

There are strategies in God's Word for avoiding this downward spiral of spending time on what doesn't matter and, as a result, depleting our best resources for what does matter. Isaiah reminds us that our true calling or purpose in life is to glorify God. God created us for His glory, honor, reputation, or splendor. Therefore, we must seek the Lord's face to determine our calling for this season of our lives. God will reveal His purpose for us, instructing and teaching us in the way we should go, counseling us with His eye upon us (Psalm 32:8).

The challenge lies in choosing to say yes to the activities that align with His purpose and no to those that do not. We must remember that when we say yes to a *good* activity, we are implicitly saying no to a *best* activity. . .time with our family or time doing what is truly our calling. This doesn't come easy, but it may help to remember that motherhood of a preschooler is for a short season, gone forever before we know it.

Lord, I invite You to reveal Your purpose for me.
Align my days, raising my preschooler with activities that glorify You.

Rainy Day Love

Flood waters can't drown love, torrents of rain can't put it out.
Love can't be bought, love can't be sold—it's not to be found in the marketplace.
Song of Solomon 8:7 MSG

*F*ew brides and grooms struggle with the concept of love at their weddings. Nothing seemed easier than loving that handsome guy in a tuxedo, waiting at the altar. His eyes lit up as you, dressed like a princess, walked slowly down the aisle. You wanted to promise him the world.

Sometime during the first years together, a rainy season sets in— as it does for all couples. The cloudbursts don't feel like showers of blessing! Bills, in-law complications, and job or education pressures flood our days. Now we wish instant love could be found on sale at the nearest Wal-Mart. We would stock up for the difficult times that come with marriage and parenting small children.

But God gives us something much better. Not only did Jesus demonstrate His passion for us on the cross, but He, our true Love, wants to fill us with His Spirit every day and teach us how to love each other and our little ones. Occasionally, He parts the waters for His children. More often, He gives us daily love that will keep our marriages and families afloat.

Dear Lord, sometimes I feel like we're drowning!
But You have promised to supply all we need. I'm counting on
You for the love I lack. Thanks for rescuing me and my family. Amen.

Fear Not

For God hath not given us the spirit of fear;
but of power, and of love, and of a sound mind.
2 Timothy 1:7 KJV

The mother's breath caught as she saw her preschooler balancing on a rock at the edge of a drop-off. She didn't want to startle the child, fearful her daughter might tumble over the side. This wasn't the first time her toddler had wandered into danger without the slightest sign of fear.

As our children develop, they learn many important lessons from their mothers. They come to know danger and how to respect the many perils in life. However, we can also impart unnecessary trepidations to our children, ones that will hinder them as they grow.

We can allow life's experiences to keep us from serving the Lord in whatever capacity He has for us. Sometimes we fear the unknown, the power of rejection, or even the fear of failure. If we aren't careful, we can forfeit great blessings by ignoring God's urging to serve in the work He has designed for us.

What an exciting gift we could give God if we were to stand on the proverbial edge of the cliff, ready to step out in power and love to serve God. Let us have a mind set on God, not on our own inadequacies. Let's be content wherever His path leads.

Thank You, Lord, that You can take all fear from me.
Give me the desire to serve You in any area You want. Amen.

A Rocky Start

Then Jesus got into the boat and started across the lake with his disciples.
Suddenly, a fierce storm struck the lake, with waves breaking into the boat.
But Jesus was sleeping.
Matthew 8:23–24 NLT

Jo and her husband, David, were beyond excited. It was the first family vacation in a long time. Their three oldest remembered the favorite vacation spot, but their youngest child had never been there. As the family van neared the lake, the children began bouncing in their seats, clearly ready to go swimming before even unpacking.

"Can we swim now, before lunch?" their oldest asked.

David winked at his wife and made his own puppy face.

"Oh, fine," Jo said, laughingly.

After reaching their cabin, hauling a few bags inside, and changing, everyone made their way down to the water. The three oldest dove right in, but their youngest, Josh, held back. At three years old, the most water he'd ever seen was in the bathtub. Now, as he stared at the water rushing in over his toes, he began to cry.

"Help, Mommy! Daddy!"

Jo and David kept eyes on the other three while paying special attention to their youngest. David waded toward Josh, lifted him up in his arms, and bounced so the water made them both wet.

Jo sat on the sand and called to Josh. "See, Josh, you're safe with Daddy!"

Jesus' disciples felt the same way as Josh: alone and terrified. But Jesus was right there and would never have abandoned them in their fear.

God, thank You for protecting me.

Have a Hannah Heart

For this child I prayed; and the LORD hath given me my petition which I asked of him: Therefore also I have lent him to the LORD; as long as he liveth he shall be lent to the LORD. And he worshipped the LORD there.
1 Samuel 1:27–28 KJV

In her sorrow of barrenness, Hannah prayed for a son and promised him back to God. When God answered her prayer, Hannah kept her word.

She gave Samuel back to the Lord when he was just a boy. Instead of keeping him by her side, as most mothers would, Hannah left Samuel in the care of an old prophet who couldn't control his own children.

Hannah had a heart of faith, as her song of praise in 1 Samuel 2 shows. She knew the God who gave her a son could and would protect him.

Hannah also had a heart of worship, and she taught her small son to do the same. Scripture says he worshipped before Eli instructed him. Apparently, his mother had instilled a fear of God in him and shown him how to respond.

Oh, to have a heart of faith and worship!

Then we would take our babies to church despite any criticism, and we would not fear when our children head off to some forgotten mission field.

Lord, give us hearts that trust.

Give us Hannah hearts!

Father, I want a heart like Hannah's. I want to know You as she knew You. As I invest time in Your Word and prayer, make these desires become reality. Amen.

Out of Our Comfort Zones

Indeed, in our hearts we felt the sentence of death. But this happened that we might not rely on ourselves but on God, who raises the dead.
2 Corinthians 1:9 NIV

*F*our strangers had said yes to God's call. They met for the first time at Miami International Airport before heading to Guyana, South America, on a medical mission trip. Their assignment: Perform surgeries for a week in archaic conditions among tremendous obstacles. Forced out of their comfort zones, they learned to rely solely upon the Lord. The result: His ability was manifested in and through them in amazing ways.

We all enjoy familiar surroundings and predictable outcomes. Friends are chosen over strangers. Home is preferred over hotels. When our environment is somewhat controlled, *we* feel more in control. But when we step out of our comfort zone, anything can happen! It's scary. It's intimidating. It's humbling.

Many times God calls us out of our comfort zones for that very reason. He wants us to venture out of the boat, like Peter. He knows that we will have to trust Him alone and not rely upon ourselves. He wants us to become God-sufficient, not self-sufficient.

The next time God takes you to an uncomfortable place, view it as an opportunity for spiritual growth. Rely totally upon Him. Then, watch God work in amazing ways!

Dear Lord, help me follow You when I am called out of my comfort zone. Teach me to rely upon You and not myself. Amen.

Perfect My Prayers, Lord

Likewise the Spirit also helps in our weaknesses. For we do not know what we should pray for as we ought, but the Spirit Himself makes intercession for us with groanings which cannot be uttered.
Romans 8:26 NKJV

*E*xhausted, Kim walked through the door of her home. Children's clothing, books, and toys filled the floor. The babysitter had piled clean clothes on the couch to be folded but evidently hadn't gotten back to them. Kim proceeded to the kitchen where a sink full of dirty dishes awaited her. After working a ten-hour day, the last thing she wanted to face was a dirty house, dirty children, and a confrontation with the babysitter.

Why wasn't the Lord listening to her prayers? She'd asked Him repeatedly to help her make the babysitter understand that she needed help with the house as well as the kids.

As she began picking up the toys, she thought that maybe she wasn't approaching the Lord in the right manner, and that was the reason for the unanswered prayers. Kim prayed and asked the Holy Spirit to help her.

Three days later, she was amazed at the change that had taken place in her home. The house was tidy, the kids were clean, and dinner could be smelled cooking on the stove. Her husband came out of the kitchen, hugged her, and said, "I'm sorry, honey. I should have been helping out all along. I promise, you'll never have to carry this all alone again."

Lord, please intercede for me when I don't know what to pray. You alone know my every need. Thank You for knowing me better than I know myself. Amen.

Keep Going

And let us not be weary in well doing:
for in due season we shall reap, if we faint not.
Galatians 6:9 KJV

*A*my collapsed into the recliner. She just needed to catch her breath. A minute later she heard the padding of little Zoe's feet.

"Mommy, I'm still thirsty. I need another drink." The little girl grinned at her mother.

Amy sighed. It had already taken her half an hour to get the kids into bed for the night, and that was after they'd brushed their teeth and had their drinks. Still, she gave the child another small drink and walked her back to her bed. "Zoe, stay in your bed now. There will be no more drinks."

Just then, from the room next door, she heard her child Evan cry, "Mommy, Cody won't quit snoring. I can't sleep if Cody's snoring!" to which Cody began to giggle from beneath his blanket.

Amy thought she might scream. This seemed to be the nightly routine in her house. She tried to keep in mind that her children wouldn't be small forever. She wanted to enjoy them. Sometimes she just wished she had as much energy as they had.

"Help me, Lord," she prayed. "Help me be patient and to have enough strength." Amy knew she would be busy for many years, but if she stuck with it, the results would be beautiful.

O Giver of Strength, let me not be consumed by weariness.
Help me joyfully work toward the goal.

No, dear brothers and sisters, I have not achieved it, but I focus on this one thing:
Forgetting the past and looking forward to what lies ahead.
Philippians 3:13 NLT

In a game of tug-of-war, there are two sides, each pulling on one end of a rope, hoping to pull the other side across a line. Our enemy wants us to remain in a never-ending battle with our past, because it keeps us from moving on to the future. Our enemy is relentless; he will pull and pull until he entraps you in the game.

Let go of the rope and watch your past flail as it falls on its back. Its effects on you are crippled when you don't play the game. Let go, turn your back, and walk away. It may taunt you a bit and try to lure you back—just keep walking.

As parents, we need to learn from the past, but then we need to take our growth into the future. Staying mired in a battle with the past is defeat, not victory. Letting go of regrets and failures, while we take what was meant for evil and use it for good, will help us to make wise parenting decisions and train up our children in the way they should go.

Father, forgive me for the things I have done that disappointed You. Help me to receive Your forgiveness and move on, fully, into the future, having learned from my past and now able to apply it to today and the days ahead. Amen.

Strength in Grace

You therefore, my son, be strong in the grace that is in Christ Jesus.
2 Timothy 2:1 NKJV

The young mother watched her child take his first hesitant steps. After tumbling to the ground, his eyes turned to his mother, seeking her reaction. Her bright smile and obvious joy at his success, not his fall, encouraged the child to try again. Each time he tried, he grew stronger. Before long, the child's steps were no longer hesitant, but confident.

By not displaying anger or concern, but showing understanding and encouragement, the mother gave her son the strength to climb back up and try again. The boy trusted her for his well-being. He continued to learn to walk, and then to run.

As Christians, we often fall or make mistakes. God's grace is always there to demonstrate His forgiveness. He urges us to climb to our feet and try again. Every time we attempt to walk in faith, we are resting in God's grace and drawing strength from Him. On our own, we would fall and not be able to try again. With God in charge of our well-being, we can not only have the ability to walk, we can learn to run with confidence in God.

*Dear Father, thank You for Your grace, which encourages me to grow
stronger in my faith and in my walk. Continue to help me
find strength and confidence in You. Amen.*

Smile!

Why art thou cast down, O my soul? and why art thou disquieted in me?
hope thou in God: for I shall yet praise him for the help of his countenance.
Psalm 42:5 KJV

*A*lthough we cannot see God's face with our physical eyes, our spiritual eyes can perceive His countenance. As we spend time in His presence, our agitation is calmed; our anxiety, eased; our anguish, alleviated.

As we are helped by the countenance of the Father, so children are helped by the countenance of the mother. As the Father's ambassador to her children, a mother can encourage a child with just a loving look. Or she can discourage her children with a knit brow, a slight frown, or a quiet sigh.

The best defense against a sad countenance is a smile. Not a Mona Lisa smirk, but a wide ear-to-ear grin. It is impossible to knit your brow when you're smiling.

Watch what happens when you smile at your little ones. They will naturally smile back. If they aren't accustomed to seeing you smile, they may laugh, wondering what you're up to. But soon everyone will be cheerful.

"When Mom ain't happy, ain't nobody happy."

But when Mom is smiling, the whole house will be full of light.

Father, thank You for shining Your face on me. Let me lift up my little ones daily with a bright countenance. Help me to smile through the storms of life, knowing that You are always with me, holding my hand and guiding my feet. Amen.

Break That Snake

Hezekiah trusted in the LORD, the God of Israel. . . . He held fast to the LORD
and did not cease to follow him. . . . And the LORD was with him;
he was successful in whatever he undertook.
2 Kings 18:5–7 NIV

*K*ing Hezekiah was described as being held fast—or "glued"—to God. He led his country as a godly example. God was pleased! Then scripture said Hezekiah broke the bronze snake that Moses had made.

Wouldn't God have wanted that snake to remain in the temple, like a museum piece? It was meant to be an object lesson of how God healed the Israelites. In fact, that very snake on the pole is used as a modern symbol for the medical field. Why would God have wanted Hezekiah to get rid of such a valuable piece of history?

The Israelites had been offering incense to it, deifying the snake as did their Canaanite neighbors. That bronze snake was intended to point the Israelites to God. Instead, it replaced Him and became an object of worship.

We are all guilty of having bronze snakes—something given to us by God, for our good, which ends up replacing Him. We want a lovely home for our families, but decorating it takes up our time and energy. We want security for our kids, only to become obsessive about our work. There is danger in letting anything displace God as the object of our attention—anything!

Lord, help me to identify my bronze snakes and break them into pieces.
Teach me to hold fast to You alone!

Peaceful Parenting

You will keep in perfect peace him whose mind is steadfast,
because he trusts in you.
Isaiah 26:3 NIV

𝒟o you see the glass as half-full? Do you tend to keep your eyes on Jesus, viewing the world from an eternal perspective? Do you trust that the Lord knows best? Do you have an overflowing peace that transcends the situation?

God's Word directs us to set our minds and hearts on things that are above (Colossians 3:1–2). We need to be deliberate in concentrating or focusing our minds on God's eternal perspective, not on the temporal earthly perspective. God tells us that when our minds are steadfast or fixed on the Lord, we will have peace. When our hearts and minds turn to the Lord for wisdom, guidance, and instruction in parenting, the Lord will sustain us. We will receive peace not because we understand fully what is occurring in our world or will happen in the future, but because we trust the Lord. We have confidence in the Lord that He is sovereign; He is in control of all that is allowed to happen to our families and us. We are secure in Him. In parenting, as we have this eternal perspective, we can know the Lord's perfect peace. We can be free from our fears, inadequacies, insecurities, and worries about our children, parenting, and the future, knowing the Lord has a plan for our welfare that provides a future with hope for our family and us (Jeremiah 29:11).

Lord, direct my mind to be steadfast on You. I praise You for
the peace provided in parenting as I trust in Your eternal perspective.

Censored Potty-Talk

A time to tear and a time to mend, a time to be silent and a time to speak.
Ecclesiastes 3:7 NIV

*N*icole never went anywhere without her small notepad. As a mother to three small children, her life carried daily stress, but it was also accompanied by unending giggles. Not a day went by in which at least one of her children didn't say something just too cute or funny not to write down.

At the same time, however, Nicole was trying to lovingly remind her children that there were appropriate and inappropriate times and places to speak. The children were coming to understand that when Mama was speaking on the phone, they needed to play nicely with each other and not scream and shout. What Nicole hadn't thought to mention was that potty-training comments were not appropriate at church.

When her youngest strolled up to a church elder and his wife and proudly announced his oncoming bowel movement, Nicole thought she might collapse from embarrassment. The elderly couple stared at her in bewilderment before bursting into hysterics and congratulating the bright-eyed toddler.

With her other two children in tow, Nicole scooped her vocal son into her arms and headed for the nearest restroom. She had to be careful not to sound upset with her son, but at the same time, she needed to correct his social blunder. Then—and only then—would she add his statement to her notebook.

*Lord, help me to remember that these childhood
times are learning experiences for me, too.*

The Best Investment

Don't you see that children are GOD's best gift?
the fruit of the womb his generous legacy?
Psalm 127:3 MSG

*W*hen viewed in terms of dollars and cents, children do not represent a great financial return. Even before birth, parents deal with the high cost of prenatal care. They buy insurance, set up payment schedules for labor and delivery charges, and purchase cribs, car seats, and strollers. When little "Her Majesty" or "His Highness" arrives, neither comes with an owner's manual. However, an endless list of required items soon appears, including onesies, formula, and diapers by the ton. As children grow, the cost in dollars, time, and energy escalates, leaving parents with only a cluttered house and yard to show for a huge investment, and their child, of course, who continues to eat them out of house and home.

Yet God considers children one of His most precious gifts. Lovely homes with clean carpets will not last. The status of new cars and big bank accounts shrinks compared with hugs from chubby little arms and warm, messy kisses that melt the heart. Even more, material possessions lose their significance when we realize the muddy little souls that stain the new sofa not only will make a unique impact in human history, but will live eternally. In a child, God creates a being who can reflect His image forever.

And He lets us imperfect moms help.

Father, why would You entrust such treasures to me?
Still, with Your help, my children will become the people You
planned before time began. Thank You for this privilege. Amen.

Take It to the Lord

Come to Me, all you who labor and are heavy-laden and overburdened, and I will cause you to rest. [I will ease and relieve and refresh your souls.]
Matthew 11:28 AMP

*V*ictoria looked at her calendar. "Parent-Teacher Meeting 6:00 p.m." glared up at her in red ink. She sighed, wishing she didn't have to attend. But her daughter Kimberly's preschool teacher was expecting her. As she dressed for work, her mind raced with all the things she needed to do that day. After work, dinner had to be prepared and cleaned up. After the conference, she would rush home and bake cupcakes for her daughter's class, do some laundry, work on her Sunday school lesson, and begin drafting the design for the invitations to the fund-raising event for the teens at church. On top of her regular job, getting the kids to school, going to work, keeping the house, and doing laundry, her time was evaporating in front of her eyes.

When had her life become so full? Why hadn't she said no to some of the demanding things that awaited her?

Victoria bowed her head and prayed.

Heavenly Father, some days I feel overburdened with all the things I need to get done. I thank You that I can come to You, and You will make me feel so much better. Please teach me to say no sometimes so that I will stay refreshed. In Jesus' name, amen.

Sustained in Times of Drought

"He will be like a tree planted by the water that sends out its roots by the stream. It does not fear when heat comes; its leaves are always green. It has no worries in a year of drought and never fails to bear fruit."
Jeremiah 17:8 NIV

$\mathcal{D}$ry. Parched. Withered. The results of a drought-laden land are obvious. Water has ceased to saturate the soil. Rain has failed to nourish the plants. Drought conditions are serious because life depends upon an adequate water supply. Mature plants survive drought conditions because their deep roots tap into underground reservoirs.

Most of us have experienced times of drought in our lives. Physical trials may assail us. Financial woes may burden us. Heartache may envelop us. Life threatens to be snuffed out. In those desert times, we experience intense heat and insatiable thirst. However, God has provided a source of nourishment for our souls. Jesus is the Living Water. As we reach out to Him, our thirst is satisfied. Our life is sustained.

Our spiritual roots grow deeper in times of testing as we acknowledge our need and seek Jesus, the Living Water. We can even flourish during those times. Spiritual maturity results as we endure hardship by depending upon the Lord's sustenance. Because our roots have found the eternal source of spiritual water, we need not fear times of drought.

Dear Lord, help me become deeply rooted in You, knowing that it is Your Living Water that sustains me. Amen.

Sunday Morning Values

Fix these words of mine in your hearts and minds; tie them as symbols on your hands and bind them on your foreheads. Teach them to your children.
Deuteronomy 11:18–19 NIV

If you attended Sunday school as a child, you most likely recall hearing the stories of Daniel in the lions' den, David and Goliath, and Noah and the ark. You probably also sang songs such as "This Little Light of Mine," "Jesus Loves the Little Children," and, of course, "Jesus Loves Me."

God told the Israelites to remember His teachings and to teach them to their children. They did so, and throughout the ages, the following generations were also obedient in teaching their children. It is up to this generation to continue the family tradition.

Moms (and dads, too!) are to be instructing kids in the ways of the Lord. However, regularly attending a place of worship is a wonderful supplement to effectively training them. Many Sunday school teachers give of their time to prepare Bible lessons and share them with preschoolers each week. If you already have a class where your children can learn more about Jesus, remember to thank their teacher this Sunday. If you don't currently attend a place of worship, consider finding one where your children can grow in their knowledge of Jesus.

Lord Jesus, thank You that Your words have been passed down through the generations. I pray for knowledge and for clarity as I teach them to my children. Amen.

How Much More?

If ye then, being evil, know how to give good gifts unto your children, how much more shall your Father which is in heaven give good things to them that ask him?
Matthew 7:11 KJV

*W*hen we pray, what do we expect?

Do we truly believe that God hears and answers prayers, or do we think He has a heavenly voice mail system that He ignores?

That latter idea may seem preposterous to a child of God. Yet how often do we approach prayer thinking that God won't answer, or worse, thinking that He may send us an answer that will be hard for us to accept?

We have not, James says, because we ask not (James 4:2). And sometimes we don't get what we ask because we ask with wrong motives (James 4:3). Or we ask in unbelief (James 1:6–8), not knowing the heart of God.

God loves us, in the same way and perhaps more than we love our children. As we would never give our children anything bad, God will never—ever—give us anything bad. As James 1:17 (KJV) says, "Every *good* gift and every perfect gift is from above, and cometh down from the Father of lights" (emphasis added).

So ask. Believe. And receive so much more.

Father, I believe in You and trust You to answer my prayers,
knowing that You will give me so much more than I could ever ask for or
imagine. Thank You for being such a good and wonderful Father.

The Mind of Christ

Let this mind be in you, which was also in Christ Jesus.
Philippians 2:5 KJV

*W*e know Christ loved children. We also recognize that He always did the will of the Father. As Christians, we are expected to be Christlike and to develop a thinking pattern like that of the Savior. It isn't a suggestion or even an option. God commands us to have a mind like Christ's.

This involves everything we do. When we are making a decision about our child or family, we must ask, "How would Jesus handle this?" When we are faced with a difficult situation at work, we must consider what Christ's response would be. When we are tempted to sin, we must remember that the Lord also was tempted, but He did not give in. He is our example. We are to follow His steps.

This will not always be easy. There will be times that human nature will kick in, and we will want to do our own thing. At other times, we might be unsure of just how Christ would respond to a situation. There will be days when we are discouraged that we are not becoming like Christ more quickly. But we cannot give up; we cannot lose hope. Developing the mind of Christ is a lifelong process. We can get to know Him more fully through Bible study and prayer. We can open our hearts and let Him tell us what's in His mind.

Dear Jesus, I want a mind like Yours. Give me patience to develop it.

Godly Role Models

And Jesus grew in wisdom and stature, and in favor with God and men.
Luke 2:52 NIV

When Lisa prepared to be a mother for the first time, she was a bit nervous, but she was also confident that she knew what she was doing. She'd purchased all the latest parenting books, had the safest child-proof amenities, and had even been trained in infant CPR. What more would she need?

The evening the baby arrived, however, Lisa realized she didn't have a clue what she was doing. Not only was a life painfully emerging from her body, but reality was setting in. What if she wasn't a good parent? What if her child grew to be one of those wanted people on the evening news? Such thoughts and fears seemed silly to her before, but now they bombarded her already fatigued mind.

Tired and sobbing in bed one week later, Lisa stood and made her way to her bedroom closet. She found her neglected childhood Bible and began to search for the familiar story, the one about a young virgin girl who was told by an angel that she would give birth to the world's Savior. That incident, Lisa thought, had to be much more intense than the adjustment she was experiencing.

Lying in bed, Lisa drifted off to sleep. She really wasn't alone. The God she had known in her childhood hadn't changed. She realized she couldn't determine her baby's future, but she could be a loving and positive model for him. One day he would hopefully become a man whose heart's desire was for wisdom and God.

God, guide me as I guide my child.

Be a Faithful Steward

Moreover it is required in stewards, that a man be found faithful.
1 Corinthians 4:2 KJV

*A*lthough we tend to think of children as our possessions, we are only stewards of their little lives. God has graciously loaned us precious souls to prepare for eternity.

We are to love them (Titus 2:4), to provide their physical needs (Proverbs 31:21), to "bring them up in the nurture and admonition of the Lord" (Ephesians 6:4 KJV), to teach them God's Word all day (Deuteronomy 6:7), and to instruct them in God's law (Proverbs 1:8).

It's a job of eternal proportions.

Being a steward is not easy, as Joseph discovered. Yet he never shirked his duties. No matter what the challenges were before him, Joseph was never afraid. No matter what his situation, he remained steadfast in his faith, knowing God was always with him, protecting him, guiding him, leading him, providing for him. And because of his faith, things always worked out in his favor and, in turn, in favor of his family.

We, too, must have courage, remain true to our task, and exercise faith, believing that God will indeed help us as we take on this awesome responsibility, because we love Him.

Praise God for motherhood! Praise God for children! Praise God for our families!

Dear Lord! Because I believe in You and know that You are forever beside me, I can take on any challenges of motherhood that are before me. I rise up in courage and a strong faith, knowing You work out all things in my favor and the favor of my family. Thank You for giving me the privilege of caring for Your children. Amen.

Family Celebration

One generation shall praise thy works to another,
and shall declare thy mighty acts.
Psalm 145:4 KJV

*J*esus loves me, this I know!"

Several preschoolers yelled the song at the top of their lungs as they stood before the congregation. Others stared with fawnlike eyes, clutching hands of friends or siblings. A few actually followed the melody sung by their Sunday school teacher.

One mom sitting near the front breathed a sigh of relief that her boys did not stand side by side. Another mother prayed her daughter would not pick her nose. But all the parents felt like cheering God for these beautiful, bright-eyed little singers.

Other generations of Christians in the congregation celebrated Jesus' love as they listened to the children's praise. A teenager remembered meeting God in Bible school. The song happily reminded a newly married couple that God had given them each other. A middle-aged woman hurting from divorce took refuge in the knowledge that God still loved her. A husband and wife in their fifties felt God's comfort, knowing their parents rested in His loving arms in heaven.

"The Bible tells me so!" The kids gave it their all.

An elderly man realized afresh the God of his childhood still kept the promises in His Word.

The children wandered off the platform to enthusiastic applause.

Up in heaven, God clapped His hands, too.

Lord God, how great You are! How wonderful to celebrate Your love as a church family. Some day all generations will worship you together forever! Amen.

Deadly Traps

*If you respect the LORD, you and your children have a strong fortress
and a life-giving fountain that keeps you safe from deadly traps.*
Proverbs 14:26–27 CEV

When we feel the most secure in ourselves, that our doctrine is
the most sound, and that our morals are the purest, we should be on
guard. Sometimes the weakest Christian is in less danger than the
strongest one, because strong virtues can become great vulnerabilities.

Genesis 3 reveals the deadliest trap of all. Satan contradicts God
and tells Eve to disobey God in order to be like Him, having full
knowledge of good and evil. Satan even tempted Christ with similar
ideas. He went to some of the people who were closest to the Father.
Adam and Eve walked and talked with God, and Jesus Christ was the
Son of God. The difference was in the preparation. Adam and Eve
weren't prepared for Satan's lies, so they hadn't girded up a resolve to
withstand the temptation. But Jesus knew exactly what to expect of
His enemy, so He never faltered.

In order to protect our families and avoid the deadly traps
of Satan, we must respect the words of the Lord. God desires
our obedience because He wants the very best for us. We must be
prepared to withstand the attacks of our enemy, and stand with
resolve to respect God in all things.

*Father, help me to recognize the traps of my enemy. Protect me
and my family within Your safe fortress, and give me the
strength and resolve to withstand temptation. Amen.*

Freed Captives

*O give thanks unto the LORD, for he is good. . . . Let the redeemed of the
LORD say so, whom he hath redeemed from the hand of the enemy.*
Psalm 107:1–2 KJV

*Y*oung children often do something wrong that requires
punishment. As mothers, we are usually the ones who deal with each
infraction. The toddler never wants to face up to what he or she has
done. They might fold their arms as they sit in a chair for time-out,
or cry huge tears to garner sympathy as they act like they are being
imprisoned.

Most of the time when the chastisement is completed,
preschoolers will run to the mother wanting comfort. They are
seeking affirmation that they are still loved, despite what they have
done. As we hug our child and tell him how much we love him, we
can see his relief at a restored relationship.

Before we were Christians, we were held captive by sin. We
couldn't set ourselves free; we could only receive a pardon by
accepting Christ as our Savior. When we did, the change in our lives
was dramatic. Our whole outlook on life was different. We knew
we were loved by the God who created everything. The freedom we
have in Christ is so overwhelming that we can't help but be thankful.
We can praise Him for redeeming us from sin and have a grateful
attitude that is evident to all.

*Lord, I can't say enough about how You paid the price for my sin.
Thank You, Jesus, for redeeming me. Amen.*

Wisdom

When pride comes, then comes disgrace, but with humility comes wisdom.
Proverbs 11:2 NIV

Wisdom is a coveted virtue. When the Lord asked King Solomon what he most desired, King Solomon chose wisdom. God granted him a wise and discerning heart. Although worldly wisdom may come with age, spiritual wisdom does not. Many young women are more spiritually discerning than their mothers or even grandmothers. How is that possible?

Spiritual wisdom comes with spiritual maturity. Spiritual maturity comes from an intimate walk with the Lord. Since God is the source of wisdom, we must humbly ask that He impart His wisdom to us. Wisdom is gleaned as we admit to God our lack of wisdom. We must acknowledge that He knows best.

Preschool mothers can easily become overwhelmed. Preschool choices, discipline issues, and sibling rivalry all require wisdom that we may not possess. Chapter one of James encourages those that lack wisdom to ask God. We must not doubt, but believe that God will impart His wisdom to us. Although we may be young mothers, we can obtain godly wisdom. It is available when we ask. Do not try to tackle motherhood alone. Humble yourself before the Lord and His wisdom will be yours.

Dear Lord, You know there are some days I feel so inadequate.
Help me humbly come before You so that I can receive Your wisdom. Amen.

Help Me Raise Them Right!

But the fruit of the [Holy] Spirit [the work which His presence within accomplishes] is love, joy (gladness), peace, patience (an even temper, forbearance), kindness, goodness (benevolence), faithfulness.
Galatians 5:22 AMP

*T*iffany hoped that the church counselor would be able to help her teach the boys how to love and treat each other better. With tears in her eyes, she explained, "My boys fight over the blocks, they fight over the cars, they fight over the puzzles, and they even fight over their books. I don't know what to do about the twins. Everyone told me when I was pregnant that the babies would be so close and loving. Boy, were they wrong."

"So your boys never get along?" The counselor asked.

Tiffany sniffed. "Well, I wouldn't say *never*."

Later, she left feeling better. One of the things she took away from the meeting was that the boys were expressing themselves, and that with a little loving care from her and a lot of help from God, they would grow into the young Christian men she envisioned.

Heavenly Father, be with me and help me to raise my children so that they will be women and men of God. Please, fill them with Your spirit. Amen.

A Good Example

Care for the flock that God has entrusted to you.
Watch over it willingly, not grudgingly. . .because you are
eager to serve God. . . . Lead them by your own good example.
1 Peter 5:2–3 NLT

*C*an you think of someone who was a good example to you when you were younger? How about a bad example? Hopefully the good example comes to mind faster than the bad example.

As a mom, God has given you the opportunity to be an example to your little one. Sure, we all fall short. . .especially when yet *another* cup of milk spills, or when the wall is "decorated" with crayon. But overall, you are vital in the development of that little human being. . . his health, his education, his emotions, and most of all, his spiritual training. What you do will be absorbed—and most often imitated— by him. Your choice to be a good example will have long-lasting benefits.

In 1 Peter, there is a charge to church leaders to care for those under them. However, as moms, this applies to us, as well. We have our own little "flock" to care for—those wonderful children God has entrusted to us. We should have the same spirit of watching over them "willingly," because we "are eager to serve God."

Heavenly Father, I pray that I will reflect You today as I
strive to be a good example to the ones whom You have entrusted to me.
Help me to lead them well, with a good attitude. Amen.

Renewed Mind

Whatever you do, work at it with all your heart,
as working for the Lord, not for men.
Colossians 3:23 NIV

Claire recalled the past few years of her life—the infinite number of diapers changed, loads of laundry completed, dishes washed, house cleanings, meals prepared, times of instruction with her children—and thought to herself, *Isn't there more to life than this?*

The Lord tells us, "YES!" The Lord provides a renewed mind-set for how we are to embrace these tasks as mothers. He instructs us that whatever our task (e.g., cleaning toilets, grocery shopping, teaching our children), we need to put our entire being into it as if we were polishing the pearly gates for the Almighty! We are, in fact, serving Him, because everything we have—the house, the car, the children, and the bank account—belongs to God. When we have the privilege of changing diapers, washing laundry, and cooking meals, we are engaging in the very tasks the Lord has specifically called us to do for this season of our life. We can choose to complete His work with an attitude of drudgery and boredom, or we can reframe the task as an act of service to the Lord, giving back to the One who has blessed us with a place to live and children who call us "Mother."

Lord, renew my mind to complete every task for Your glory in
obedience and thankfulness for the blessing of being a mom.

Things That Go Bump in the Night

*"I am the LORD, your God, who takes hold of your right hand
and says to you, Do not fear; I will help you. Do not be afraid,
O worm Jacob, O little Israel, for I myself will help you," declares
the LORD, your Redeemer, the Holy One of Israel.*
Isaiah 41:13–14 NIV

Everything seems spookier at night—house creaks, wind rustling the trees outside of windows, the hoot of an owl. When a child has a bad dream or faces a fear-filled night, he seeks the safest place on earth—sleeping right between Mom and Dad.

God understands how defenseless and small young ones can feel.

Israel was a tiny nation trying to get established among ferocious giants. Imagine how that little army felt when it saw its enemies. Taller, mightier, fiercer, and far more experienced warriors! Yet over and over, God protected Israel from her enemies, helping her overcome outrageous odds. He constantly reminded Israel that He was the One who saved her. He was always present.

At bedtime or during the night when fears arise, we can lead our children to give God their knots of worries. We can teach them that God is always with them, holding their hands tightly. *"Do not be afraid, for I am with you,"* God promises. He will protect our children from their enemies—real or imagined—in the daytime or in the night.

Lord of our nights, may my children experience Your promises for themselves, knowing they are wrapped securely in Your perfect love that casts out all fears.

Immersed in God's Word

I will delight myself in thy statutes: I will not forget thy word.
Psalm 119:16 KJV

*I*n today's fast-paced world it is difficult to truly find delight in much of anything. We just don't have time. We might look forward to something and even enjoy it a lot, but so often our minds are already rushing to the next thing on our agenda.

So how can we really delight in God's Word? Many days we read it because it's the "right thing" to do. We want to set the right example for our little ones, or we want God's blessing on our family. We figure that's the best way to get it.

It's true that God does bless those who recognize the importance of His Word and of spending time with Him, but we shouldn't be using our devotions as a magic formula to get something from Him. Our desire should be to become more like Christ. The only way to do this is to walk with Him daily. We must learn more about Him and put into practice what we observe. Then we not only reap God's blessing, we become one of His blessings. That's the best legacy we can give to our children.

*Thank You, Lord, for giving me Your Word that
I might know You more fully and become more like You.*

Rules

But speak thou the things which become sound doctrine.
Titus 2:1 KJV

Four-year-old Allen slammed the door to the car then buckled up his seat belt. He looked at his mom and announced, "I don't want to go to school anymore." He crossed his arms and stared straight ahead.

"Why not? Did you have a bad day?" Laura watched her son's eyes fill with tears.

He burrowed his head in his hands and refused to answer.

Laura put the car into gear and drove toward home. "Do I need to go to class with you tomorrow and talk to the teacher?"

"No."

Laura wanted to press Allen further but knew he needed to work through his thoughts. In a few minutes, she was rewarded for her silence.

"They have too many rules at school," he blurted out.

"I agree," Laura answered. She prayed for the right words to help her explain the importance of rules.

Allen perked up. "You do?"

"Sure. You can't talk while your teacher is talking because you might miss something important. You can't go down the slide backward because you might hit your head on the ground. I know they won't let you run with pencils—you might stab yourself or someone else. Those are horrible rules," she finished.

He uncrossed his arms. "Well, those aren't bad rules. I don't want to get hurt."

"What rules don't you like?" Laura asked as she pulled into their driveway.

Allen unfastened his seat belt. "Never mind. What are we having for a snack?"

*Thank You, Lord, for giving me the right words
to use when teaching my children. Amen.*

Giving Preference

Be kindly affectionate to one another with brotherly love,
in honor giving preference to one another.
Romans 12:10 NKJV

Preschoolers have a mind of their own. They want to do everything their way, even if that way isn't the most expedient. This is very evident when they're playing with other children. We can listen to them make up new rules to adapt the game to their advantage. Without realizing what they are doing, they can manipulate everyone around them to do their will.

Sometimes mothers get frustrated because their children will throw a fit when they don't get their way. Toddlers will refuse to play the game or cry to try to get their way. They have to be taught that they can't change the guidelines to suit their needs alone. They must consider others.

As Christians, we often think our way is the right way: God's way. We justify our method and can sometimes act like two-year-olds when others don't agree with us. We should always consider what God's way is, but remember that there may be different roads to the same goal.

Instead of insisting on our preferences, we should pray that we can see through other's eyes. Let's be willing to honor others in matters where there might be more than one way to accomplish a goal.

Lord, help me to see when to stand firm and when to be pliable.
Help me to love and honor others above myself. Amen.

Happy Days

Is any among you afflicted? let him pray. Is any merry? let him sing psalms.
James 5:13 KJV

$\mathcal{D}$on't go into the street," Charity warned her three-year-old while raking last year's dead leaves from the flower beds.

"I won't, Mommy." Cami scribbled on the driveway with chalk.

As Charity worked, she prayed silently for her friend Danielle's troubled marriage.

Her daughter's happy little voice broke into her thoughts. Charity leaned on her rake and watched Cami celebrate the lovely spring day with her favorite song: "If You're Happy and You Know It." Cami didn't worry about staying on-key or leaving out a few words. She clapped her chubby hands, stomped her feet, and yelled "AMEN!" at the top of her lungs. When even that didn't express her gladness, Cami sang louder and danced like a daisy in the wind, her nearly white hair glowing in the sunshine.

How God must enjoy this! Charity felt her own heart lift.

"*Yes, I do. Would you sing for Me, too?*" The still, small Voice sounded wistful.

Charity caught her breath. She had learned to pray constantly. . . so many needy people! But Charity never thought God might want to hear *her* song of joy on a perfect day like this. She threw down her rake.

"Cami, want me to sing with you? Let's do all the verses!"

Lord, Thank You for the privilege of prayer. But help me also exercise the privilege of praise. I want to sing Your song! Amen.

Filter, Don't Fret

*Finally, brethren, whatsoever things are true, whatsoever things are honest,
whatsoever things are just, whatsoever things are pure, whatsoever things are
lovely, whatsoever things are of good report; if there be any virtue,
and if there be any praise, think on these things.*
Philippians 4:8 KJV

Mothers are notorious worriers.

Faster than a baby can cry, a mother can worry why he is.

We worry if the baby doesn't sleep or if he sleeps too much. We
worry if he nurses weakly or if he drains us dry.

Worry has been defined as taking on a responsibility God never
intended us to have. So let's give the responsibility for our lives and
those of our children back to God. Let's leave our worries at His
door, knowing that He can handle everything far better than we ever
could. After all, He's God!

What a privilege to be able to cast our cares upon the Lord,
knowing that He cares for us. He and His angels are watching over
both us and our babies—while we sleep and while we're awake.
There's no need to fret. Instead, we have faith!

And if, in those unguarded moments, we find a worry begin to
creep into our mind, we have the privilege of taking that thought
captive to Christ. We can do that by filtering our minds as Paul
directs. Are the thoughts we think true, honest, just, pure, lovely, of
good report, virtuous, or praiseworthy? If the answer is no, we can
discard those thoughts, leave them at Jesus' feet, and replace them
with His pure, lovely, praiseworthy Word.

What an awesome God we have!

*Oh Father, I cast all my cares upon you and allow Your peace
to settle upon me. Fill my mind today and every day with
praise and joy for all You have done for me. Amen.*

Open the Door

Here I am! I stand at the door and knock. If anyone hears my voice and opens the door, I will come in and eat with him, and he with me.
Revelation 3:20 NIV

*J*esus is knocking on the door of our hearts. He will not barge in uninvited. What is our response? Do we eagerly invite Him in? Or would we prefer that He leave us alone? If we yearn for His help, we beckon Him to enter. If we desire to know Him more, we hasten Him in. But if we think we can handle life on our own, we ignore the knocking. Or perhaps we feel unworthy to receive such a noble visitor.

Whether we care to admit it or not, we desperately need God's daily presence. His guidance, wisdom, and counsel are invaluable because He is omniscient. When we open our heart's door and invite Him in, He walks with us throughout the day. Guidance is given. Peace is imparted. Strength is obtained.

You may feel that you are handling life just fine without His help. Are you really? You may feel unworthy of His presence. Yet you are His valuable creation! God loves you so much that He gave His life so that you can enter into a personal relationship with Him. He's standing at the door and knocking. Why not invite Him in?

Dear Lord, thank You for pursuing a relationship with me. May I gladly open the door and enjoy fellowship with You throughout the day. Amen.

Quiet Resting Place

"Come with me by yourselves to a quiet place and get some rest."
Mark 6:31 NIV

$\mathcal{T}$iffany had not slept well the night before. Her mind raced with all there was to do. The daily pressures of raising a preschooler and fulfilling life's many demands were wearing her down. It was even beginning to dampen her joy in living.

Jesus came to give us life and to have it in abundance (John 10:10). A key to living this abundant life is regular rest. Our heavenly Father and our Savior, Jesus, demonstrated that we must make time to rest. God, after creating the earth and heavens, rested (Genesis 2:1–3). Jesus encouraged His disciples to have a quiet resting place. As mothers of preschoolers, we must have a quiet resting place that we regularly spend time in. This place may be in our closet, bathroom, or a special corner with a cozy chair. The place is a sanctuary, a place of refuge where our children know that when Mom is in her quiet resting place, she is not to be disturbed. In our quiet resting place, we are able to fall before the glorious throne of God, pray, meditate on scripture, reflect on God's goodness, and be filled by the Lord. A basket of tools such as a Bible, devotional, tissues, journal, and pen will help facilitate our experience with the Lord in this quiet resting place.

Father, I thank You that from the beginning You have modeled an abundant life filled with rest. Help me to diligently make time to retreat to my quiet resting place.

God Gives Patience and Joy

Strengthened with all might, according to his glorious power,
unto all patience and longsuffering with joyfulness.
Colossians 1:11 KJV

You've heard the saying "no pain, no gain." It's really almost a cliché, but there's a good bit of wisdom packed into those four small words.

When your child was born, she came with a mind of her own. Apparently, newborns come with the belief that they alone rule the world and that you exist for the sole purpose of answering their demands. It's true that when they are tiny you really do have to meet those needs. As they grow, however, they begin to develop personalities. They learn the fine art of manipulation, and the job really begins. Battles of the wills become part of the daily routine, especially if the child tends to have very strong opinions.

Now you really have the opportunity to help your child become what God wants her to be. It might be exasperating at times. You have to decide if you will joyfully embrace this chance of a lifetime or if you will wallow in the difficulties. God knows it won't be easy. That's why He offers to give you the strength and patience for each task. Accept His offer, and look forward to each day with joy.

Thank You, God, for granting me the strength and patience to
joyfully raise my children. I want to accept these gifts daily.

A Resting Place

Find rest, O my soul, in God alone; my hope comes from him.
Psalm 62:5 NIV

It's been jokingly suggested that people in the business world should take afternoon naps the way toddlers do. Imagine what those afternoon naps would do to stress levels!

Babies and small children need rest throughout the day. Mothers are interpreters of their children's crankiness and can determine what their children need at that time. The smaller the child, the more likely the mother will say, "Oh! It's getting closer to nap time."

Babies need naps because they are not as developed and require rest. Preschool-age children need rest for the same reason, but also because their boundless energy requires it. Still others say that neither the infant nor the toddler needs the actual downtime. In reality, it's the mother!

God knew that our bodies would get tired and that we would require not only rest but sleep.

And not just on a daily basis. We need to rest from our daily activities, one day each week. The Bible says that God rested on the seventh day of creation. This wasn't because God needed a quick breather; He wanted to demonstrate and give us permission to rest. He designed our lives so that we could take one day each week to find much-needed rest from our daily activities. If we are willing, resting will allow us to be refreshed by God. Unlike us, God never sleeps. We can turn to Him 24-7. And it is through His strength that we can find true rest.

*Lord, I am amazed by You! You hear my cries
and have provided for my spiritual refreshment.*

Builder or Vandal?

Every wise woman buildeth her house:
but the foolish plucketh it down with her hands.
Proverbs 14:1 KJV

*A*nyone who has built a house knows the process doesn't take place overnight! Months of planning, gathering resources, and doing hard physical labor all go into this project. Poor weather may slow things down. Expenses may surpass the original estimates. Finally, however, a beautiful new house stands, complete with bedrooms where owners will rest, a kitchen from which delicious smells will draw hungry stomachs and hearts, and a living room where loved ones will open gifts around the Christmas tree. No owner would think of knocking holes in the walls or smashing the windows. Instead, we spend large amounts of money, time, and effort in caring for our homes.

A family is hard to build, too! Ask any woman who has spent years nurturing those she loves. Yet we sometimes find it easy to undermine the foundation of family faith by neglecting God's Word or His command to meet with other Christian believers. We may tear down our husbands and children with thoughtless words and actions—or let our moods blast them through the roof! When we have invested so much in building our families, why join Satan's efforts to vandalize the precious structure God has designed for His glory?

Lord Jesus, sometimes I forget how important my family is in Your plan.
Thank You for these people, so valuable in Your sight.
Help me be a fellow builder with You. Amen.

Lost Identity

Since you are precious in My sight, since you are honored and I love you.
Isaiah 43:4 NASB

*A*s Karen drove home, she reflected on the conversations among the women at the luncheon. . . .

"What do you do?" they had asked her.

Karen stumbled over her words, hesitating to admit she was "just a mother." The Lord led her to surrender her professional career to stay at home with her children. Now, in conversations like these, Karen felt unsure of who she truly was, as if she had lost her identity.

God's Word provides our identity. Our identities are not comprised of being a mother, wife, attorney, or doctor. Rather, these are *roles* we may fill for a season of our lives. Our *identity* is in the labels Christ provided us in shedding His blood on the cross: created and formed by God, redeemed, called by name, belonging to the Lord, saved, precious, honored and loved (Isaiah 43:1–4).

The world provides a false identity to our preschoolers, encouraging them to accept the culture that says we are what we do. However, we must counter this deception of focusing on our role by grounding our children in their true identity. In living joyfully for who we are in Christ, we can teach our children a godly identity that cannot be lost. Our children can know they are called by Christ's very own name in being a Christian.

*Lord, I praise You for my identity as one You created and formed,
redeemed, called by name, belonging to You, saved, precious, honored,
and loved. Enable me to teach my children their identity in You.*

Putting the Pieces Together

We are assured and know that [God being a partner in their labor] all things work together and are [fitting into a plan] for good to and for those who love God and are called according to [His] design and purpose.
Romans 8:28 AMP

*K*ellie smiled down at her little girl, Dani. They were working on a puzzle of Noah's ark. The little girl tried to shove a piece into the wrong space. When that didn't work, she tried turning it over.

After many more tries, the four-year-old finally handed the piece to her mother. "Here ya go," she said.

Kellie pretended to think about where the part would go. She looked at the puzzle piece and then tried it in what she knew was the wrong spot. "This is a hard one, isn't it?"

Dani chewed her lower lip and studied the puzzle. "Uh-huh."

Once more Kellie watched her child. She knew Dani would figure out that the piece went on the elephant's leg in just a few moments.

Sure enough, Dani gave a little squeal. "Give me the puzzle piece, Mommy! I know where it goes now!"

With a great feeling of satisfaction and pride, Kellie watched her daughter put the piece into place.

Lord, thank You for loving me and for helping me teach my children how to put the pieces of life into order so that they can become great men and women for You. I can't do it without You. Amen.

Human Weakness
Reveals God's Glory

*For we who are alive are always being given over to death for
Jesus' sake, so that his life may be revealed in our mortal body.*
2 Corinthians 4:11 NIV

It is easy to praise the Lord when life is going well. Our newborn
baby is healthy. The job offer comes through. Our stock portfolio
hits new highs. But what is our attitude when life does not go
according to our plan? The doctor discloses congenital birth
defects. The door closes on our dream job. Our portfolio plummets.
Disappointments and trials have a way of humbling us. In those
moments of human weakness, we have a choice to make. We can feel
sorry for ourselves and blame God. Or, we can turn to Him, asking
for His strength to persevere.

When we are at our weakest, God can reveal His strength. We are
not in control. We desperately need God. We run to Him. Cling to
Him. Rely upon Him. When we get to the end of our ropes, the Lord
can work mightily. His power and strength uphold us. His peace
sustains us. He carries us when we cannot go on. Human weakness is
an opportunity to personally experience Christ's strength. Others will
also observe His strength in our lives. May our weakness be turned to
strength for His glory.

*Dear Lord, when I feel weak, help me lean upon You.
May others see Your strength in me during times of weakness. Amen.*

Make Me an Instrument

Never take your own revenge, beloved, but leave room for the wrath of God,
for it is written, "VENGEANCE IS MINE, I WILL REPAY," says
the Lord. . . . Do not be overcome by evil, but overcome evil with good.
Romans 12:19, 21 NASB

*W*e know that revenge is up to God. Yet don't we often wish that He would make us His instrument as He carries out that revenge? Taking revenge on others, in unforgiveness and anger, is usurping God's authority with disobedience. He exacts the necessary revenge, on our behalf, so that we can keep our hearts free of bitterness and unforgiveness. His desire for us is that we walk in peace and exhibit forgiveness to our brothers and sisters, as instruments of His mercy, not His wrath.

The trick to the seemingly impossible task of laying aside the desire for revenge and retribution is to not just wait around for a wave of forgiveness to sweep over us, compelling us to act lovingly. But, in obedience to God, we need to be willing to act immediately, saying to the person who has wronged us, "I forgive you." Even if it still hurts, and even if we think we're not ready. Forgiveness offered in obedience will be rewarded with a heart softened over time.

Heavenly Father, please make me an instrument of Your love and forgiveness.
Forgive me for my bitter thoughts and for my desire for revenge against those
who have wronged me. Help me to lay my anger at Your feet and allow
You to work things out according to Your will. Amen.

True Hope

Which hope we have as an anchor of the soul, both sure and stedfast.
Hebrews 6:19 KJV

It was Saturday morning. Julie wasn't ready to get out of bed. Her alarm clock hadn't even gone off yet, and Julie was not ready to be awake. All she wanted was to burrow beneath the warm covers and hug her pillow.

"Mommy? Are you awake yet?" Julie's four-year-old, Elizabeth, climbed onto her bed and poked at Julie's eyelids. Julie mumbled something that didn't even come close to the English language. Opening her eyes, Julie stared at her daughter. Elizabeth now sat cross-legged on the bed, her head turned slightly in thought, her brown curls messy.

Julie prayed silently. It hadn't been that many hours since she'd gone to bed. What would it be like to return to childhood and be as carefree as her daughter? Still, Elizabeth's presence reminded Julie that she could have hope for the new day because of God's promises. God had Julie at this point and age in her life for a reason. God had blessed her not only with hope and a beautiful daughter, but with a Savior who loved her unconditionally, even if Julie wasn't always excited at the beginning of each day.

Sitting up and hugging Elizabeth, Julie thanked God for Jesus. She thanked Him for the sacrifice He had made. Julie knew that heaven would be her home one day, but for now, she thanked God for today and the day's treasures she hadn't even lived yet.

Jesus, my hope is in Your sacrifice.

Gifted Kids

And that special gift of ministry you were given when the leaders of the church laid hands on you and prayed—keep that dusted off and in use.
1 Timothy 4:14 MSG

A gifted child. Ah, such a coveted label! Having that tag on our child means better classes at school, additional opportunities, probably a guaranteed admission into an exclusive university, most likely a solid profession, too. Doesn't it?

Maybe. But maybe not. New studies are finding that many kids identified early in elementary school as gifted are relabeled as gifted underachievers by the time they reach high school. Studies show that children get weighed down with such a label. They stop taking risks because they're so invested in performing well.

A gifted label from God has a completely different meaning. Every believer is gifted. God's gifts are not quantifiable by a series of tests, and they're not intended to boost an individual's value in the eyes of the world. God's gifts are intangible, generously given, and meant for the benefit of others. Gifts like teaching, service, encouragement, comforting others.

God made each of our children unique, with different passions and talents. Our job is to be the kind of encourager that our children need to help them make the most of the gifts God has given them. May we be like Paul, who urged his young friend Timothy to not neglect the gift God had given to him.

Thank You for Your promise, Lord, that whatever good work You begin in my child, You will continue to bring to fullness.

The Yoke of Rest

Take my yoke upon you, and learn of me;
for I am meek and lowly in heart:
and ye shall find rest unto your souls.
Matthew 11:29 KJV

*W*hen it comes to the Christian life, things are not as they seem.

The weak things of the world confound the strong. The poor in spirit possess the riches of the kingdom of God. If you lose your life, you keep it.

And here in Matthew, Jesus said if we work, we will find rest.

How can this be?

It happens as we are yoked with Christ.

For two oxen to work together in a yoke, one must lead and the other follow. If the weaker ox decides to go in a different direction, there is tension, and the work stops. But as the weaker learns from and submits to the stronger, the work goes more smoothly.

As the stronger ox, Jesus carries the greater burden. If we try to go our own way, the yoke will pull against our necks, and the work will be hindered. But if we submit to His leading, we will learn more of Him, and the work He wants to do in our lives will go more smoothly.

As we meekly follow His leading, the tension ceases and we find rest.

Father, I will follow where You lead, knowing therein I will find rest.
Thank You for working in my life. Amen.

Thankful Purpose

Continue stedfastly in prayer, watching therein with thanksgiving.
Colossians 4:2 ASV

*W*orry is like an invasive weed that creeps into our minds as we think about the myriad ways something can go wrong with our children. Sickness. Dog bite. Injury. The list goes on and on. Before we know it, the invasive worry becomes pervasive and consumes our thoughts. We lose our delight in our children because we are so concerned for their welfare.

Worry should not consume us and drive us from God. Instead, it should draw us to Him through prayer for each concern. Instead of dwelling on what could happen, we need to turn to Him and give thanks for His sovereignty and loving care.

We will always have concerns that involve our little ones. Our response is what makes the difference. As we come before God each time, He will give us peace for our children. Worry that sends us to our knees before the Lord is a good way to continue to present our babies to Him. Our apprehension brought before God can turn to praise. We can once more enjoy the gift of our children.

*Thank You, God, for turning my doubts and fears into praise
and replacing my worry with Your peace. Amen.*

The Hardest Part

Chasten thy son while there is hope, and let not thy soul spare for his crying.
Proverbs 19:18 KJV

*B*ig tears rolled down Jana's cheeks, and her little lip trembled. "But Mommy, I really wanted ice cream, too." At that moment Renee nearly gave in. Her little daughter looked so pathetic and vulnerable. After all, Jana was only three. Maybe she was too young to be expected to clean up her books.

As Renee wavered, she knew what she had to do. She pulled her child into her lap. "I wanted you to have ice cream, too, Jana, but you knew the deal. Daniel and Britney picked up their things. It wouldn't be right if I let you be rewarded along with them," Renee explained. "I want you to remember this the next time I tell you to do something."

Jana's tears turned to sobs as she realized she would indeed miss out on her favorite treat. Renee prayed that she had done the right thing and that Jana truly would learn from the experience.

Discipline is the hard part of parenting, but it is necessary, and if properly handled it is quite effective. It's often difficult to be consistent or to know the best solution, but God is wise and shares this wisdom with us even in the area of child rearing.

Dear Father, I do not like disciplining my children.
I know that I must while they are young.
I only ask for wisdom to do this properly.

Follow the Leader

Be imitators of God, therefore, as dearly loved children
and live a life of love, just as Christ loved us and gave
himself up for us as a fragrant offering and sacrifice to God.
Ephesians 5:1–2 NIV

$\mathscr{K}$ids love to play follow the leader. One child is designated the leader, and the others dutifully line up behind her as she leads them wherever she wants them to go. They follow without question or argument. They don't even make a suggestion as to where the next step should be. They are content to play the game well, by following their leader. When the leader stops, everyone stops; when the leader sits, everyone sits. Whether in action or inaction, the leader is in charge.

That is exactly how we are to live our Christian walk. We, as followers of Christ, have designated Him as our Leader. Now, we need to get behind Him and follow where He leads. We need to do this without question or argument, and without getting in His way by thinking we may have a better plan.

The only way to successfully follow our Leader is to recognize Him and know His voice. We can only hear our Leader's voice by making a practice of listening for it. Studying scripture, actively praying, and listening for Him will guide us to the steps we must take as we follow Jesus Christ, our Leader.

Jesus, I want You to be my Leader in all things. Whether You lead me to
move or to be still, help me hear Your guidance and obey Your will. Amen.

Praying for Safety

We prayed that he would give us a safe journey and protect us,
our children, and our goods as we traveled.
Ezra 8:21 NLT

$\mathcal{S}$ometimes in the hurry of travel—whether on a road trip or just around town, running errands—we don't think to ask God to protect us on the journey. In the midst of buckling the kids into car seats, handing out sippy cups and Cheerios, having everyone keep their hands and feet to themselves, and generally keeping tears at bay, we just assume that we will make it to and from the destination without any incidents.

But have you ever taken just a moment before driving off to ask that God protect you and your vehicle from danger? Better yet, each time you set out on a trip, take turns with your children, asking God to give you safety in your travels. It's always a joy to hear the prayers of children, and what better way to instill in them full dependence on God than to have them request His protection? He is able to safeguard you against a blowout, a careless driver, or an unavoidable object in your path. Take just a moment today to ask your Father to protect you as you travel.

Lord, thank You for Your protection.
Thank You for Your safety as we travel.
Please protect us once again today. Amen.

Perfect or Perfectionist?

Mark the perfect man, and behold the upright: for the end of that man is peace.
Psalm 37:37 KJV

*M*otherhood is a high calling. Sometimes the height of that calling makes mothers anxious. We want to do it right. We want to be perfect, and we want our children to be perfect.

Although it is a noble goal, as we strive toward perfection, we may become perfectionists. We may become intolerant of the mistakes and messes of our little ones. Instead of patiently enduring their childishness with a laugh, we may become harsh and critical, creating anxiety in the home.

Fortunately, we don't need to be perfectionists, because we're already perfect. A *perfect* mother is one who is "blameless," "complete," or "has integrity." Such a mother is one who has been saved, who is blameless before God because she is in Christ.

Because she has received and understands grace, a perfect mother will understand her shortcomings and those of her children, and she will be able to impart grace to her household. A perfect mother's household will have joy and peace.

Father, thank You for making me complete, whole, and perfect in Christ. Thank You for the grace and patience You have given me. Enable me to share this grace with my children. Let me give them a peaceful home. Amen.

So Much More

I am come that they might have life,
and that they might have it more abundantly.
John 10:10 KJV

As a teenager, she had accepted Jesus Christ as her Savior. Tucking her ticket to heaven in her back pocket, she carried on with life as if nothing had happened. Unbeknownst to her, she had received so much more than a heavenly home. A treasure chest full of spiritual riches had been placed before her. Abundant life on earth could be realized. Yet sadly, she never knew how spiritually rich she truly was.

Jesus came and died on the cross to give us the gift of eternal life. But He wants to give us abundant life on earth as well. He has given us the Holy Spirit as His indwelling presence to guide, comfort, and lead. He has given us everything we need for victorious living. We can have power to rise above any situation. We can have peace in the deepest of valleys. We can experience His presence at all times.

Realize that you have not only been given eternal life, you have been given abundant life. Enjoy the blessings that Christ has in store for you. Don't be content to live in spiritual poverty. Open the treasure chest!

Dear Lord, thank You for giving me eternal life. Help me appropriate
all the blessings that are mine so that I can experience the
abundant life that You desire for me. Amen.

Peaceful Fruit of Righteousness

*No discipline seems pleasant at the time, but painful. Later on,
however, it produces a harvest of righteousness and peace
for those who have been trained by it.*
Hebrews 12:11 NIV

$\mathcal{M}$eredith remembers too clearly the early days of her preschooler's relentless crying as she trained her to take naps. Now, her preschooler doesn't fight her naps. She knows that after lunch she takes a nap and even tells Meredith, "Mommy, it is time for my nap!"

Like Meredith's preschooler fighting discipline in the early days of learning to take naps, we often fight our heavenly Father's discipline. Discipline is the patient instruction that lovingly fosters order, peace, and a right relationship. Through conversing with the Lord, invite Him to reveal areas of your relationship with your preschooler that need to be brought into submission to yield the peaceful fruit of righteousness. Maybe the areas of training for your preschooler are back talk, temper tantrums, or whining. Preschoolers need structure, stability, dependability, routine, and consistency. They need to know what they can expect for the day and be able to count on a mother who consistently and lovingly fosters obedience.

Our heavenly Father disciplines us to yield the peaceful fruit of righteousness—a right relationship with Him as Father; likewise, we need to gently and firmly teach our preschoolers a right relationship with us as mothers. As we persevere in what is often painful and unpleasant, the peaceful fruit of righteousness will be born.

*Lord, reveal to me areas in which I need to lovingly instruct
my preschooler to yield the peaceful fruit of righteousness.*

Forgotten

*Why sayest thou, O Jacob, and speakest, O Israel, My way is hid from the
LORD, and my judgment is passed over from my God?*
Isaiah 40:27 KJV

*T*hat's it. I've *had* it!"

Chelsea shut her screaming three-year-old in his room, placed her
howling baby in his crib, and fled to the bathroom. Chelsea slammed
the door behind her and locked it, gulping air as if she had escaped
an enemy. Her children wailed. She didn't care. For sixty seconds, she
would give herself the luxury of not caring if they yelled themselves
blue. Maybe she could cough alone and treat herself to blowing her
nose without her toddler's "help."

The week had pushed Chelsea past her limits. Her boss
demanded overtime. Her husband griped about the cluttered house.
Chelsea caught a virus from her children—how guilty she felt,
dumping sick kids on her mom when the sitter wouldn't take them.

The pastor said God would never give Chelsea more than she
could bear, but she'd like to see *him* change places with her! Tears
dripped down her cheeks. *Even God has forgotten me. . . .*

The phone rang. Chelsea sighed, unlocked the door, and picked
it up.

"Chelsea?" Her Bible study leader's warm voice sounded anxious.
"Are you all right? God's put you on my mind all day. Can I help?"

*Father, when I have nothing left to give, I somehow think You have
nothing left to give, either. Please pardon my lack of faith—
and show me how much You love me! Amen.*

Learning Curve

Do not think of yourself more highly than you ought, but. . .
in accordance with the measure of faith God has given you.
Romans 12:3 NIV

*E*ach child learns at a different rate. The doctor gives us a standard to go by when watching our toddler develop, but each child is unique. Some walk and talk early, while some walk and talk much later. If we try to hurry our children or force them to do activities they aren't ready to do, we can cause more harm than good.

When we are patient and let our toddlers go at their own pace, except for special cases, most children will be healthier and more balanced as they grow. They have confidence in their abilities instead of always trying to do more to please their mother.

Christians grow at different paces, too. Some new Christians seem to take off and mature almost overnight. Others take years to show any maturity and growth in Christ. We can't compare one believer to another because all are distinctive. If they are encouraged in their faith, instead of being criticized, Christians will become more certain of their abilities and beliefs.

Those who have been Christians a longer time or are more mature in their faith must be careful not to judge others or put themselves on a pedestal. We should remember that we all have different amounts of faith. Let us love one another as we are, not as we think each other should be.

Thank You, Lord, that we are all special to You. Amen.

Fight or Flight?

"We have no power to face this vast army. . . .
We do not know what to do, but our eyes are upon you."
2 Chronicles 20:12 NIV

A vast army was approaching from Edom to wipe out King Jehoshaphat and the army of Judah. What did King Jehoshaphat do? Instruct the military to prepare to fight the enemy? Or did he panic and run for the hills?

Most of us choose one of two options when faced with a crisis: fight or flight. King Jehoshaphat did neither. "Alarmed, Jehoshaphat resolved to inquire of the LORD, and he proclaimed a fast for all Judah. . . . Then Jehoshaphat stood up in the assembly. . .and said: 'O LORD, God of our fathers. . .we will stand in your presence. . .and will cry out to you in our distress, and you will hear us and save us' " (2 Chronicles 20:3, 5–6, 9 NIV).

Was Jehoshaphat frightened? You bet! But the very first thing he did was stop and pray. He took his concerns to God, he led his people by example, he acknowledged that he didn't have all of the answers, he listened to guidance—which came immediately—and he praised God! Before the outcome of the battle was evident!

Talk about faith under fire! What a wonderful example of godly leadership. The next time we are faced with a crisis, remember that we are setting the example to our children of how to respond: Stop, pray, listen, and thank God for His answers.

Lord, Jehoshaphat knew that he could call upon You during any crisis and that You would be His rescuer. Help me to have faith as bold as Jehoshaphat's.

But Why?

Then Joseph said to his brothers, "Come close to me." When they had done so,
he said, "I am your brother Joseph, the one you sold into Egypt! And now,
do not be distressed and do not be angry with yourselves for selling me here,
because it was to save lives that God sent me ahead of you."
Genesis 45:4–5 NIV

*C*hildren sometimes seem irrational—especially when they ask
questions about concepts they can't yet understand. If a poll was
taken and mothers were asked what question their children ask the
most, the answer would be a resounding *"why?"*

The reason children ask "why?" is probably because children
crave new information, but it's also because they're still too young
to make logical connections between cause and effect. More than
a few mothers have become frustrated after these long, child-led
interrogations. Their responses to "why" questions can quickly
become "because I said so" answers.

When Joseph was sold into slavery and then sent to prison after
being falsely accused, his "why" probably sounded like a broken
record. But just as the child who cannot yet understand the meaning
behind concepts, so Joseph could not fathom the purpose God had in
store for him in Egypt.

As mothers, we can also look at situations and not understand
why God has allowed events to happen or not happen. Going directly
to God and asking is a 24-7 gift we have. Waiting on God's timing is
another.

Lord, please be patient with me when I question You.
Help me to see the Truth.

Listening Wisely

Hear instruction, and be wise, and refuse it not.
Proverbs 8:33 KJV

*E*veryone has advice for mothers. From the time we are pregnant we hear how to feed, discipline, teach, dress, and love our child. The list of well-meaning advice is endless. Each person has a different experience or slant on what is best for us to do. Everyone is convinced that his or her opinions represent the truth.

There comes a point where a mother tunes out recommendations simply because she has no idea what is best anymore. She can be overwhelmed with the variety and conflict in the various methods of child rearing. If she listens to one person, then another will be offended. No one seems to want to consider the mother's desires as she raises her child.

When this happens, we must learn to listen wisely. Study God's Word and see what He says is important in child rearing. The Bible has many good things to say to a mother. We need to hear what our friends and family are saying, but sift their counsel through scripture. Find the nuggets of truth that are good and will help in each situation, and put away the rest. We shouldn't disdain anyone's pointers, but we can know that God will guide us, and He will be the final counselor.

God, thank You for giving me wise counsel. Help me to be patient,
and to truly hear what I need to know. Amen.

Judge Deborah

Deborah, a prophetess, the wife of Lappidoth, was leading Israel at that time.
She held court under the Palm of Deborah between Ramah and Bethel in the hill
country of Ephraim, and the Israelites came to her to have their disputes decided.
Judges 4:4–5 NIV

*B*ible scholars know only a few things about Deborah, Israel's
only female judge: She was married, familiar with family life. She
listened to people's problems and gave them God's wisdom. She
was highly respected, considered one of Israel's best judges. She had
an assurance that she was appointed by God. "Village life in Israel
ceased, ceased until I, Deborah, arose, arose a mother in Israel"
(Judges 5:7 NIV).

Oh, wouldn't it be wonderful to have a woman like Deborah
in our lives? Imagine how helpful it would be, after a difficult day
with a cranky two-year-old, to push our strollers up the hill to visit
Deborah, sit in the shade under a palm tree, and ask her for God's
wisdom to deal with our child!

There are many older women at church who can be our mentors
and guides, pointing us to God's wisdom. Pray that God will
open your eyes to a Deborah-like woman. Finding such a friend is
a blessing from the Lord, just as important today as it was four
thousand years ago.

Lord, help me find a woman like Deborah. You appointed someone, You believe
in mentoring, but I don't know where to look for her! Open my eyes to a
woman—or women—who can share Your wisdom with me.

Seeking Praise

"His master replied, 'Well done, good and faithful servant!
You have been faithful with a few things; I will put you in charge
of many things. Come and share your master's happiness!' "
Matthew 25:23 NIV

*H*ot meals miraculously appear at dinnertime. Clean clothes are folded neatly in dresser drawers. The clutter around the house mysteriously vanishes. Who is responsible for such occurrences— an elf or secret helper? As mothers, we all know the answer to that question! However, many times these acts of love are taken for granted by family members. Our efforts seem to be in vain. Motherhood can often be a thankless job!

However, we should not become discouraged. Our husband and children may not always express thanks and appreciation, but the Lord will. We will receive a heavenly reward for our behind-the-scenes acts of service. God's approving voice will sound sweeter than that of any standing ovation. May we yearn for God's approval, not man's applause.

When we serve our family, we are ultimately serving the Lord. Regardless of how menial the tasks appear, do them for Him. We will never be disappointed when our actions are an outward expression of our love for the Lord. We will hear Him whisper, "Well done." We will experience joy in our hearts. Live for His praise alone.

Dear Lord, help me serve my family out of my love for You.
May I yearn for Your approval. Amen.

Choosing to Rejoice

Rejoice evermore.
1 Thessalonians 5:16 KJV

*Y*ou wake up to a beautiful morning. Freshly fallen snow sparkles in the morning sunlight. Everything is so pure and perfect. It is easy to rejoice. Then you hear a croupy cough that pulls you from the frosted windowpane to the side of your young child's bed. A quick touch to the forehead reveals what you already instinctively knew. His fever is high. You are sure it will be a trip to the doctor.

Suddenly the snow looks more like foe than friend. Will you still rejoice? You already had your day parceled out. How will you react to this change of plans? As a believer, Christ lives in You. None of this came as a surprise to Him. He allowed it for a purpose. He might choose to reveal His reasons, but only if it's important for you to know them. One thing is certain: You have received the challenge to rejoice evermore. Be assured that God is with you through any trial you will face. That not only gives you a reason, it gives you the ability to be joyful in every circumstance. After all, the trials and joys of this earth are but for a season. Heaven awaits, and what rejoicing that will bring.

O Lord, it is You alone who fills my heart with joy.
Thank You for sunshine in the midst of rain.

The Waiting Game

So humble yourselves under the mighty power of God,
and at the right time he will lift you up in honor.
1 Peter 5:6 NLT

*H*igh school and college reunions had been the worst. Not only was Jana five, ten, or fifteen years older, but it seemed she'd had to answer the same two questions that many times, too.

Yes, she was married, but no, she and her husband had no children. Everyone eventually chalked up her childlessness to the desire for career advancement, but that belief wasn't exactly true. The truth was that they'd tried almost everything. . .and hadn't been able to get pregnant.

Until now.

Jana walked into her twenty-year high school reunion, one hand in her husband's and her other on her protruding abdomen. It would have been one thing to walk into the crowded, old gymnasium and be excited for having proved her friends wrong. Such retaliation, however, was not the case. Instead, Jana flitted from table to table and friend to friend, eager to share and tell about God's faithfulness.

She had no idea why God's timing wasn't her and her husband's timing. Nothing had seemed right during those painful reunions and friends' baby showers. But maybe God was glorifying Himself through the testimony Jana was now excitedly giving her friends and family. Within days of learning they were pregnant, Jana had received more exciting news. Their adoption efforts were finally coming to an end.

If their calculations were right, they would adopt a three-year-old girl just weeks after Jana gave birth to their newborn daughter.

Father, Your faithfulness astounds me. I will praise You for Your timing.

Grown-Up Love

When I was a child, I spake as a child, I understood as a child,
I thought as a child: but when I became a man, I put away childish things.
1 Corinthians 13:11 KJV

*P*astors often read 1 Corinthians 13, the "Love Chapter," at weddings. Even unbelievers feel drawn to the rich poetic language, vivid imagery, and most of all, to that magic word: love. Christians, upon hearing the powerful Word of God, recommit their lifestyles to Christ.

But God uses families to help us understand our lack of love!

"I thought I was a mature Christian; then I had children!" Brianna shook her head while other mothers at the Bible study laughed with her.

A mom can read all day about long-suffering, but when her four-year-old uses lipstick to paint the living room walls, she stops theorizing about patience. We mothers consider ourselves kind women until our toddlers hide the car keys. And we're far too spiritual to harbor envy—until an old high school friend shows up, looking great in her size 4 business suit without a single spit-up stain.

Fortunately, God knows we, too, are still children. Believers won't mature completely until "that which is perfect is come" (1 Corinthians 13:10 KJV). We may find the road to true love a long one. But with the help of God's Spirit, we will see ourselves, more and more, in the Love Chapter.

Lord Jesus, when I feel the least loving, remind me how it is done.
Thank You. Amen.

Whose Yoke Are
You Bearing?

For my yoke is easy, and my burden is light.
Matthew 11:30 KJV

$\mathcal{D}$espite living in a world with so many conveniences, women seem to be under a greater burden now than ever before.

Mothers seem especially stressed. They are constantly on the run for their families and themselves. They are frustrated because they can't meet the maternal standards of their mothers and grandmothers, nor can they achieve the exhilaration of "liberation" touted by the world.

Christian mothers are especially stressed, because we look at the struggle in light of scripture. And often, we cry out to God saying, "I can't do this, Lord! It's too much!"

If the burden *is* too much, then maybe we're carrying the wrong one.

If the yoke is too heavy, it may not be the one He's fashioned for us. It may be one we've made ourselves. Jesus said *His* burden is light.

We can sometimes make our yokes heavier by expecting perfection, by trying to please others rather than God, and by seeking fulfillment outside of God's plan.

A woman's yoke is spelled out in Titus 2:4–5. We are to be humble women who love and obey our husbands, love our children, and work at home. The more we add, the heavier the yoke will be.

Of course, Jesus will help us carry our burden, even if we've added more to it. But better to take His yoke and lighten the load.

*Father, I know I have added to the burden You want me to carry. Give me the
strength to drop the nonessentials so I can carry Your lighter yoke. Amen.*

Counted Faithful

And I thank Christ Jesus our Lord, who hath enabled me,
for that he counted me faithful, putting me into the ministry.
1 Timothy 1:12 KJV

It is true that in this passage Paul is talking about being a minister of the Bible, but what he says here can be applied in so many ways to motherhood. We certainly should teach the Gospel to our children. Those are the most important lessons they will ever have, because that training will impact their eternity.

Still, we minister to our children daily in many ways. There are those areas that are typically considered, such as providing meals and clean clothes. We must also meet emotional needs by providing love and attention in lavish doses.

These are obvious ways mothers care for children, but there are subtle ways as well. We must be careful how we respond to each situation in life, because our kids are watching and learning. We are always teaching them, even when we don't realize it.

It is an awesome task, but Christ enables us. He saw something in each of us that said, "This woman will be faithful." His strength will never fail us. Through Him we can be worthy of our call to motherhood.

Dear Jesus, I am honored that you find me worthy to be a mother
to Your little ones. Help me always be faithful in this ministry.

But the wisdom that comes from heaven is first of all pure; then peace-loving, considerate, submissive, full of mercy and good fruit, impartial and sincere.
James 3:17 NIV

As each day of rearing a preschooler passed, Laura felt more and more inadequate. She thought to herself, *As my child got older, I thought it would be easier.* Laura's conversations with the Lord often reflected her feelings of failure and need for the Lord to provide wisdom on how to raise her child. *God provided the child,* Laura thought, *shouldn't He also provide the instruction book?*

God does provide the instruction book: the Bible. King Solomon pleased the Lord in that he asked for wisdom (1 Kings 3:9). Just like Solomon, we can please God by asking the Lord to give us what He gave Solomon: "a wise and discerning mind" (1 Kings 3:12). James 1:5 (ESV) tells us "If any of you lacks wisdom, let him ask God, who gives generously to all without reproach, and it will be given him." When we struggle with feelings of inadequacy and failure as a mom, we can study God's instruction book, converse with God regarding the areas where we need wisdom, and then enjoy the wisdom the Lord will provide that is "first of all pure; then peace-loving, considerate, submissive, full of mercy and good fruit, impartial and sincere" (James 3:17).

Lord, thank You for the child You have given me. Please provide me with wisdom in the specific areas in which I feel inadequate as a mom.

Grasp His Love

And I pray that you, being rooted and established in love,
may have power, together with all the saints, to grasp how
wide and long and high and deep is the love of Christ.
Ephesians 3:17–18 NIV

*N*obody likes me. Everybody hates me. Guess I'll go eat worms."
Although this is a silly children's song, many of us have felt this way
at some point in our lives. (Except the part about eating worms!)
The whole world seems to be against us. Abandoned by family or
friends, we sense that we're all alone. Although intellectually we may
concede that we haven't been totally forsaken, our emotions tell us
otherwise.

When we find ourselves in that lonely state, we must grasp
the truth about love. God is love. God's love will never fail. He
demonstrated that love by laying down His life for us. How great
is that love! Nothing will ever be able to separate us from God's
love. He loves us in the good times as well as the bad. He loves
us when we're walking with Him or when we go astray. His love
is unconditional. He cannot love us any more or any less than He
always does. How awesome is God's love? It is wider, longer, higher,
and deeper than we can fathom! May we truly grasp and experience
His amazing love.

Dear Lord, thank You for your unfailing love! Help me fully receive Your
unconditional love so that I will never feel unloved again. Amen.

Who's In Charge Here?

*Sin will not be your master, because you are
not under law but under God's grace.*
Romans 6:14 NCV

$\mathcal{S}$in is a tough boss to please. We sometimes hand him our relationships, our minds and talents, our money, our entertainment. We may dedicate all our time and energy to him—even weekends and holidays—but he's not content until we hand over our very souls. Like sheep, we go where he pushes us. When he threatens or cajoles, we do what he says. Sin hurts us and those we love. Yet we humans still harbor the idea that we are free and independent.

Sometimes sin chooses a different disguise. Merciless as ever, he dangles a legalistic carrot before our eyes and tells us *if* we live extra good lives and *if* we follow his never-ending list of rules, we will become like God. So we either fail and stay in the pits of self-hatred or live in a fantasy world of self-congratulation because we're perfect or close to it.

Sin wants to control us and our kids. But God's grace says, "No! I'd rather die than see you live like that!"

If we lose our old boss and turn to God, we freely choose life and blessing forever. And when sin whispers at us from dark alleys, we can tell him we no longer work for him.

Lord Jesus, though I love You and appreciate all You've done, sin still tries to run my life. Help me say a loud no to the tempter and an even louder yes to You! Help me to walk in Your light. Amen.

Crabby Days

We don't have a priest who is out of touch with our reality. He's been through weakness and testing, experienced it all—all but the sin. So let's walk right up to him and get what he is so ready to give. Take the mercy, accept the help.
Hebrews 4:15 MSG

*J*esus grew up in a tiny home in an ordinary Palestinian village. His parents lived paycheck to paycheck. When it was time to sacrifice at the temple, they purchased a dove—a sign of low income. And there was probably a new baby added to that house every few years, wailing in the night and waking everyone up.

Jesus had typical siblings: jealous, eager to point out flaws and assume the worst. He knew what a bad day felt like—when the hammer hit his thumb and caused a blood blister, and when his brothers were in bad moods and fought with each other through dinner.

We don't have to hide our bad moods or grouchy feelings from God. He gets it! He knows that some days are just plain hard. But He doesn't leave us stuck there. Scripture tells us that we can boldly approach the throne of grace and find help in our time of need. Right at 5:00 p.m., when the three-year-old wants dinner. And at 10:00 p.m., when the baby winds up like a siren. We can call upon the Lord for His grace, to survive the crabbiest of days.

Lord God, be here! In the kitchen at dinnertime. . .in the nursery during the wee hours of the morning. . . Be here in our midst.

Counterfeit Fillers

So God created man in his own image, in the image of God he created him;
male and female he created them.
Genesis 1:27 NIV

*R*oberta felt empty. She was loved by God, blessed with a family, and well provided for; however, she couldn't shake how bored with life she truly was. Roberta felt a void in her heart that was just not completely and permanently filled with anything that she had or enjoyed.

Motherhood can sometimes foster feelings of emptiness, particularly when many of the tasks we do day after day for our preschooler can become chores or drudgery. In fact, we may even try to run from the void inside by doing more—joining every playgroup, doing every service project, filling our day with more and more doing, busyness, frenzy. Or maybe we try to fill our lives with material things to escape the lonely feeling inside. Or maybe we dwell on the future and how life will be better when our preschooler is older, and we have more time for ourselves! However, these activities and acquisitions are counterfeit fillers. At best, counterfeits provide only brief, fleeting satisfaction.

The Lord is the only permanent and genuine filler for the emptiness we feel. God created us in His image with the intent that we would need Him to fill any emptiness we may have. God promises that He will fill us (Matthew 5:3, 6; Isaiah 29:19; 55:1–3) when we seek Him. Reject counterfeits. Seek Him alone.

Lord, in this season of raising my preschooler, help me to be aware
of counterfeit fillers and seek You alone. Come fill me.

Dependable as
the Sunrise

It is of the LORD's mercies that we are not consumed, because his compassions
fail not. They are new every morning: great is thy faithfulness.
Lamentations 3:22–23 KJV

*P*ilar, please get into your car seat. Hurry, I have to get to work!"

"Look, Mommy!" The four-year-old wriggled free from Elena's grasp in the early morning chill and pointed toward the east. "God likes to finger paint, too!"

For a few seconds, Elena almost forgot they were running late, as usual. The glorious rose, lavender, blue, and peach clouds formed a canopy fit for the golden sun, which was enthroned on the horizon like a king. *Oh, Lord, you are such an artist!* How long had it been since Elena had stopped during the morning rush to enjoy the sunrise God designed? She picked up her daughter; together they savored the magnificence of the morning.

What if God decided to close down the dawn every time His work went unnoticed? The earth and its inhabitants would not survive long. Yet despite our failure to love and worship Him, God does not waver in His compassion for His people. Even when we do not appreciate His mercies, fresh and new every morning, He sends the warmth and beauty we take for granted. Where would we be without God's faithfulness?

Lord Jesus, thank You for the beautiful sunrise. You are the faithful Sun of
Righteousness, who makes salvation possible for my family and me. Amen.

A Gentle and Quiet Spirit

*Clothe yourselves. . .with the beauty that comes from within,
the unfading beauty of a gentle and quiet spirit, which is so precious to God.*
1 Peter 3:4 NLT

"*G*entle" and "quiet" are not words we as moms typically have spring to our minds. In fact, some days are spent trying to block out the noise of the two-year-old singing the ABCs at the top of her lungs, or repeatedly reminding the three-year-old to stop pulling the cat's tail. To attempt to convince our children to be gentle and quiet is most often an impossible task.

God's Word instructs us to focus on the beauty within us—a "gentle and quiet spirit," which has a beauty that will never fade. What a joy it would be to be known by our children and by others as one who has a gentle and quiet spirit, but mostly as "precious to God."

The next time you get dressed, remember to also "clothe yourself" with this spirit of beauty on the inside. The more we work on developing a gentle and quiet spirit, the easier those days will seem when the four-year-old "helps" by watering the plants—a little too much—or the baby has lost her pacifier *again*.

*Lord, please help me put on a gentle and quiet spirit today.
In a world that focuses so much on outward beauty, remind me to
emphasize the inner beauty, which You consider "precious." Amen.*

No Excuses

*For you have need of steadfast patience and endurance, so that you
may perform and fully accomplish the will of God, and thus receive
and carry away [and enjoy to the full] what is promised.*
Hebrews 10:36 AMP

It was a small argument this time, but Barbara knew it was one her
son shouldn't have heard. He sat quietly, playing with his blocks. She
sighed. At the age of four, Andy had heard his parents arguing way
too often. Barbara recognized that she had to learn to control her
temper. The things she and her husband fought over were silly. Why
couldn't she just cool her temper and discuss things calmly with her
husband, maybe give in every now and then?

Barbara wanted to blame her stubbornness on her past, but she
knew that was just an excuse. She gathered Andy up into her arms
and hugged him close. It was time to get help.

Hadn't her husband joked with her last Sunday that maybe
they should take the anger management class offered at the church?
Barbara decided that now was as good a time as any to start agreeing
with her husband. She kissed Andy's forehead and then returned him
to his toys. Barbara picked up her cell phone and dialed the church
office.

*Heavenly Father, thank You for my church family.
Thank You for helping me to learn patience as I walk down
this road of life. Without You I would be lost. Amen.*

One Flesh, First and Last

Therefore shall a man leave his father and his mother,
and shall cleave unto his wife: and they shall be one flesh.
Genesis 2:24 KJV

*S*omething happens to a wife once she becomes a mother.

Where once she was totally devoted to the care of her husband, she suddenly has someone new to care for, someone who needs and demands her attention every hour of the day.

Her focus often shifts to the baby, sometimes to the exclusion of her husband.

As more children come along, her attachment to her husband can get more and more tenuous. She sees herself as a mother first and a wife second.

This is not God's plan. While children are an integral part of His design, when God gave Eve to Adam, the first family was complete. The children would come and go, but they would be one flesh, first and last.

Forget not the husband of your youth. God gave you to him.

During those hectic years when the children are small and demanding, set aside time for your husband, and teach the children to honor that time. He needs your support and encouragement even more as a father than he did when he was a husband only.

And you need him just as much.

Father, my husband is precious to me, but sometimes I forget him
as I get consumed with the needs of these little ones You've given me.
Help me to keep him first, so our love will last. Amen.

Quiet Time

*In the morning, O LORD, you hear my voice; in the morning
I lay my requests before you and wait in expectation.*
Psalm 5:3 NIV

*S*atan wants to spoil the quiet times we have with God. One woman tells of how her young child woke every morning at precisely 6:30. So, in order to ensure that she would be able to have a private time of prayer and meditation on God's Word, she determined to awaken each morning at 6:00. The first morning she tried this, her daughter woke at 6:05, just five minutes into her prayer time. The next morning, she woke at 6:05 again. This mom envisioned a minion of the devil, poking her daughter awake just to disrupt her time with her Lord.

She read, in the book of Psalms, where David wrote of the beauty of morning worship and prayer. David knew just how busy the day would become and how important it was to start it with the proper focus. So, he rose each morning and prayed expectantly, waiting on the Lord in anticipation of what was to come.

So that young mom began to earnestly pray that God would help her fulfill her desire to spend time with Him, by protecting her daughter's sleep. Day by day, the child slept longer and longer, until that desperate mom was finally able to pray and study for a full hour each morning.

*Jesus, please help me find time to be with You in the midst of my busy day.
Protect me against Satan's attempts at distracting me from my time with You.
Help me to hear Your voice each day. Amen.*

Not Mine

And the multitude of them that believed were of one heart and of one soul. . .
they had all things common.
Acts 4:32 KJV

One of the first words our children learn is "mine." We notice it
especially when they are playing with another child. Our sweet little
toddler can turn into an ogre as she grabs onto her toy and refuses to
share. This is her possession, and she doesn't want anyone else to touch it.

Teaching preschoolers to share can be a long, arduous task. They
get angry when any other child wants their toy. Our children don't
understand the concept of letting someone else have a turn. They
don't realize how much fun they will have when they learn to play
with someone else.

Sometimes Christians act like toddlers over what they consider
theirs in the body of believers. "Nobody sits in my pew." "This is my
area of ministry, and I'm the best for the job. How could she try to
barge in and do what I do so well?"

God wants us to share all things as a group. We need to take
turns doing jobs, and we should not be offended when someone
sits where we normally sit. When we allow others to share and work
alongside us, we have a real peace and joy because we are behaving in a
godly manner. Let's learn to rejoice in others and not be possessive.

Lord, thank You for making us a body that fits together and works together.
Amen.

What's the Truth?

He writes the same way in all his letters, speaking in them of these matters. His letters contain some things that are hard to understand, which ignorant and unstable people distort, as they do the other Scriptures, to their own destruction.
2 Peter 3:16 NIV

Shawna was exasperated. "Tell me what happened," she said.

"He started it!" her two twin boys shouted at the same time. They both pointed their index finger at the other.

Shawna tired to remain calm. She had only been on the telephone for a minute before the ruckus began. Promising to call her friend back, Shawna had hung up and set the phone down.

"One at a time! One at a time!" she commanded, feeling as though her services as a mother would have prepared her well for a Supreme Court seat.

Both boys began talking, their sentences running together and their explanations conflicting. Shawna didn't know what had happened, and there was no way she was going to find out until she separated the two. Maybe then she would be able to understand the truth.

Today's world, its beliefs and opinions, are a lot like fighting twin boys. The truth is hard to distinguish apart from God's wisdom. When Paul wrote his letters, he wrote with wisdom, but those who did not believe were not able to understand.

Ask God for wisdom, understanding, and discernment as you study the scriptures and seek Truth.

God, help me to understand Your Truth.

Hope Is a Reality

*Hope maketh not ashamed; because the love of God is shed
abroad in our hearts by the Holy Ghost which is given unto us.*
Romans 5:5 KJV

*M*ommy, will God take care of me while I sleep?"

We parents hop up and down with excitement at our preschoolers' first word! But they learn to ask questions—hard questions. Can we in good conscience answer, "Yes, He will"?

Even Christian adults catch hopelessness as if it were a disease. Television, movies, books, and plays all push the idea that positive outlooks and happy endings are for those who have lost touch with reality and/or aren't too bright.

But the Bible's viewpoint does not match this dark notion. Certainly the Old and New Testaments do not mince words about people's cruelty to each other. They paint all-too-vivid pictures of human sin and a graphic portrayal of our Savior's tortuous death to atone for it! Yet this realistic Book explodes with hope and joy, because Jesus arose and laughed in death's face. We can, too, if we welcome Him into our lives.

So when little ones ask us if God will take care of them while they sleep, we don't have to tell loving lies. We don't have to duck questions about evil. Instead, we can truthfully assure them that God will keep them safe forever. They'll get a good night's sleep.

We will, too.

*Heavenly Father, I thank You for the hope Your Spirit lights in us.
And for the happy ending that is no fairy tale. Amen.*

Friends of Jesus,
Friends of Others

I have called you friends.
John 15:15 KJV

*A*preschooler typically has many playmates that he would consider friends, whether they be at preschool, church, a library reading class, the playground, or around the neighborhood. Moms often set up playdates with these little ones so that their child can interact with others.

It may seem too early to choose good friends for your youngster, but this is the perfect time to begin teaching him the importance of selecting positive influences. Of course, he cannot do it by himself yet, but he can recognize good traits when they are pointed out. "I really like the way Alex shares," you may say, or, "Isn't Shawn good at waiting for his turn?" There are many valuable life lessons to be learned, beginning at an early age.

Even more important than growing earthly relationships is developing his relationship with his heavenly Father. Remind him, "Jesus is your very best friend." Daily Bible reading and prayer time will strengthen his bond with this Best Friend. Share with him the importance of this Friend in your life, too. By establishing this relationship, he will have a Counselor who can guide him in choosing his associates throughout life. Many playmates will come and go, but Jesus will be his Friend forever.

Father, thank You for being my best friend. Please help me as I teach my little one about You and about those he chooses as earthly friends. Amen.

Are You Content?

But godliness with contentment is great gain.
1 Timothy 6:6 KJV

$\mathscr{I}$t had been a hectic morning, and Kathleen just wanted a bit of time to straighten the house, so she allowed three-year-old Mallory some time with her favorite cartoons.

As she went about her tasks, she caught bits and pieces of the toy and snack commercials that regularly interrupted the feature program. *They sure start young,* Kathleen thought as she realized just how similar this was to prime-time programs.

She was growing weary of hearing "Hey kids, check this out," or "You've got to try new. . ." When she heard "Keep up with your friends with. . ." she knew it was time for Mallory to be otherwise entertained.

"Mallory, why don't you come on over to the table and color for a while," Kathleen suggested.

"But Mommy, all I have are boring old crayons and paper. I need some sparkly crayons and a jumbo coloring book," Mallory whined.

Well, the season of discontent has already begun, thought Kathleen. She knew her daughter was a bit young, but she tried to explain anyway.

"Mallory, Jesus knows what you really need, and He provides that and much more. Let's thank Him for all He's given us," she said.

O God, You do provide abundantly.
Thank You for Your many wonderful gifts.

Being Held

*So do not fear, for I am with you; do not be dismayed, for I am your God. I will
strengthen you and help you; I will uphold you with my righteous right hand.*
Isaiah 41:10 NIV

The beach was desolate. Waves gently lapped against the sand. In
the distance, a father could be seen running. A little boy followed
close behind. Yet as time went on, the distance between them grew.
The youngster became tired and had difficulty keeping up with his
father's pace. The boy slowed down. Discouraged, he finally stopped
altogether. Sensing that his son had all but given up, the father
stopped, turned around, and went back to him. Kneeling down, he
spoke to his son. Then he scooped him up and carried him home.

We may see ourselves in this scene. Closely following the Lord
is difficult at times. A barren stretch is before us. Discouragement
sets in. As we have trouble keeping up, the gap widens. We fear being
lost forever. Do not be dismayed. The Lord knows your struggle. He
knows when you are falling behind. He will never leave or forsake
you. He will stop and come to you. He will speak encouraging words
to your heart. He will pick you up and carry you like a child. He will
help you by imparting His strength to you.

*Dear Lord, thank You for helping me when I am weak.
May Your strength uphold me in my greatest hour of need. Amen.*

Creating Habits

Do not be deceived: "Evil company corrupts good habits."
1 Corinthians 15:33 NKJV

Claire was frustrated. She wasn't ever able to get the housework done—her lack of organization was spilling over into every area of her life. And her preschooler, Abby, had begun to demonstrate bad habits she'd learned from none other than Claire herself. The child's toys were strewn all over the house, her dirty clothes rested on her bedroom floor where she'd dropped them the night before, and lately she'd begun leaving her fruit-snack wrappers on the living room floor. Claire knew their bad habits had to change.

She prayed about it, and the very next morning a woman from church called and invited Claire to a "mothers of preschoolers" group. Claire hurried to the first meeting. When she entered the fellowship hall, she received a notebook full of tips and tools to help her get more organized. There were pamphlets that provided a cooking and cleaning schedule, with helpful suggestions to make her family healthy and happy.

It didn't take long for Abby to notice a change in her mother's day-to-day routine and become interested in what her mommy was doing. Claire decided to create a notebook for Abby, too. Mother and daughter sat down and began to work on their new and improved lifestyle. The notebooks were fun for both of them, and soon they had done away with bad habits and developed new ones. Claire thanked the Lord for supplying the answer she had so desperately needed.

Heavenly Father, thank You for helping me recognize my bad habits and for helping me to develop new—and better—ones. Amen.

Interruptions!

Then some children were brought to Him so that He might lay
His hands on them and pray; and the disciples rebuked them. But Jesus said,
"Let the children alone, and do not hinder them from coming to Me;
for the kingdom of heaven belongs to such as these."
Matthew 19:13–14 NASB

*J*esus was constantly interrupted. By a woman touching the hem of His garment, hoping for healing. By a crowd hungering for miracles. By wily Pharisees looking to trap Him. And He continues to be constantly interrupted today, by parents longing for His blessing on their children.

No wonder the disciples felt it was their job to shoo people away. Jesus was a busy man! They felt Jesus needed them to act as bodyguards, keeping unimportant people from distracting Him.

The disciples got it all wrong, Jesus pointed out. He loved children! Children were the most welcome interruption of all and the real business of heaven. Jesus delighted in their childlike faith, trust, and simple joy. Children were important to Jesus. This snapshot of His day etches in our minds the example of never turning away a child.

Oh, if only we could respond to our child's interruptions as Jesus did! Instead, interruptions seem like annoyances. Our lives feel littered by so many unfinished conversations and half-done tasks.

There will be time for finishing things later, Jesus suggests. For now, children are our priority.

Lord, make me thankful for these interruptions. Remind me that
childhood flies by. My children will be gone soon. Let me respond to
them as You would, by stopping and opening my arms, offering time.

Lasting Fruit

"I am the vine, you are the branches; he who abides in Me and I in him,
he bears much fruit, for apart from Me you can do nothing."
John 15:5 NASB

*L*ara doesn't think about starting the day without spending quiet time with the Lord. She remembers too often how those few moments of extra sleep, in lieu of having a quiet time, made her impatient and hot-tempered with her preschooler. Today, she experiences the outflow of the fruit of the Spirit—"love, joy, peace, patience, kindness, goodness, faithfulness, gentleness, self-control" (Galatians 5:22–23 NASB)—during the time she spends with the Lord, which reflects in the time she spends with her preschooler.

God desires us to be totally connected and dependent on Him for every moment of every day, particularly as we raise the gifts the Lord has given us, our preschoolers. The Lord describes this intimate union in John 15:1–11, as He explains how our heavenly Father is the vine grower, deliberately growing us into the image of Christ. Jesus is the vine and we are the branches. The purpose of this union is to bear much fruit; "fruit that will last" (John 15:16 NIV) in the lives of our preschoolers to glorify God, which is what we have been created to do (Isaiah 43:7). When we as mothers model the fruit of the Spirit, our preschoolers will hunger and thirst to know the Lord, the only lasting fruit.

Lord, I praise You for the close union with You that allows me to bear lasting fruit—a personal relationship with You for my preschooler and me.

Quiet in Chaos

*And Jesus answered and said unto her, Martha, Martha, thou art careful
and troubled about many things: But one thing is needful: and Mary
hath chosen that good part, which shall not be taken away from her.*
Luke 10:41–42 KJV

We hear it in sermons.

We read it in books.

"Be a Mary, not a Martha. Don't get so busy serving the Lord
that you don't have time to enjoy Him."

But where is there time in a house with toddlers to enjoy the
good part? How can we sit at Jesus' feet when there isn't time to sit
at all?

Perhaps our frustrations come from thinking that "sitting at
Jesus' feet" is synonymous with "quiet time."

There was nothing quiet about Martha and Mary's house. Jesus
came with at least twelve followers. The house was crowded and noisy
as Mary listened to Christ.

Like Mary, we can find the better part, even when surrounded
by noisy preschoolers. We can share our time in the Word—our
"quiet" time—with our little ones. We can keep a Bible open on the
kitchen counter so we can read it all day long. We can pray constantly
throughout the day.

We don't need a silent house to hear the Lord.

And we can sit at his feet even when we're on the run.

*Father, speak to me through the din of my day.
Tune my ears to hear You always. Amen.*

There is a lad here, which hath five barley loaves, and two small fishes.
John 6:9 KJV

Carrie sliced Colton's sandwich into perfect diagonals, knowing he might fuss if they weren't equal. Carrie sighed. She should help her four-year-old son learn more flexibility.

As they walked to the park for a picnic, Colton's mood matched the sunshine. On the swings, Carrie cheered his attempts to pump his legs. They went down slides and explored the log cabin where the county's first pioneer lived.

Colton spotted an elderly man sitting on a bench with a nearby grocery cart full of odds and ends. "Who's that man?"

Carrie led Colton out of earshot to a picnic table. She told him to stop pointing—it wasn't nice—and explained that the man probably lived in the park; he didn't have a house; and no, he couldn't live in the log cabin.

"Is he poor?" Colton asked.

"Yes." Carrie opened his lunch box. "Here's your sandwich."

"I don't want it."

"Colton." Carrie gritted her teeth. "The two halves are the same."

"I know they are." His next words blew her away. "I don't want the sandwich because I'm going to give it to the poor man. Doesn't my Bible say Jesus wants us to share?"

Colton darted toward the man, sandwich in hand.

"Colton!" Carrie yelled. He stopped, and she took his hand. "I'll go with you."

Father, You can accomplish great things through small children.
Help me open my heart to Your lessons as well. Amen.

Anxiety-Free Contentment

*And He said to His disciples, "For this reason I say to you,
do not worry about your life, as to what you will eat;
nor for your body, as to what you will put on."*
Luke 12:22 NASB

According to Proverbs 31, mothers were to feed and clothe their families.

These tasks took a woman's time and energy, especially when she had to plant the garden, haggle with vendors at the market, and make clothes by hand. Without the benefit of modern conveniences to deliver and preserve food, and given the threat of famine and pestilence, feeding a family could cause a mother much anxiety.

Imagine the reaction of the women of Palestine when Jesus said, "Don't worry about what you're going to eat and wear. God will give you these needs as you seek Him." What relief they must have felt!

Have we forgotten this simple truth? Even though we feed and clothe our families with relative ease compared to our foremothers, do we still get stressed because our children wear hand-me-downs or eat leftovers twice in one week?

God promises to meet our basic needs. If our families need more than hand-me-downs and leftovers, God will provide them. Tap into the joy of this guarantee.

Be content with what you have, and believe God. If you really *need* more, He'll give it.

*Father, help me to see my situation clearly. I may not have the world's best,
but my needs are met. Thank You for giving us all we need and so much more.
Amen.*

Take This Cup

"Father, if You are willing, remove this cup from Me;
yet not My will, but Yours be done."
Luke 22:42 NASB

*H*as the Lord ever handed you a cup that you were unwilling to
drink? Catching a glimpse of what the future might hold, you did not
want to take another sip. Perhaps a parent's terminal illness has cast a
shadow on tomorrow. Or maybe an upcoming surgery is looming on
the horizon. Your heart cries out, "Lord, take this away!"

Jesus can relate. In the Garden of Gethsemane, He was
distraught, sorrowful, and troubled. His sweat, like drops of blood,
fell to the ground as He begged His heavenly Father to intervene.
Jesus wanted to forgo the excruciating pain of being nailed to a cross
and the spiritual agony of taking on the sins of the world.

Yet He willingly submitted. He trusted that God would provide
by giving Him strength to endure. He saw victory on the other side
of the cross. Because Jesus has been there, He can help us in our
"Garden of Gethsemane." Model His behavior. Pray. Allow your heart
to speak honestly to God. Then submit.

We, too, can experience spiritual victory. We, too, can receive
supernatural power and strength to endure what we never thought
possible. The same resurrection power that raised Jesus from the
dead is available to us. May His will be done.

Dear Lord, many times the future is too difficult to face.
Give me Your strength to walk the path that You have laid for me. Amen.

Wise Choice

I have set before you life and death, blessing and cursing:
therefore choose life, that both thou and thy seed may live.
Deuteronomy 30:19 KJV

The toddler chortled as she slipped the plastic bucket over her head like a hat. The bucket fell past her eyes. When she started forward, she ran into the wall and tumbled to the floor. As she began to cry, her mother lifted her up, explaining why she couldn't run with something over her eyes. The child repeated the behavior with the same result several times before she understood the lesson.

This mother could have forbidden the child to put the bucket on her head, but she chose to let her daughter learn from her mistakes. She wanted the girl to grasp the necessity of making wise decisions.

Throughout life there are many choices facing us. One of the most important is that of choosing God, and life with Him, over the lure of the world. Even after opting to follow God, we often allow a blindness to send us back into an old lifestyle. When we fall, we have to remember that it was a result of our choosing.

When we shrug off the former self and walk forward with our eyes on God, we can walk in confidence. Our determination will not only affect us, but our children and grandchildren. Each time we choose God, we are closer to His perfection.

Lord, I'm so glad You are a forgiving God.
Forgive my past, and lead me to a life with You. Amen.

The Best Wardrobe

Strength and honour are her clothing; and she shall rejoice in time to come.
Proverbs 31:25 KJV

*H*ow many times have you stood in your closet, staring at the array of sweaters, pants, and skirts, thinking, *I really have nothing to wear?* You don't feel like ironing what's there. The season is changing, and you're tired of summer outfits, but you aren't ready to pull out the fall clothes. You try on one thing after another and feel unattractive in all of it. It's usually not the best way to start your day, but Proverbs 31:25 has the answer.

Strength and honor are the clothing of a virtuous woman. They never become wrinkled. They are always stylish, and they make any woman attractive. Best of all, instead of being purchased in an expensive department store, they are obtained and renewed by walking regularly with Jesus.

It may be true that as a mother of a preschooler you don't often feel clothed in strength, and after a battle of wills you might not feel especially honorable, but it's not your own strength and honor you should consider. It's God's. Let Him wrap you in godly garments, and you'll be the best-dressed mom around.

Dear God, remind me that being clothed in godliness is so much more effective than the new and expensive but fading garments of this world.

The Perfect Mother

"My grace is sufficient for you, for my power is made perfect in weakness."
2 Corinthians 12:9 NIV

Suzanne desired to be the perfect mother. She worked around the clock, preparing gourmet meals for her own family and others who had a need, cleaning the house, doing laundry, washing dishes, and providing church and community service. Suzanne soon felt weary, discouraged, and depressed. Her joy for life was gone.

This is not the life God calls us to. John 15:5 (NIV) describes the type of living God planned for us: "I am the vine; you are the branches. If a man remains in me and I in him, he will bear much fruit; apart from me you can do nothing." We are not expected to live any moment of life without the Lord. God desires for us to be in such close union with Him that the Holy Spirit in us lives *through* us. It is God in us that will enable us to not be perfect but to glorify God as a mother. God requires us to lay down our inadequacies at the foot of the cross—our desperate pleas for help. It is then that God will make His grace sufficient for us. It is in our acknowledged weakness that God's power is made perfect and complete. God promises, in this state of union with the Lord, "[His] joy may be in [us] and that [our] joy may be complete (John 15:11 NIV).

Lord, I desire to be in constant union with You.
Holy Spirit, live life through me as I parent my child for Your glory.

Use Your Manners

And a servant of the Lord must not quarrel but be gentle to all, able to teach,
patient, in humility correcting those who are in opposition.
2 Timothy 2:24–25 NKJV

*H*ey!" a toddler shouted at the pastor's wife in an attempt to get
her attention while she was at the pulpit, welcoming visitors to the
church. The boy's mortified mother quickly scooped him up and
headed for the back door, scolding him for his rude outburst.

"Hey!" that same mom shouted at her little boy, trying to get
his attention in their backyard. She was shocked as she immediately
remembered scolding him in church for shouting the same word in
effort to get someone's attention. She had scolded him for doing
something he had learned from her.

Parents quickly correct their children's bad manners, but
sometimes their correction is delivered impatiently and can be rude.
Children learn from their mothers how to treat others and what type
of behavior is acceptable. We can enforce our rules and impose our
desires on our children, but it would be much better to use our own
good manners to model appropriate behavior.

Second Timothy 2:24–25 teaches us to be gentle to all and
patient in our teaching. This includes when we teach our children,
training them to be good and effective servants of God.

Jesus, please help me to be gentle and patient when correcting my child.
I want to be a good model and not just a dictator in my home.
Let me be an example of You. Amen.

Lying Tongues

He that speaketh truth sheweth forth righteousness:
but a false witness deceit.
Proverbs 12:17 KJV

The mother was more than a little rushed. The little one was just beginning to teethe. The dog that her husband insisted wouldn't be a problem just made a mess on the new carpet. And bake-sale cookies needed to be made and ready to send with her preschooler within thirty minutes.

Superwoman might manage her missions better, but Superwoman had obviously never directed this household! So rather than remove the bulky baking ingredients from the cabinet or even making the slice-and-bake cookies from the refrigerator, this mother went to another cabinet and reached high on tiptoes until she found the hidden store-packaged cookies. She quickly removed the wrapper and arranged them on a plate. *No one will ever know,* she thought.

"Mom," the child said after bounding into the room and accepting the cookies, "these aren't your famous homemade cookies, are they?"

With only limited hesitation, the mother responded, "Of course they are, silly!"

Her child's face sank. "They don't look like your special cookies, Mom."

The mother dropped to her knees and embraced her child. "I'm sorry, honey, you're right. These came from the store," she said.

"That's okay, Mom. I love you anyway!"

Like the forgiveness our children extend to us when we're less-than-perfect mothers, isn't it wonderful that our heavenly Father extends His grace to us when we're less-than-perfect children of God?

Lord, You know that my busy schedule doesn't allow time
for everything. But please help me to always be truthful
about what I have and haven't accomplished.

Mother Hen

*"How often I have longed to gather your children together,
as a hen gathers her chicks under her wings."*
Luke 13:34 NIV

A pastor told a story of how he felt as a father when a new babysitter was hired. He would quietly pull the babysitter off to one side and remind her that all of the stuff he owned—the house, car, flat-screen television—could disappear while he and his wife were out. But if anything happened to his children, he said in all seriousness, well, she wouldn't want to know what would happen. His children were *that* valuable to him.

That is exactly how God feels about His children! Young and old. He wants us all under His wing, safely cared for and lovingly protected. We are God's most prized possessions. So are our children. And our neighbor's children. And every child in the preschool and nursery. Lost children. Lonely children. Struggling children. Even happy, well-adjusted children. God wants them all, every last one, under His wings of care. "He will cover you with his feathers, and under his wings you will find refuge" (Psalm 91:4 NIV).

Let's remember to pray regularly for the children in our lives. Nieces, nephews, neighborhood kids. Keep a preschool class list handy to pray for those kids, too. God wants to bring them under His wing for all eternity.

*Lord, teach me to care for others as You do. Help me not to grow weary
or bored in praying for those around me. Some of these kids might not
have anyone else praying for them. At least they will have me.*

Patient Endurance

We ourselves glory in you. . .for your patience and faith
in all your persecutions and tribulations that ye endure.
2 Thessalonians 1:4 KJV

Teaching preschoolers something new can be a trying experience.
Their fingers fumble at the task. They make mistakes and have to
start over. Precious time is passing while we wait for them to learn,
all the while knowing we could have performed the task in a fraction
of the time. Yet if they don't try and work at it, our children will
never learn. They will always be dependent on us to do everything for
them.

God allows us to go through trials and struggles for a reason. He
could do all things for us, but He has chosen not to. He knows we
learn the most when the task is tough and we persist. God wants us
to grow through our difficult experiences. Through these times our
faith deepens, and we have more appreciation for our Lord and who
He is.

Our perseverance through tribulation also encourages others to
know God and trust Him. When we look for the easy way out, we
don't grow spiritually. We need to learn to have patience with our
children as they practice and comprehend each new undertaking, and
we need to have patience with God as He allows us to grasp more
understanding of Him.

Jesus, You are the One I look to as I go through difficulties.
Help me to have patience and endure as You did. Amen.

Remember the Joy

A woman when she is in travail hath sorrow, because her hour is come:
but as soon as she is delivered of the child, she remembereth no more the anguish,
for joy that a man is born into the world.
John 16:21 KJV

There's no place in the brain that remembers pain," the surgeon told his patient, "which is why women can have more than one baby."

While there are physiological reasons we cannot feel a given pain again, Jesus said we forget labor because of joy. The intense joy that a baby is born overcomes the pain of the birth.

When the baby is laid in our arms, we think we will never forget the happiness. But as the years of motherhood pass, we do.

We forget that these little ones who get us up at night, who fight with each other from sunrise to bedtime, who talk back, who send us to bed crying, were our little miracles not many years earlier.

Among the household hubbub, we often forget they are blessings. We forget the great privilege we have of bringing them up for God's glory. The Father could have sent that sassy toddler to anyone. But He sent him to *you* because He trusted *you* to care for that precious soul.

When you are ready to send them to Grandma, take a step back.

Recall the day they were born.

And remember the joy.

Father, thank You for entrusting these children to me. Remind me how happy I
was when they were born, so that that joy will still be mine today. Amen.

I Love You the Most

"Love one another, even as I have loved you."
John 13:34 NASB

At the close of each day, when tucking in their little ones, moms all over the world say, "I love you." What sweetness meets her ears when the small voice responds with, "I love you, too, Mommy." Those five words can melt a mother's heart, erasing the hardships of even the worst of days.

How wonderful of our heavenly Father to give us earthly examples of love. He, of course, is love itself, giving His only Child to die for people who didn't love Him in return. God the Father even had to turn His face from His Son, who took the sin of mankind on Himself. What unimaginable love!

Some children and mommies play a game together. One will say, "I love you," with the other replying, "I love you more," and the first finishing, "I love you the most" (although with preschoolers, it often comes out "I love you the mostest"). We tell Jesus we love Him, but He responds, "I love you more." He then commands us to love others in the same way that He loves us. How can we do any less for the One who loves us and gave His life for us?

Lord, I thank You for loving me with such an awesome love.
Help me show others my love for You by loving them more. Amen.

Friendship

If one falls down, his friend can help him up.
But pity the man who falls and has no one to help him up!
Ecclesiastes 4:10 NIV

Julie grew up an Air Force brat. Yearly summer moves displaced family vacations. Acquaintances were the norm. Long-lasting friendships were rare. In her forties, she was finally able to put down roots. She pondered the sacrifice that yearly moves had cost. While other people had established long-term relationships over their lifetime, Julie was starting from scratch.

God created us to be social creatures. We were made for relationship, with one another and with our Creator. Investing time in people results in having friends. Friends experience life together. They share joy and laughter, sorrow and pain. They celebrate victories and rejoice together in good times. They help carry life's burdens and lighten the load. Friends drop what they are doing to offer assistance. Friends put friends first. Friends lay down their lives for one another.

Take time to cultivate relationships. Get involved in your church and community to meet others. Make friendship a priority. Be the kind of friend to someone that you would desire for yourself. Life is richer with a friend. It's never too late to begin establishing meaningful relationships with others.

Dear Lord, sometimes life is so busy that I don't take the time to nurture relationships. Help me make friendship a priority. Amen.

Going into Battle

Thou therefore endure hardness, as a good soldier of Jesus Christ.
2 Timothy 2:3 KJV

Karen Miller and her family didn't believe in celebrating Halloween. She wasn't looking forward to the meeting she'd set up with her son's preschool teacher, Mrs. Stuart, but knew she had to stand up for what she believed in. As she pushed through the school doors, Karen prayed silently, asking God to help her express herself without causing either of them to become angry.

Karen took a deep breath and entered the classroom. Pumpkins and other harvest vegetables decorated the room. She'd expected to see ghosts, goblins, jack-o'-lanterns, and witches.

Mrs. Stuart welcomed her. "I am so glad that you came in to talk to me, Mrs. Miller. Won't you have a seat?"

Karen sat down, and soon she and Mrs. Stuart were discussing the witch paper.

Mrs. Stuart apologized. "Yesterday, I wasn't here, and my substitute teacher thought she'd do an art project with the children. As you can see there aren't any Halloween decorations in this room. I don't allow it, but she didn't know that and thought she was helping me. I really am sorry that you were offended."

Karen left the school pleased that God had given her the courage to go speak to her child's teacher with gentleness and grace.

Lord, You are my strength, and I thank You for helping
me to stand up for what I believe in. Amen.

Chosen Satisfaction

But if we have food and clothing, we will be content with that.
1 Timothy 6:8 NIV

The mother sighed and closed her eyes, fighting impatience. Her child had whined all day. Nothing had satisfied her. She wondered again if her daughter was coming down with something. Every time the girl was tired or getting sick, she was impossible to please. Even if she asked for her favorite snack, by the time it was ready, the preschooler didn't want to eat it.

Picking up her child, the mother held her close. Normally, she was a delight and easy to care for. The mother began to rock, hoping her daughter would forget her discomforts. The girl relaxed against her.

We are often cranky with God. The weather is too hot or too cold. Nobody likes us. We don't have enough money. People expect us to do everything. Work is piling up, and we don't have time to get our chores done. The complaints are endless.

Being satisfied, or content, is a choice. Our focus has to change from ourselves to God. We have to remember all He has done and given us. Often the worst times of discontent are when we are tired, sick, or our routine is somehow thrown off. Each time we must choose to focus on God and be satisfied with Him. We can lean back and relax in His arms.

Thank You, God, for all You have provided. Help me see the positives of You and not the negatives of the world. Amen.

In His Time

He hath made every thing beautiful in his time: also he hath set the world in their heart, so that no man can find out the work that God maketh from the beginning to the end.
Ecclesiastes 3:11 KJV

There's a really fun children's song entitled "He's Still Workin' on Me." It has wonderful lyrics for both children and adults to claim. The only problem is that we tend to sing the words while ignoring the message.

You see, it tells us not to judge our little ones yet because they're an incomplete work. God is still molding them just like He is us. No one is perfect yet, but that day is coming for those who have trusted Christ as their Savior. Only God knows when that day will be. Right now we need to allow Him to do His work in our lives, and we should point our little ones in the right direction, too.

Too many times we expect our children to be flawless in the here and now. We want them to do just what we say, and if they don't, we become frustrated. We refuse to acknowledge that frustration as part of our own imperfection.

It is important to teach and discipline our kids, but we must do it with love and patience. Let's let God work in His time.

Father, I am imperfect and sometimes impatient, but I want to let You work in Your time. Give me patience, O God, as I strive to follow You.

What Will
Heaven Be Like?

*"In my Father's house are many rooms; if it were not so,
I would have told you. I am going there to prepare a place for you."*
John 14:2 NIV

*T*his verse makes heaven seem like a gigantic hotel, filled with rooms. And Jesus sounds like the hotel manager, doling out keys. But the Greek word used for "rooms" in this scripture means dwelling or abiding place, implying permanence. Hardly a hotel!

Jesus gave us hints of heaven, but not the full picture. We're all naturally curious about heaven; after all, eternal life is a challenging concept to grasp. It boggles the mind to think of living forever.

Trying to understand heaven with our limitations would be like trying to explain to a fetus about life outside the womb. "Well, little baby, your lungs will fill up with air, and you will start to breathe! And you'll be hungry and want to eat. Oh, and you'll feel hot and cold, too. Trust me! You'll love it!" How could a fetus possibly understand? It's a realm beyond him. Given a choice, he might even prefer to stay where he is.

But we know more than a fetus knows. Jesus knows more about heaven than we can know. He gave us all of the information that we need: We belong in heaven, and a place is being prepared for us. We will live in God's presence forever.

If it were not so, Jesus would not have told us. Trust Him! You'll love it.

Lord of heaven, thank You for wanting us to be with You for all eternity!

A Pure Heart

Everyone who has this hope in him purifies himself, just as he is pure.
1 John 3:3 NIV

The stifled whimpers were coming from Paul's room. Maria and her husband, Tom, glanced at the clock and saw it was only 2:00 a.m.

"Do you want to go, or do you want me to go?" Tom asked through a bearlike yawn.

Maria rolled over and stretched. "I don't remember whose turn it is. Let's both go."

Over the past few weeks, Paul had been having nightmares. They began after Paul went to a friend's house to watch a movie. Maria and Tom had no idea that the preschoolers would have their movie choice overridden by the friend's junior-high-age brother. Paul had come home, talking about dinosaurs eating people. Maria had called over to the house. The friend's mother had apologized profusely, but that hadn't stopped the nightmares.

Maria and Tom were just about to enter Paul's room when they heard and saw a sight that caused them to back away slowly from the door frame. Paul was leaning beside his bed, his hands clasped in prayer. "This is silly, God, because I know there are no monsters under my bed. I got brave enough this time and decided to check. Still, You have to protect me, okay? I'm just a boy. Thanks."

Paul climbed back into bed. Less than a minute later, he was snoring.

"He may be a boy now," Tom whispered to Maria, "but I have a feeling that boy is going to be quite a man."

Father, I praise You for giving me a confident hope in You.

I'm Ba-a-ack!

"If you grasp and cling to life on your terms, you'll lose it,
but if you let that life go, you'll get life on God's terms."
Luke 17:33 MSG

*J*esus wanted His disciples to understand that many people will focus on business as usual on the day of His return, just as their predecessors did before Noah's flood swept them away. Workers will be plowing fields, carrying on commerce, and doing lunch as did the people of Sodom and Gomorrah before hellish fire and brimstone destroyed their cities. Jesus emphasized that His return to earth will be sudden and obvious, like lightning across the sky. He warned His disciples to drop everything when He returns. No one should worry about their possessions.

Why did Jesus say that? After all, if He appeared out of the blue, we would forget all about our homes. Our clothes. Our cars. Our businesses.

Or would we? Jesus reminded His followers of Lot's wife. Even with molten brimstone falling from the sky, threatening to burn her family to a crisp, Lot's wife couldn't resist the thought of returning to her house and her way of life. As a result, she turned into an immovable pillar of salt.

If we have been worshipping our possessions when Jesus comes, will our idolatry become obvious as we find ourselves earth- instead of heaven-bound?

Father, please do not allow my possessions to own me.
Let me model this attitude to my children so that when You return,
their eyes will be fixed on You alone. Amen.

Faith Is. . .

Now faith is being sure of what we hope for and certain of what we do not see.
Hebrews 11:1 NIV

Faith is not wishful thinking, grasping at straws, or our last resort. Faith is being sure and certain. Faith is taking God at His word. It is knowing that God will bring to pass that which He promises. By faith, Noah built an ark, even though it had not yet rained. By faith, Abraham left his homeland and ventured to a foreign country, even though he could not see it. By faith, Moses led the people out of Egypt, even though he felt unqualified as a leader. These men of faith did not know what the future would hold, yet they knew the One who holds the future.

Faith requires a leap, a jump. Everything is not neatly figured out. If we had all the answers, faith wouldn't be required.

In response to what the Lord is asking us to do or believe, in faith, we simply say yes. Like Peter, we decide to step out of the boat as we keep our eyes on Him. We trust God, knowing that He will keep His promises.

When we step out in faith, we are given a glimpse of the spiritual realm. We "see" the invisible. We can be sure and certain because our trust is placed in the Lord. He will remain faithful. We can stake our lives on His trustworthiness. Let's step out and believe Him. Let's exercise faith.

Dear Lord, give me faith to trust You when I cannot see.
Increase my faith. Amen.

Calgon, Take Me Away!

*News about Jesus kept spreading. Large crowds came to listen to
him teach and to be healed of their diseases. But Jesus would
often go to some place where he could be alone and pray.*
Luke 5:15–16 CEV

Several years ago, the Calgon Company aired a commercial
portraying a frantic, busy mom in her chaotic home. Kids are yelling,
dogs are barking, the phone is ringing, and it is apparent that she is
past her limit! She utters that still-famous line, "Calgon, take me
away!" and she is instantly soaking in a luxurious bubble bath, in a
silent bathroom.

Even Jesus needed escape from the chaos of constantly having
throngs of people around Him. He needed to find a quiet place to
pray and think. That doesn't make Him a bad Friend or Master; it
simply proves that He, the Son of God, was also human. He knew the
importance of protecting Himself both mentally and emotionally.

We need to be sure to get our Calgon moments. It doesn't make
us bad or insensitive to others. We must find that quiet place to be
alone with our thoughts and spend time in reflection and prayer. The
chaos of life is often too loud to hear the Savior's voice. By seeking
out silence, we will be better able to hear Him when He calls.

*Lord, I know I need more peace and quiet, and believe me, I want it.
Please help me to establish some order to the chaos and to
make room for quiet times of prayer. Amen.*

Faithful Words

She opens her mouth in wisdom, and the teaching of kindness is on her tongue.
Proverbs 31:26 NASB

*F*rom morning till night, Catherine spends the day interacting with her three young children. Her words, seasoned with grace, reflect patience, kindness, and gentleness. Unlike children who wilt under the stormy wrath of their parents, Catherine's children, like flowers turning toward the warm sunshine, experience daily nurturing through their mother's gentle assurance and guidance.

Catherine models Proverbs 31:26. Whether Catherine corrects or praises, she speaks in patient, quiet tones, words of faithful instruction. She has insight and good judgment because she is spiritually centered. She spends quiet time before the Lord each day before the children wake up. In addition, she seeks Him for wisdom throughout the day. Catherine's growth is also attributed to another mom who has slightly older children and who models the type of godly mother Catherine strives to be. This more seasoned mother mentors Catherine in her early years of child rearing.

Do you desire to guide your children with words of wisdom, kindness, and faithful instruction? Then spend time with the Lord, pray, connect with other moms, and find a mentor. You will become that life-giving sunshine that reflects the source of true Light from our Savior.

*Holy Spirit, I invite you to fill me with Your words of wisdom,
kindness, and faithful instruction to my children.*

I Don't Know How!

*If any of you is deficient in wisdom, let him ask of the giving
God [Who gives] to everyone liberally and ungrudgingly,
without reproaching or faultfinding, and it will be given him.*
James 1:5 AMP

*B*ut Mommy, I don't know how!" Davy dropped his shoelaces back
onto the floor. Tears filled his blue eyes as he looked up at her.

His mother, Sharon, had watched her son try over and over again
to get his shoes to tie just right. She smiled. "I know it's hard right
now, Davy, but you will get it, and then you can teach your little
sister, Sarah, when she's old enough to tie her shoes."

Sharon laid the baby in her crib and then knelt down beside her
three-year-old son. She knew it would be easier just to buy him shoes
with Velcro closures, but Sharon wanted Davy to learn patience as
well as to learn how to tie his shoes.

She'd recently asked God for patience and wisdom in dealing
with her two small children. It was times like this that she needed
both. Sharon helped Davy tie his shoes and then gave him a big hug.

He stood up and smiled. "Thanks, Mommy!"

Sharon smiled as she watched him run happily from the room.

*Thank You, Lord, for answering my prayers. I thank You for sharing
Your wisdom with me and for teaching me how to deal with my children.
Help me, Lord, to be a good example to them. In Your holy name, amen.*

Proper Diet

Jesus said to them, "My food is to do the will of Him who sent Me,
and to finish His work."
John 4:34 NKJV

The mother sighed in frustration. Once again her child wasn't hungry at mealtime because she had had some unhealthy snacks earlier. She was beginning to think that giving her preschooler the right nutrition was impossible. The nagging thought that she might be allowing irreparable damage to her toddler wouldn't leave her alone.

Our children love to snack. Chips. Candy. Cookies. They love foods that are tasty and quick to pop in their mouths. They don't stop to consider the problems that come from indulging in unwholesome fare. The young child only cares about eating what tastes good at the moment.

We are often enticed into doing something other than God's will. Sin can be very enticing, and some sins can seem so small we don't realize we're "partaking" of an unhealthy food. Just like our young charges, we can be so caught up in our daily busyness, we don't stop to consider that we aren't putting the right nourishment in our minds, spirits, and bodies.

Let's make sure we're eating the right bread of life by putting aside the temptation and getting the proper diet—mentally, spiritually, and physically.

Jesus, You have set the example for me. Thank You.
Help me to always do the Father's will and not my own. Amen.

Big Kitties

Calves and lions will eat together and be cared for by little children. . . .
Lions and oxen will both eat straw. Little children will play near snake holes.
They will stick their hands into dens of poisonous snakes and never be hurt.
Isaiah 11:6–8 CEV

*M*ost people know the story of Daniel in the lions' den. Daniel spent the night with those big hungry cats, punished for civil disobedience. Much to the astonishment of those who sought to harm him, he emerged unhurt! There wasn't a tooth mark on Daniel. . .not a scratch from a claw. Those lions had no interest in making a meal of Daniel. They acted like kittens.

How could that be? Lions are carnivores. Lions are on the top of the food chain! Where was their prey instinct? After all, nature is nature.

Obviously, a miracle occurred that night in Babylon. Miracles don't happen very often, but doesn't it sound amazing? To lie peacefully in close proximity to those majestic beasts, up close and personal?

Daniel's night in the lions' den gives us a peek through the window into our eternal destiny. Heaven will be a place without sin! Without vicious prey instincts or evil decrees from authorities. It's good to remember what we have to look forward to as children of God.

We have such hope! One day, we will live in perfect safety and peace, surrounded by the presence of God the way sunshine surrounds our day.

Lord of all creatures great and small, thank You that
someday my children and I will finally see You!

Thankful Hearts Pray

[I] cease not to give thanks for you, making mention of you in my prayers.
Ephesians 1:16 KJV

There is a tenacious link between prayer and thankfulness.

When Jesus raised Lazarus, He began by praying, "Father, I thank thee that thou hast heard me" (John 11:41 KJV). He said this even before God heard and granted His request!

Paul admonishes believers to not be anxious, but "in every thing by prayer and supplication with thanksgiving let your requests be made known unto God" (Philippians 4:6 KJV).

In the future, the angels and elders will sing: "Blessing, and glory, and wisdom, and thanksgiving, and honour, and power, and might, be unto our God for ever and ever" (Revelation 7:12 KJV).

Thankful hearts pray. When we understand that all that we have in this life comes from God, in whom "we live, and move, and have our being" (Acts 17:28 KJV), we will eagerly and gratefully run to Him.

On the other hand, if there are situations in our lives for which we are not thankful, we may be less likely to go Him for help. If we have bitterness or unforgiveness or are discontent, we may not pray as we should.

Do we pray for our homes, even when they're cluttered? Our husbands, even when they are thoughtless? Our children, even when they misbehave?

We need to stop and be thankful for everything in our lives—the good and the not so good. And then lift up our requests, knowing He will answer our prayers and bless us, over and over again.

Thank you, Father, for these little children You have given me. Thank You for entrusting them to me. Please give me wisdom to direct them today. Amen.

The Promise Fulfilled

And so, after he had patiently endured, he obtained the promise.
Hebrews 6:15 KJV

God can be trusted to keep His promises in every area of our life—from meeting our needs, to giving us wisdom as we raise our children, to everything else. We know all of this, but too often we struggle because although we know He'll fulfill His promises, He doesn't always do it in our time frame.

Like Abraham and Sarah, many of us struggle with letting God work according to the schedule He has planned. We try to take matters into our own hands only to wind up with disastrous results. Think about all the trouble that Israel would have been spared had Abraham and Sarah not chosen to bring a baby boy into the world through their own time and means.

They are certainly not the only biblical examples, yet how often do we fail to learn the obvious lessons from the myriad of people God reveals to us through scripture?

We must recognize that God really is God. He created and controls this universe. He sees the big picture and plans accordingly—and He always fulfills His promises.

Great God, You've never failed me. I know You'll keep Your promises.
Help me to accept the timing You know is right.

Writing on the Wall

I have heard of you, that the Spirit of the holy God [or gods] is in you and that light and understanding and superior wisdom are found in you. . . . Then Daniel answered before the king, Let your gifts be for yourself and give your rewards to another. However, I will read the writing to the king and make known to him the interpretation.
Daniel 5:14, 17 AMP

*F*inding a child scribbling on the wall in red crayon is every mother's nightmare! The child gets punished, while Mom angrily scrubs the wall and wonders how she will ever restore it to its original, pristine condition.

Perhaps she should consider what her child may have been writing. Was he simply being naughty, or was he drawing a picture and trying, in his simple way, to write "I love you, Mommy"? He may have recently seen his mother lovingly hang pictures on the wall and then stand back to admire them. Perhaps he was simply adding his own masterpiece for her to admire.

Sometimes, situations aren't what they seem, and wisdom is required for an accurate interpretation. Daniel was called upon to decipher some writing on the wall that happened to be a message from God. In his wisdom, he knew right away that it was of God. May we each be so spiritually astute that we can decipher the situation from God's point of view every time.

Lord, grant me wisdom that I might hear Your voice and understand what You are saying to me. Help me see things clearly so that I act with wisdom in all things. Amen.

Made for His Glory

And the LORD said unto him, Who hath made man's mouth? or who maketh the
dumb, or deaf, or the seeing, or the blind? have not I the LORD?
Exodus 4:11 KJV

The woman smiled encouragingly at the tiny baby with "special
needs."

"Perfect in God's eyes," she told the mother.

Later that night, as the mother was rocking her daughter to
sleep, the woman's words echoed in her mind.

Putting her lips next to her baby's ear, the mother whispered,
"You, my angel, are perfect in God's eyes."

Her daughter had been created by a perfect, loving heavenly
Father, who had made her the way He chose so that she would
fulfill His perfect will. She was fearfully and wonderfully—and
differently—made for His Glory. And she would glorify Him most
just the way she was.

All children—those who have special needs and those who
don't—have been designed for a special purpose. Through children
and the challenges and joys they bring, imperfect mothers are molded
into the image of Christ.

It's not always easy to accept our difficult situations, but it is
God's sovereign plan.

And it is perfect.

Dear Father, although this situation is sometimes difficult to accept,
I thank You for this child and Your perfect plan. Let Your Spirit flow
through me to my child, so together we will bring You glory. Amen.

Grow Up!

*"O unbelieving and perverse generation," Jesus replied, "how long
shall I stay with you? How long shall I put up with you?"*
Matthew 17:17 NIV

To Jennifer, this particular Sunday morning seemed the least holy
morning of the previous week. Her husband, Brent, left early for
a church committee meeting. Her son, Nick, hid the only pair of
shoes he had not worn out in the sand box. While she refereed a fight
between three-year-old Madison and four-year-old Nick in the back
bedroom, Jennifer smelled smoke. The sweet rolls she'd been baking
for Sunday school nearly set the oven ablaze. After hauling teary
children to church alone, Jennifer made the usual pre–Sunday school
restroom stop. The morning exploded with Madison's hysterical
screams. The church janitor had used bright blue freshener in the
toilet!

"How long will I have to put up with you?" Jennifer gritted her
teeth. "When are you ever going to grow up?"

As the words echoed, Jennifer hung her head. How could she say
such a thing to her children—at church, no less?

Many moms experience similar irritation and guilt when little
ones act like—well, little ones! Jesus Himself, human as well as
divine, sometimes struggled with immature, petty disciples. But He
knew if He persevered, His followers would indeed grow up—and do
great things for God!

*Lord Jesus, thank You for understanding my frustrations.
Help me see my children with Your eyes and trust You
for the energy to love them at this stage. Amen.*

God Is Great. . .Pass It On!

"Be careful never to forget what you yourself have seen.
Do not let these memories escape from your mind as long as you live!
And be sure to pass them on to your children and grandchildren."
Deuteronomy 4:9 NLT

At times, it's easy to refrain from sharing things with our children: We may not have the patience to explain it, we may think they're too young to understand, or we may just be too tired from a long day to verbalize what we're thinking. But we are instructed to pass on the good things that God has done—telling our children and our grandchildren.

Think back over the last week. Can you recall something that God has done for you? Share it with your kids! Did you score and get that "prime parking space" at the grocery store? Thank Jesus, right there in the car. Did God give you the food that you needed today? Praise Him for meeting your nourishment needs. Has someone for whom you've been praying been healed? Celebrate his or her restoration. Tell your kids how great God is!

We see many awesome works of God. Pass the excitement on to your kids as you thank Him for His goodness. Through your example, your children will learn to give thanks to God and will one day pass on the good news to their children.

Dear heavenly Father, thank You for all of the great things You have done for me!
Please help me to remember to share them with my children,
to bring You the glory You deserve. Amen.

The Lord:
An Everyday Experience

These commandments that I give you today are to be upon your hearts. Impress them on your children. Talk about them when you sit at home and when you walk along the road, when you lie down and when you get up.
Deuteronomy 6:6–7 NIV

A preschooler, Mary, sat at the kitchen table, demanding more grapes be placed in her already half-filled bowl. Her mom knew from Mary's past behavior not to fill the bowl too much or all the grapes would end up on the floor. As Mary persisted, her mom saw the perfect opportunity to apply scripture to this teachable moment. Mom encouraged Mary that when she was faithful with a few things, she could be trusted to be faithful with more (Matthew 25:21, 23).

Deuteronomy 6:4–9 provides the framework for making the Lord an everyday experience for our preschoolers. As the Lord is placed at the forefront of our minds and hearts, we are more readily able to apply scripture to their lives. The Christian market provides a number of helpful ways—CDs, DVDs, books, and Bibles for children—to make the Lord an everyday experience. Also, we may point out God's beautiful creation and pray at set times (e.g., before meals, naps, and bed) and spontaneous times (e.g., as we learn of a friend in need) throughout the day. We can also sing praise songs as a part of our nap time or bedtime routines. Soon, our preschoolers will be making the Lord an everyday experience, through prayer, praise, and song.

Lord, enable me to make You an everyday experience as I teach my preschooler Your character and Word.

Two Different Mothers

"Be careful not to do your 'acts of righteousness' before men, to be seen by them.
If you do, you will have no reward from your Father in heaven."
Matthew 6:1 NIV

*L*ydia's mother, Ashley, was good at pointing out all of Lydia's imperfections as a mother. She talked about how the house could be oh-so-much cleaner, how macaroni and cheese was not its own food group, and how Lydia should have waited longer before having children. Lydia usually brushed aside her mother's comments, until one struck her as perhaps being true.

"I love you," Ashley said to her daughter. "But I want to tell you something about yourself, and I want to apologize about something."

Lydia set her coffee mug on the table and offered raised eyebrows and a surprised smile before asking, "What are you talking about?"

Ashley continued. "I think we act one way toward our children in public and another way at home. I see you pretending, just smiling and laughing with your children and the other school mothers, but when you get home, you're so quick to get upset or yell at the children for something. Until today, I didn't realize that I did and still do the same to you. I'm sorry."

Lydia was shocked and a bit insulted, but then thought about the three times she'd already yelled at the children that day. Maybe, just maybe, her mother had a point.

Lord, help me to be kind yet real in my interactions with my children.

The Barking Child

Every good and perfect gift is from above.
James 1:17 NIV

*H*eidi has always been passionate about animals. Now that she's a teen, Heidi's mother doesn't want to encourage this interest because she doesn't think there are enough career opportunities for an animal lover.

God has made each one of our children a unique package, with different passions and talents. Often, a gift might be apparent as early as preschool years, like Heidi's. As a four-year-old, she used to pretend she was an animal, driving her mom to distraction with barking dog sounds and cat meows.

But God set that passion for animals in Heidi's heart for a special reason. He's an animal lover, too. When the prophet Jonah wanted Nineveh destroyed, God objected. He had a desire for the people to repent *and* He was also concerned for the cattle (Jonah 4:11)!

It's possible that we may undervalue something God has set in our child's heart. Are we encouraging our children to persist in their areas of talent? Or do we try to steer them to what will pay the bills or provide security? Or maybe even fill a gap left over from our own childhood longings?

We need to help our kids make the most of the gifts God has given them—to practice those gifts and learn to employ them with patience and diligence. We want them to have a lifelong desire to use any talent—bug collector, cookie maker, tricycle racer—to serve God.

Thank You, Lord, for creating such a unique package of talents and abilities in my children! Help me to recognize Your ongoing work in their lives.

When Yes Means No

*The Lord says: "These people come near to me with their mouth
and honor me with their lips, but their hearts are far from me."*
Isaiah 29:13 NIV

A young mother was desperate to curtail her two-year-old's
negative responses.

Regardless of her question, his answer was always no! Becoming
weary and exasperated, she calmly told him, "We do not use the 'no'
word in our family." A few days later, he responded to a question by
stomping his feet and yelling, "Yes!" It was quite apparent that his
"yes" meant "no"!

Although we may smile at this story, are we ever guilty of the
same offense? Our mouth says one thing, but our heart speaks
another. We may fool others, but God is not deceived. Man may look
at the outward appearance, but God looks at the heart. He sees right
through our words. If our words and heart don't match, He knows it
instantly.

Our hearts reveal our true treasure. Does the treasure chest of
our heart contain spiritual riches or worldly priorities? Although we
live "in the world," we should not be "of the world." It is impossible
to follow the world and Christ at the same time because they are
diametrically opposed to one another. Let's come near to the Lord
not only with our mouths, but with our hearts as well.

*Dear Lord, I confess that many times the attitude of my heart and the
words that I speak do not match. Help me honor You in every way. Amen.*

Foundation of Righteousness

All Scripture is God-breathed and is useful for teaching, rebuking, correcting and training in righteousness, so that the man of God may be thoroughly equipped for every good work.
2 Timothy 3:16–17 NIV

Concetta excitedly showed her mom the picture of the "burning bush" she colored in church that morning and told her, "Like Moses, I will obey God." It delighted Concetta's mom to hear her child desiring to please the Lord. She felt as if the consistent application of God's Word in raising her preschooler was having a positive effect in establishing a foundation of righteousness in Concetta.

God's Word provides the tools we need to establish a foundation of righteousness in our preschoolers' lives. Second Timothy 3:16–17 tells us that we can use God's Word to teach, reprove, correct, and train in righteousness. This begins with a mom who knows God's Word, who searches His Word for the particular scriptures to use when correcting or praising her preschooler's behavior, and who consistently applies scripture in her own life. For example, we can use God's Word in replacing a preschooler's complaining, whining, and negative attitude by fostering and modeling thankful hearts (Philippians 2:14; Colossians 3:17; 1 Thessalonians 5:18). By using scriptures in ways like these, we can raise our preschooler "in the training and instruction of the Lord" (Ephesians 6:4 NIV). Thus, God's Word establishes a foundation of righteousness in our household.

Heavenly Father, help me to be a student of Your Word. Reveal to me how to apply scriptures in developing a foundation of righteousness in my preschooler.

Love Your Children

That they may teach the young women to be sober,
to love their husbands, to love their children.
Titus 2:4 KJV

*M*rs. Emerson, I don't know how you do it," Liz said. "I've seen families who are really tight-knit, but there's something about yours that always amazes me."

The older lady smiled. "It's a little thing called love, Liz. True, genuine love. When you truly love your children with the love of Christ, your children will know it, and they'll begin to love you the same way."

It all sounded so simple, but Liz knew that it wasn't. Oh, she loved her little ones, but it was sometimes hard to show them.

Apparently, Mrs. Emerson could tell that the younger mother was struggling with this idea, for she followed up her initial comments by explaining further.

"It's not always easy, dear, and it doesn't mean that you always give in to them and let them have their way. You must discipline when necessary, but not out of anger. Use it as an opportunity to teach. Sincerely praise and encourage your little ones. And learn to laugh as much as possible.

"As they grow, give them responsibilities. Realize, though, that as you do this, you are preparing them to be independent. There will come a time when you'll need to let go. It'll be tough, but if you've shown them you love and trust them, they'll always be glad to come back."

Liz pondered this woman's advice. She knew she'd learn a lot more from her.

Thank You, God, for wise mentors in my
life who encourage me as I raise my children.

Sneaky God

If ye then, being evil, know how to give good gifts unto your children: how much more shall your heavenly Father give the Holy Spirit to them that ask him?
Luke 11:13 KJV

*W*hen good things happened to Madeleine, she always suspected God would sabotage them to teach her a lesson. If He bestowed a job bonus upon her, she expected car trouble. If her child-care arrangements worked out, Madeleine knew they couldn't last. If she dared initiate a closer relationship with God, it was only a matter of time before she blew it, and He would retract His blessings.

One day while doing her required Bible reading, Madeleine stumbled on a scene in which Jesus told His listeners that God wanted to meet their needs because He loved them like His children. Madeleine adored her little daughters, Brittany and Michaela. She wanted to give them everything, including the best of herself—her most loving moments, her creative abilities, her brightest moods.

In God's Word, she discovered God her Father also wanted to give her—Madeleine!—Himself.

"Just ask!" God said. "Don't be timid!" He wasn't playing mind games with Madeleine. He wanted to meet her needs.

We laugh at Madeleine's paranoia, but many of us suspect God harbors ulterior motives. When He sends us good gifts, we look for snakes in the wrapping paper.

All the while, He longs to pour out His Holy Spirit on all who ask.

Lord, please forgive me for suspecting You of sabotage.
Help me desire more of Your Holy Spirit today. Amen.

A Rest from Work

For he spake in a certain place of the seventh day on this wise,
and God did rest the seventh day from all his works.
Hebrews 4:4 KJV

As a mother, you probably feel that you have enough responsibilities to keep you busy twenty-five hours a day, eight days a week. Most of us have caught ourselves saying, "If only I had a few more hours. . ." Truthfully, if we had those hours, we'd quickly fill them and wish for more. There will never be a shortage of work for mothers.

Perhaps that is why we hesitate to take time to rest. Many moms are the first one up in their household and the last to go to sleep. Otherwise it would be difficult to complete some necessary tasks. But God knew we couldn't go on and on without ever taking a break, so He instituted a day of rest—a day for us to be physically and spiritually refreshed. It's tempting to fill those hours with draining activities, too, but we have to take time to realize that if we refuse to rest, the quality of our work, as well as our parenting, will suffer. We must rest. We must fellowship with God or our efforts will be in vain. Acknowledge this real need, and find a way to accommodate it. Everyone will be better off when you do.

Father, it's not easy for me to take time to rest, but it's needful.
Help me add it to my to-do list.

Heaped with Blessings

Blessed be the Lord, who daily loads us with benefits, the God of our salvation!
Psalm 68:19 NKJV

The young toddler cooed with pleasure each time his mother spooned up a bite of ice cream. When he turned to look at something else, the mother balanced the remainder of the frozen treat on the spoon in an impossible heap to fit in a mouth. When the toddler turned around to take another bite, his eyes widened. He let out a scream of delight and leaned forward, not caring that the amount would never fit between his lips. The mother couldn't help laughing at his obvious joy.

Every day, God loads us with benefits. From sunrise to sunrise, we have at our fingertips enough blessings to make us scream with delight and clap our hands. However, cares of the world and daily life can blind us to all that God has bestowed. We become weighed down with hardships, and we forget all about the wonderful aspects of being a believer in Christ.

We can choose to continue letting the negative aspects of the world steal our joy in God and His gifts, or we can turn around and see the heaping spoonful He is holding out to us. When we open our eyes to His blessings, our cares will fade away. God should have no doubt about our delight in Him.

You are my salvation, God. Thank You and praise You for all You've done.

Don't Forget

*In every thing give thanks: for this is the will
of God in Christ Jesus concerning you.*
1 Thessalonians 5:18 KJV

Linn looked up at his mother. Today was Thanksgiving, and she had just read him the story of the first Thanksgiving. His tummy was full from eating lunch, and his thoughts turned to the turkey that had tasted so good. "Did the Pilgrims say grace before they ate their turkeys, too?" He asked.

"Yes, they did," she said, nodding.

His four-year-old mind raced.

"Why?"

She yawned. "Why what?"

"Why did they say grace?"

"It had been a long, hard winter, and they were thankful that the Indians were sharing their food with them," his mother answered.

Linn felt her rest her chin on the top of his head. "Did they talk to Jesus all the time?"

Her chin moved against his hair as she answered. "I think so. They wanted to come to America so they would be free to worship God. Always remember that and be thankful that the Pilgrims suffered so that we could talk to God anytime we want to." She kissed him on the cheek.

Linn loved talking to God. He yawned. "Okay, Mommy."

*Father God, thank You for all things. Thank You that my family
is free to worship you anytime. Thank You that I am free to tell my
child about You and how You had a hand even in America's early history.
Never let me forget to give You thanks. Amen.*

Why?

For the Holy Ghost shall teach you in the same hour what ye ought to say.
Luke 12:12 KJV

$\mathcal{W}$hy, Mommy?"

That was the question of the hour. Elizabeth was worn out from her preschooler's "why" questions. It seemed as though he wanted to know everything there was to know—and all in one afternoon.

"Why what, sweetheart?" She slipped his pajama top over his head.

"You said we'd say our good night prayers after I got my pajamas on. Why do we have to do that every night?" He yawned.

"Because I said so" didn't quite fit here. Elizabeth brushed a lock of hair from his eyes. "Don't you enjoy saying your good night prayers?" She asked.

"I guess so, but why do I have to do it?" he said, pressing on stubbornly.

Elizabeth silently sought the Lord for the right answer. She'd never really thought about why she prayed every night, she just did. "We say our good night prayers and ask God to watch over us, and we pray that He will bless those we love. Talking to God at the end of the day and telling Him our problems makes it easier for us to have a happy life." She didn't know if it was too much for her son to grasp or not.

"Oh, okay." He knelt by his bed and said his prayers. As soon as he was finished, he climbed under the covers and whispered, "I love you, Mommy."

She kissed his forehead and whispered back, "I love you, too."

Thank You, Lord, for sending the Holy Spirit to help me say
the right words when my child asks the hard questions. Amen.

Paper Turkeys

Give thanks to the LORD, for he is good. His love endures forever.
Psalm 136:1 NIV

*A*s a former elementary schoolteacher, Elizabeth's mind was still overflowing with craft ideas. But now she was a stay-at-home mom, and instead of having twenty-plus children, she cared for her own two children 24-7.

Thanksgiving was approaching, and as she thought about the large meal her family would have, she also thought about ways to include her children in the holiday events. A pastime her school children had loved was creating paper turkeys.

Now, sitting in the house's playroom with William and Brianna, it was time to pass on the paper turkey tradition. Both children were thrilled when their hands rested on the construction paper, and Mama traced them to make turkeys. As Elizabeth cut the turkeys from the paper, she explained that the thumb was the turkey's head, and all the other fingers were feathers meant to write on. They represented the people or things in life the children were thankful for.

Taking the crayons from their box, William and Brianna began to write what they were thankful for: God, Mommy, Daddy, macaroni and cheese. . . Eventually, each finger had one thankful thought. Elizabeth thought they were done with the project when William began to whimper.

"Mommy," he cried, "I ran out of fingers, but I'm still thankful for more!"

About to reach for more construction paper, Elizabeth had a better idea.

"How about we pray to Jesus and tell Him the rest?"

Lord, thank You for life's blessings.

Hot Potato

*Get rid of all bitterness, rage and anger, brawling
and slander, along with every form of malice.*
Ephesians 4:31 NIV

*R*emember the childhood game, hot potato? Participants tossed a ball to one another, pretending that it was a hot potato. The object was to get rid of the ball as quickly as possible. Holding on too long would result in your hands supposedly getting burned.

What things in life do we hold on to? We can cling to an insult. We can dwell on an unkind word spoken by another. We can wallow in pain. Yet the Lord knows that holding onto these negative emotions can produce bitterness, rage, and anger. We may find ourselves fighting back in retaliation, desiring to hurt those that have harmed us. Yet in reality, we are the ones that eventually get burned.

So, like a hot potato, get rid of those negative thoughts as soon as you receive them. Give them to the Lord. Lay them at His feet. Choose to let go. Ask Him to restore your emotions by His grace. By doing so, the healing process can begin. Do not hold on and get burned. Get rid of the hot potato!

*Dear Lord, help me to quickly get rid of those things that can harm me.
May I release my hurt and pain to You. Amen.*

The Call to Home Missions

*But ye shall receive power, after that the Holy Ghost is come upon you:
and ye shall be witnesses unto me both in Jerusalem, and in all Judaea,
and in Samaria, and unto the uttermost part of the earth.*
Acts 1:8 KJV

Throughout her Christian life, the young mother had often heard
the verses calling God's people to spread the Word: "Go ye into all
the world" (Mark 16:15 KJV).

"Ye shall be witnesses. . .unto the uttermost part of the earth"
(Acts 1:8 KJV).

Yet she could go nowhere. With a preschooler, a toddler, and one
more on the way, she could barely make it out of the house to shop,
let alone go into all the world to witness.

She called her mother in the faith. "How can I go up the road
to witness to the neighbors when I have my hands so full with little
ones?"

The older woman answered wisely. "This is the time in your life
when you are called to home missions."

The young mother understood. Her home was her Jerusalem; her
children, her personal disciples. Their souls were entrusted to her to
nurture and guide.

She was on the mission field already—the most important one
of all.

*Faithful Shepherd of my soul, make me a tender and loving shepherd
to these little lambs You have given me. Let me lead them to You while
they are young so they will love You and serve You all their days. Amen.*

God's Divine Power

I have learned to be content in whatever circumstances I am. . . .
In any and every circumstance I have learned the secret of being filled
and going hungry, both of having abundance and suffering need.
Philippians 4:11–12 NASB

$\mathcal{D}$iane longed to be working outside the home, but when she was in the workforce, she longed to be home with her children. Does this sound like you? Are you content? Are you satisfied with the season and circumstances of life God has placed you?

The apostle Paul reminds us that, just like him, we can be content in any and every circumstance. Paul was able to be content in whatever situations he endured (e.g., hungry or filled) because of his relationship with the Lord. Paul had a renewed mind that focused on the eternal, not the earthly (Colossians 3:2). He also trusted and experienced God meeting every need (not want) that he had. Second Peter 1:3 (NIV) reads, "His divine power has given us everything we need for life and godliness through our knowledge of him who called us by his own glory and goodness."

We have the ability to remain content by abiding in a daily relationship with the Lord, staying grounded in His Word, and communing with Him in prayer. As a preschool mom, God will meet your needs and provide an eternal perspective on your circumstances. Trust His power for your contentment, and view your circumstances through His divine lenses.

Lord, please forgive me for being discontent. Help me to trust You to meet all of my needs and provide an eternal perspective on my current circumstances.

God First, Me Second

But more than anything else, put God's work first and do what he wants.
Then the other things will be yours as well.
Matthew 6:33 CEV

𝓜oms are incredible! Have you ever stopped to think about how many different types of tasks you perform in one day? You make certain that others are fed and clothed, then you clean the house, answer and return telephone calls, run errands, chauffer, others. . .and the list continues.

Even more difficult than performing those tasks can be prioritizing them. Should you swing by the post office before stopping for the loaf of bread? Will you have enough time to make that phone call when you return home? The mental stress can be harder to manage than actually getting everything accomplished!

Jesus tells us that above all else, we need to "put God's work first and do what he wants." He follows that direction with a promise: "Then the other things will be yours as well."

Start your day by taking some time with God. Thank Him, express your love for Him, and then ask Him to bring to mind what He wants you to do. Sure, you'll still have some frazzled days, but if you prioritize according to what God wants, He will help you with those "other things," too.

Jesus, please help me to learn to prioritize, doing what You would have me to do.
Be the Lord of my schedule, so that You will be glorified. Amen.

Familiar Love

Herein is love, not that we loved God, but that he loved us,
and sent his Son to be the propitiation for our sins.
1 John 4:10 KJV

*W*e don't keep a record of accounts for our children. They don't owe us for dirty diapers changed, meals fixed, clothes washed, cuts cleaned and bandaged, long nights of rocking when they are sick, or any of the other myriad of ways mothers are there for their toddlers.

Our love for our children does not depend on their behavior or their gifts to us. We don't ask anything of them as payment for caring for them or loving them. Instead, we look at each child as a gift from God, bestowed on us. We love with a depth of emotion impossible to describe.

Likewise, God loves us more than we can comprehend. He doesn't require anything in return. He loved us before we even knew Him, before we understood the true definition of love.

As we idly played or went on with our lives, God reached out in love. He sent His Son, Jesus, to pay the penalty for our sins, all because of the depth of feeling God has for us.

As we stop and watch our children and consider how much we care for them, we can remember God does the same with us. His heart is full as He gazes at us.

Thank You, God, that You love me more than I can ever fathom. Amen.

Confession Is Good
for the Soul

Confess your trespasses to one another, and pray for one another, that you may be healed. The effective, fervent prayer of a righteous man avails much.
James 5:16 NKJV

*S*ometimes I get so angry with Amber, and then I find myself yelling at her," Vonda confessed to her weekly prayer partner, Lou. "It seems I am angry all the time, and the sad thing is I know it isn't Amber's fault I feel this way. I feel horrible for yelling at her." She wondered what Lou would think of her now that she'd told her how she'd been behaving.

Lou's voice came over the telephone line, calm and sweet. "I know how you feel. When James was a preschooler, I felt the same way."

Vonda was glad to find out she wasn't alone in these feelings. "What did you do to keep your anger in check?" She asked.

"It wasn't easy, but when I felt anger rising up, I would try to remember to pray, asking Jesus to help me. And He would. But those times when I'd forget to pray, and my anger got the best of me, I'd go to James afterward and tell him I was sorry. "

"Really?"

Lou laughed. "Yes, really. I'd had a prayer partner that had gone through the same emotions. She prayed with me, and that helped loads. Want to pray about it now?"

"That would be wonderful."

Vonda couldn't believe how much better she felt after praying with Lou.

Lord, it is so hard to confess my sins to other people. But I know that is what Your Word says to do. Please, help me, Father God, to learn to confess and pray over my sins. Amen.

Just a Handful

*Better is an handful with quietness, than both the
hands full with travail and vexation of spirit.*
Ecclesiastes 4:6 KJV

$\mathcal{N}$ora set down the morning newspaper and sighed disgustedly.
"Celebrities have everything but common sense," she commented to
her husband. "They have big, beautiful homes, perfect clothes and
hair, and more money than I can imagine spending; yet all they do is
party, neglect their kids, and jump from one spouse to another. What
kind of life is that?"

"Shallow," Reid replied. "Makes you glad for our nice little two-
bedroom house, doesn't it?" He grinned.

Nora smiled. Lately, she had been dropping some not-so-subtle
hints that larger living quarters were needed. With two small children
and a baby due soon, things were becoming rather cramped. Still,
Nora knew that Reid was right. She was so thankful for her beautiful,
happy children and her loving, faithful husband. She realized that
God knew what was best when He designed His plan for her life. It
might be true that she really didn't enjoy stepping on her children's
toys, but having the opportunity to spend time with them and to
have an impact on more than made up for the disarray. Nora
thanked God for what her family had and for the joy and peace that
filled their home.

*Thank You, Lord, for all Your blessings on my family. When I'm
tempted to complain, help me to remember that Your gifts are perfect.*

God's Will

*Now if we are children, then we are heirs—heirs of God and
co-heirs with Christ, if indeed we share in his sufferings
in order that we may also share in his glory.*
Romans 8:17 NIV

*P*arents typically spend a lot time and money when carefully
considering what they will be able to leave their children when they
die. They might purchase life insurance or hire a financial planner to
maximize their potential. They might even write a will that directs
the fair distribution of finances and property. That way, their children
are left with no questions or doubts about what is coming to them or
how to distribute it when the time comes.

Romans 8:17 is the will that our Father has left for us. He
clearly defined how His estate would be distributed to ensure that
there would be no mistaking the truth. We share in the inheritance
with Christ. We are joint heirs with Jesus. We share as heirs in the
kingdom of God with Jesus Christ, our Lord! What an amazing
truth!

In order to reap the rewards of such glory, we must also share in
the trials and tribulations that Christ endured. Just as Jesus did, we
must also die to sin. We must take up our crosses and follow Jesus,
enduring whatever we are called to bear along the way.

*Thank You, Father, for my rich inheritance. Please give me the
strength to bear whatever I must for Your glory. Let me be Your servant,
just as Christ served You. Amen.*

It's Too Hard!

Be strong in the Lord and in his mighty power.
Ephesians 6:10 NIV

In the city of Ephesus, Paul diligently taught the people about the Lord Jesus Christ. Successfully, too! Until a large, angry mob crammed into the city theater—a structure that could seat twenty-five thousand people!—and tried to put a halt to Paul's teachings. With God's intervention, Paul made a dramatic and narrow escape.

Seldom will our children face troubles as severe as Paul's situation. But the need to persevere? That quality will be required every day of their lives, starting in toddlerhood.

Think of how many challenges a little one faces every single day! Learning new words, tying shoelaces, holding a fork, getting along with others, sharing toys. Each day brings new feats to accomplish. No wonder they are easily frustrated! Their young life is one continual learning curve. A steep one at that!

Paul gave us a powerful example of diligence: He didn't quit teaching about the Lord Jesus, despite obstacles, frustrations, and hardships. Likewise, we parents have a responsibility to help children develop diligence, even when it's hard. We quietly work with our son until each puzzle piece fits. We encourage our daughter's efforts to feed herself. We applaud a newly learned skill, like buttoning a blouse.

Those small, seemingly unimportant attempts to persevere are the first steps toward preparing our children for a future in which they can persevere under pressure. Just like Paul.

Lord Jesus, show me how to encourage my child toward diligence—
by my example and by my appropriate responses to his efforts.
Help me to be the kind of encourager my child needs.

Show Me the Money

For the love of money is a root of all sorts of evil, and some by longing for it have wandered away from the faith and pierced themselves with many griefs.
1 Timothy 6:10 NASB

After a church sermon on money management, Maggie and her husband, Richard, agreed it was time to talk to their four-year-old twin girls about helping around the house and receiving chore money.

The family sat on their overstuffed couch. Richard began to talk about the chores that he and Mommy did around the house and yard each week. Then he explained that the two girls would be doing daily chores, too. They would clean their room, dust, and help feed the puppy.

One twin spoke up. "What do we get?"

"What do you mean?" Maggie asked, clearly understanding the question but wanting her girls to explore their thoughts.

"Well," the other continued. "Daddy goes to work and gets money to buy us a house and food." Maggie and Richard nodded. "And Mommy gets money when she paints pictures. What do we get?"

Richard reached for six empty baby food jars on the coffee table. He gave each daughter three jars and four quarters. One jar was for God, one for saving, and one for spending. One quarter would go into each jar every week. The leftover quarter could be put in whichever jar they wanted.

The girls smiled and nodded as one responded, "We like that we get money, but maybe the best part is being grown-up and helping you both!"

The Word tells us that money itself is not the root of evil, but the love of and longing for it is. If we are wise, we will help our children understand that concept and frequently remind ourselves of the same.

God, help me to see money in the proper light—and not as the ultimate reward.

Your Body

*Do you not know that your body is the temple (the very sanctuary)
of the Holy Spirit Who lives within you, Whom you have received
[as a Gift] from God? You are not your own, You were bought with
a price [purchased with a preciousness and paid for, made His own].
So then, honor God and bring glory to Him in your body.*
1 Corinthians 6:19–20 AMP

$\mathcal{M}$any times we fail to see the connection between the body and
the spirit. We try to separate the spiritual from the physical, yet the
spiritual is housed in the physical. In this life, it is impossible for
our spiritual self to operate outside of our physical body; the two are
inseparable.

Taking proper care of our bodies is as essential as taking care of
our spirits. Getting enough sleep, eating nutritiously, and exercising
to maintain optimal physical health are key elements to spiritual
growth. Body and spirit are intertwined. How can we pray effectively
or read God's Word if we are exhausted? How can we have energy
at the end of the day for our children if our bodies are not properly
nourished? How can we have stamina to participate on a mission trip
if we're out of shape? Do not feel guilty for taking care of your body.
Your spiritual life depends upon it!

*Dear Lord, so much of my time is spent meeting the needs of my family.
Help me realize the importance of taking care of my physical body,
and give me time to do so. Amen.*

Set a Playdate

So they left. . .for a quiet place, where they could be alone.
Mark 6:32 NLT

$\mathcal{D}$o you consider yourself a busy mom? If you're a mom, you're busy, right? However, a fast-paced schedule can become the focus of life, rather than the little ones whom we are raising. At times it's easy to absently reply, "Uh-huh," to a little one's rambling, without taking the time to stop and listen to the question or comment.

How about setting aside a morning and having a Mommy-and-me playdate with your child? Together, enjoy planning the special time, contemplating a meal location, an activity, or both. Join in the excitement of anticipation with your little one as the playdate draws near.

When the special day arrives, mentally set this time aside for her exclusively. If you need to, turn off your cell phone. Take the time to listen to what she says, even if she does ramble. Take the time to be a kid again with her. Your full attention will speak volumes, and she will feel like the little princess that you consider her to be.

Lord, please help me to take the time to focus on my child.
As I take a few hours out of my busy schedule to give her
my full attention, bless our time together. Amen.

Dead Women Don't
Eat Cake

Likewise reckon ye also yourselves to be dead indeed unto sin,
but alive unto God through Jesus Christ our Lord.
Romans 6:11 KJV

The Christian life is one of apparent contradictions.

When we are weak, we are strong.

We are happy when we mourn.

If we make ourselves poor, we will abound.

Perhaps the most difficult truth of all is that the key to a victorious life is *death*: "I am crucified with Christ: nevertheless I live; yet not I, but Christ liveth in me: and the life which I now live in the flesh I live by the faith of the Son of God, who loved me, and gave himself for me" (Galatians 2:20 KJV).

This passage seems difficult to apply, but Paul gives us the how-to in Romans 6. Here we are told to consider ourselves to be dead to sin. In other words, think of yourself as a dead woman when it comes to a temptation.

Do you yell at your children? Dead women don't yell.

Do you get annoyed when your husband doesn't notice your new shoes? Dead women don't buy new shoes.

Do you get frustrated because you love sweets? Dead women don't eat cake.

As you repeatedly bring death to the annoying and besetting sins of life, you will see the true life of Christ blossom, so you can indeed live by faith.

Father, because You see me in Christ, I have already been crucified with Him.
That means I really can crucify my flesh. Let me be dead to the
temptations of the world, so I can fully live in Jesus. Amen.

Do Something Great for God

Therefore, I want younger widows to get married, bear children,
keep house, and give the enemy no occasion for reproach.
1 Timothy 5:14 NASB

*D*o we want to do great things for God?

Do we want to honor Him and preserve His testimony in this world?

Do we want to keep the enemy from gaining a foothold?

If the answer to all those questions is a resounding "Yes!" then we need to do our best—with God's help—in managing our household and raising our children.

Good household management—the kind that follows the tenets of scripture—is one of God's main missions and privileges for women. Having children preserves us (1 Timothy 2:15). Loving and raising those children, loving and obeying our husbands, and managing our household preserves the testimony of the Lord (Titus 2:4–5). Showing hospitality to strangers and ministering to the needs of the saints is our fundamental God-given outreach (1 Timothy 5:10).

Being a dedicated mother and managing a household well, "as unto the Lord," is full-time Christian service because it is in the home and within family that the foundation is laid for salvation and where faith is passed on to future generations.

Mothers and household managers are women with vision, faith, strength, dignity, and wisdom.

Such dedicated women do great things for God.

Father, I get so busy with these little blessings You've given me that
I often do not see the big picture. Help me to truly grasp the greatness
of my calling. Let me raise my little ones and manage my household
with a passion for my family and for You. Amen.

A Safe Haven

Unless the LORD builds the house, they labor in vain who build it;
unless the LORD guards the city, the watchman stays awake in vain.
Psalm 127:1 NKJV

Karen looked out the dining room window and sighed. Her husband, John, and their four-year-old son, Andy, were standing underneath the large oak in the backyard. Both were craning their necks and pointing upward at the tree.

"Just tell me, Daddy," Andy had said as John and he put on their fall coats ten minutes earlier. "We're building a tree house. I know we are!"

John laughed. "How did you find out?"

Andy took large hops toward the back door before opening it and saying, "'Cause, Daddy. You bought lots of wood at the store. We're going to be men and build a house together!"

Karen had given John a "be careful" look. Even now, she couldn't help looking out the window every few minutes. Hopefully, they wouldn't make the childhood haven too high. Karen could have gone on all afternoon about the safety risks. But as she looked out her house's window, she realized something.

God had blessed their family with the home she stood in now. Times hadn't always been easy, but God had never abandoned them. John was a good father, too, one who provided for and protected their family. If something like a splinter or minor fall ever did happen to Andy, it wouldn't be because John didn't love him. What it did mean was that, in more ways than one, John would always be there to catch Andy.

God, I praise You for Your provisions in my family's life.
Thank You for watching over us.

Dreary Days

He will make your righteousness shine like the dawn,
the justice of your cause like the noonday sun.
Psalm 37:6 NIV

$\mathcal{D}$reary days, especially in the middle of winter, can be trying times for a mother. The weather isn't good, but your toddlers can't understand why they can't play outside or go to the park. They get cranky and tired of staying indoors. Before long, you are as cranky as they are, praying for a day of sunshine to relieve the boredom and stress.

Without fail, the sun will shine again. When it does, both the mother and the child are ecstatic. Being out in the fresh air never felt so good. Those dismal times are quickly forgotten amid the joy of feeling the warm sun on your face.

In life we face many trials. There are times when one difficulty after another assails us. We feel battered and are unable to feel the warmth of God's joy. We long for relief, but we can't see an end to our trouble. Gloom overshadows our thankfulness, and depression can be a result.

We need to cling to the hope we have in Christ. God will make the sun to shine in our lives again as we trust Him. Trials pass. Good times come. We have hope and a reason to be thankful even in those dreary times.

Thank You, Jesus, for the hope we have in You.
We can be thankful for the hope You bring us. Amen.

Freedom

You who revere my name, the sun of righteousness will rise with healing in its wings. And you will go out and leap like calves released from the stall.
Malachi 4:2 NIV

Tori loved her family, but she couldn't draw one breath without someone demanding her attention. She and Nate hadn't planned four children under the age of six, including twin babies! After long days of nursing, diapering, and disciplining, Tori didn't feel like being touched. Nate couldn't understand her exhaustion. Instead of helping, he worked on his cars.

Tori felt so alone.

She loved Jesus, but she didn't take everyday problems to Him. One Sunday, when Nate had gone hunting, Kathy, an older woman at church, helped Tori and brought her tea while she nursed the twins. Their friendship had grown as Kathy, who had raised five children, occasionally babysat so Tori could enjoy a break. Kathy prayed for Tori daily.

"Tell God your troubles!" Kathy urged. "He cares about you. And go out with your husband, even if you eat beans for a week to pay for a sitter. You and Nate need each other."

As Tori followed Kathy's advice, she felt less trapped. Her time with Nate did not solve everything, but he seemed more willing to work out their differences. Best of all, Tori felt free to bring all her hurts to her heavenly Father. She would never lock away her feelings again.

Jesus, people surrounded You with endless demands, yet You were free in Spirit. You can liberate me, too. Thank You for the freedom I have in You! Amen.

Recounting God's Faithfulness

Posterity will serve him; future generations will be told about the Lord.
Psalm 22:30 NIV

$\mathcal{G}$inger listened attentively as Mom recounted how the Lord orchestrated Daddy and her meeting, courting, and marrying. Ginger had heard the story many times, but she desired to hear it again and again as she looked at pictures of her happy parents.

God's Word encourages us to recount God's faithfulness, particularly to our children (Psalm 78:4). It is essential for our preschoolers to hear us describe how our Lord has been trustworthy in performing wonders and miracles in our lives. As our children hear us verbalize how God has worked for His glory and our good (Romans 8:28), they will yearn to know this dependable Lord. We are to record how the Lord has worked "for a future generation, that a people not yet created may praise the LORD" (Psalm 102:18 NIV). Not only will our obedience to recounting God's faithfulness lead our preschoolers to know the Lord, but also future generations will come to know the Lord. This faithful Lord promises to keep His covenant of love "to a thousand generations" (Deuteronomy 7:9 NIV) of those who love Him and keep His commandments. We have the opportunity to influence a lineage of believers by daily recounting God's faithfulness to our preschoolers.

Lord, provide me with a heart that freely recounts Your wonders in my life. I desire to create a lineage of believers by my daily obedience to You today.

Surrounded by Witnesses

Since we are surrounded by so great a cloud of witnesses, let us lay aside every weight. . .and let us run with endurance the race that is set before us.
Hebrews 12:1 NKJV

*H*ow many times have we, as mothers, felt isolated and alone? So often, we have no other adult companionship all day. We interact with our child or children, but that isn't the same as having a conversation with a friend. This is most difficult when our toddler is ill, and we are unable to get out even to go to church.

Confinement can be tough on us. We long for company or just someone to talk to who doesn't depend on us or require anything from us. There can come a time when we are so down we don't feel we can endure the solitude anymore.

When we take the time to study all those in the Bible who have gone before us, we come to realize how much they endured. Temporary isolation doesn't look so bad anymore. These people gave up much for God. For us to sacrifice our time for a few years doesn't look like much when we read in the Bible about believers who have gone before us. When we are lonely, all we have to do is pick up God's Word and find the encouragement of the witnesses listed there.

Lord, You have provided us with the inspiration of Your followers. Thank You for them and their witness. Amen.

Jesus' Clock

*While he was still talking, some people came from the leader's house
and told him, "Your daughter is dead. Why bother the Teacher any more?"
Jesus overhead what they were talking about and said to the leader,
"Don't listen to them; just trust me."*
Mark 5:35–36 MSG

*J*esus had agreed to go to Jairus's house to heal his sick daughter.
On the way, Jesus was interrupted by a woman who boldly reached
out to touch him. "At once Jesus realized that power had gone out
from him. He turned around in the crowd and asked, 'Who touched
my clothes?' " (Mark 5:30 NIV).

Imagine Jairus's panic when Jesus stopped. Imagine the thoughts
that went through his head! *Come on, Jesus. We need to hurry! My daughter
needs You. You promised!*

Jesus wasn't in a hurry. He didn't seem to feel the urgency that
Jairus did. He took time to speak to this woman, reassuring her that
she was healed, then spoke to those around Him!

By then it was too late. Jairus's friends hurried to tell him his
daughter was dead.

But it's never too late for Jesus. Jesus' clock is different from
ours. He knew all along how this scenario would play out. Not only
would the daughter's life be restored, but the sparks of faith alive in
Jairus and his household would ignite into a flame that day.

It's never too late to invite Jesus into our homes and lives.

*Lord Jesus, come home with me today! I pray that my children
will enter into a loving and meaningful relationship with You—for life.*

Pray as a Child

Be anxious for nothing, but in everything by prayer and supplication,
with thanksgiving, let your request be known to God.
Philippians 4:6 NKJV

Christmas Day was just around the corner. Gloria dreaded this first Christmas without her loving husband by her side. Since his death in the early spring, Gloria had experienced an ever-increasing burden, as the money her loved one left behind dwindled in their bank account. Matthew, her four-year-old, couldn't wait for Christmas Day. But Gloria was sure her ten-year-old daughter, Sarah, understood the strain she was under, because she hadn't even mentioned gifts or the holiday.

A few days before Christmas, Gloria asked Sarah to help get her brother ready for bed.

"Sure, Mom," Sarah replied.

Gloria followed several minutes later to see how the kids were getting along in their bedtime routine. She stopped at the door to her son's bedroom. He and Sarah knelt beside the bed, and he prayed, "God, our mama isn't very happy, and I want You to make her happy. Thank You for giving us a good Christmas. Amen."

Tears filled Gloria's eyes as she realized that both children knew how she felt and that they were praying for her. She went to her room, knelt by her bed, and let words of praise flow from her lips.

Dear heavenly Father, please teach me to rely on You with a childlike faith.
Teach me to be thankful for what I do have, and to lean on
You when I am in need. In Your name, amen.

Make a Prayer

And every one that hath this hope set on him purifieth himself, even as he is pure.
I John 3:3 ASV

The Harrison family was often teased by friends and extended family members, but Johanna didn't care.

The family was just as enthusiastic about their children's birthday parties, with one minor exception. When the birthday cake arrived on the table and it was time to blow out the candles, the young Harrison children were encouraged to say a silent prayer instead of a silent wish. A wish didn't go anywhere, but a prayer went directly to God.

Johanna liked to watch her children's faces light up as their Superman or Barbie birthday cakes were happily devoured. However, it was the knowledge that before the candles were blown out, they had talked to Jesus.

One year, instead of "I wish for a billion ponies," Johanna's youngest had announced her prayer aloud, "Thank You, God, for my birthday and lots of people who love me."

Those few seconds gave Johanna hope as a mother. There wasn't anything really wrong with making wishes, but Johanna thought prayers might be a good way to mark birthday milestones. Hopefully, the children would one day be able to look back and see God's faithfulness traced throughout their lives.

We as adults can do the same. What's even better is that we don't have to wait for another birthday to talk with God. We have access to Him not once a year on a special day, but 24-7.

God, thank You for hearing my prayers.
Thank You for allowing me direct access through Your Son.

Endure for the Joy

*Looking unto Jesus the author and finisher of our faith; who for
the joy that was set before him endured the cross, despising the shame,
and is set down at the right hand of the throne of God.*
Hebrews 12:2 KJV

*O*ur Lord's life was one of endurance. He endured the humiliation
of becoming a man. He endured the rejection of the very people He
came to save. And He endured the ultimate rejection of His Father as
He became sin for us.

Why did He withstand so much?

According to Hebrews, it was for the *joy* set before Him. Because
He could see the ultimate victory—the salvation of man and His own
restoration to His throne in heaven—He patiently persevered in His
task on earth.

His enduring example should inspire us mothers.

A mother's life is also one of fortitude, enduring a multitude of
tiny trials every day of her life.

If we fail to see the big picture, we will get discouraged. We must
see our goal—godly children serving Christ and continuing in the
faith for another generation.

Focused on that goal, we can endure with hope and joy.

*Dear Lord, You gave up so much for me so that I could come to You. How
can I do any less for my children? Give me the patience to endure the trials of
motherhood, so I will have the great joy of one day seeing them serve You. Amen.*

My Spirit Rejoices

And my spirit hath rejoiced in God my Saviour.
Luke 1:47 KJV

*Y*ou *do* have a reason to rejoice. If you have accepted Christ as your Savior, His forgiveness is truly all that you need to have a heart overflowing with praise to God, but in His goodness our marvelous God grants us so much more. Every woman's list is different. Perhaps yours includes a godly husband, beautiful children, a comfortable home—on the other hand, it could be very different.

Mary was rejoicing in the amazing truth that she would soon give birth to the Savior of this world. That was a privilege no other woman would have. Still, God has given you the opportunity to raise up some of His other precious lambs, and that is cause to rejoice. Each one is special, and God chose them just for you.

You might be tempted to focus on the troubles you have, but counting your blessings is much healthier. Certainly, Mary's opportunity was not without consequence. Her reputation and marriage were at stake, and she would eventually watch as her precious Son was brutally murdered. Yet she still rejoiced that she was counted worthy to serve God. Are you rejoicing today?

O Great Savior, I rejoice in the great work that You do.
You alone are worthy of praise.

He Came to
the Shepherds

*And there were shepherds living out in the fields nearby, keeping watch over
their flocks at night. An angel of the Lord appeared to them, and the
glory of the Lord shone around them, and they were terrified.*
Luke 2:8–9 NIV

The shepherds received a live birth announcement! God proclaimed
the great news of Jesus' birth to lowly shepherds. Why? He could
have shouted it in the synagogues or whispered it to the religious
leaders. Perhaps He came to those with eyes to see, with ears to hear.
Perhaps, being shepherds, they would recognize the Good Shepherd.
Perhaps shepherds were humble enough to acknowledge their need.

Are we open to receive the good news? Jesus was born so that we
could live. He came to give us eternal life by paying the penalty of
our sin through His death. By faith we are forgiven and redeemed.
Do we have eyes to see our need of a Savior? Do we have ears to hear
the Gospel message?

May we learn from these shepherds. Away from the hustle and
bustle of the crowds, they had quiet time to reflect, ponder, and pray.
Humility and contentment characterized their lives. They were not
puffed up with knowledge and religiosity, judging others that did not
measure up. The Lord made a bold statement by appearing to the
shepherds. May we grasp the message and have hearts to receive Him.

*Dear Lord, may my heart be humble so I acknowledge my need of You each day.
Grant me quiet time alone with You as I revel in the good news! Amen.*

A Perfect Pregnancy?

Mary said, Behold the handmaid of the Lord;
be it unto me according to thy word.
Luke 1:38 KJV

*M*otherhood today seems a major act of faith. We often combine pregnancy, delivery, and 24-7 baby responsibility with full-time jobs. Plus, with experts' outlooks on political, economic, and environmental issues, we wonder how we will raise our children.

Centuries ago, in a bleak corner of the oppressive Roman Empire, an unmarried teenage girl also faced an impossible parenting situation. If she gave birth to God's Son, as the angel proclaimed, nobody would believe her. Friends and family might shun her and little Jesus. Who would support them financially? Her village might even stone her to death!

At best, Joseph, her future husband, would only break their betrothal, ruining Mary's future chances for marriage. What groom wanted a lying or deranged bride with her illegitimate son? If somehow Joseph retained Mary as his wife, would Jesus always remind him of her unknown lover?

Even if Joseph, by some miracle, fully accepted Jesus, how could a poor, uneducated couple raise the Son of God? Jesus was to rule forever as a king. Mary and Joseph knew nothing about royalty or thrones.

Perhaps because Mary was so young, she believed the angel when he said, "With God nothing will be impossible" (Luke 1:37 NKJV) and offered herself without reservation for His purposes.

Father, if little Mary trusted You for herself and her Child, I can trust You to
help me raise my children, even in this difficult world. Amen.

God's Valuables

They shall be mine, saith the Lord of hosts, in that day when I make up my jewels; and I will spare them, as a man spareth his own son that serveth him.
Malachi 3:17 KJV

*I*t's all about me."

Some wear this credo on T-shirts. Most of us display it on our lives. It's easy to adopt this attitude when advertisements encourage us to obsess about our desires as if they were sacred!

In Old Testament times, God's people also swallowed this idea. In fact, they believed that God had given them a raw deal. He hadn't met their expectations of prosperity. They viewed themselves as righteous victims who followed God's laws and suffered, while evildoers achieved success.

God slashed through their false veneer to reveal the truth: His people had deserted Him. They followed other gods, delving into the occult. They stole each others' spouses. They robbed God and His workers of monetary support and deprived helpless widows and orphans of justice. They mistreated people from other ethnic backgrounds.

But a few genuine believers remembered they were created to love and serve God, not indulge their appetites. They stuck together and honored Him.

God held these believers like rare, sparkling jewels in His hand. He recorded their faithfulness in a "book of remembrance" (Malachi 3:16 KJV) and promised He would spare them the total devastation reserved for their hypocritical countrymen.

Father, how easy it is to absorb the self-worship around me!
Today, please keep me in Your love and guide me in Your ways. Amen.

A Lifesong of Joy

Satisfy us each morning with your unfailing love,
so we may sing for joy to the end of our lives.
Psalm 90:14 NLT

*W*ebster defines joy as "the emotion evoked by well-being, success, or good fortune." Can you recall the last time you experienced true joy?

Some may associate joy with their wedding day, the birth of their child, the purchase of a new car, a job promotion. . .the list can go on. But joy can come in little moments with your child throughout the day: blowing bubbles, baking cookies, playing a game. . .again, the list can go on.

As a mom, joy can at times seem a distant emotion. When you are tired and have just folded the third load of laundry of the day, how can there be joy? Stop for a moment and think about the precious treasure who wore those jeans while chasing a butterfly, or who donned that sweatshirt to go jump in the leaves outside.

In 1 Thessalonians 5:16 (NLT), we are told to "always be joyful." That doesn't mean we are to be giddy when things go wrong. Rather, God desires that we maintain a spirit of joy, resting in Him.

A joyful spirit is contagious. Find delight in the "ordinary" moments, and others will catch the joy.

Lord Jesus, please be my source of joy today, even when I'm tired or things don't go quite right. Let me rest in the fact that You are in control. Amen.

Meltdowns

Cast all your anxiety on him because he cares for you.
1 Peter 5:7 NIV

*M*egan's four-year-old birthday party was well underway. She felt like a princess among the guests gathered outside. Toting an array of balloons, she proudly pranced through the crowd. Suddenly, a gust of wind caught the balloons, yanking them from her hand. As the balloons soared into the sky, her emotions quickly got away from her also. Megan was heading for a major meltdown!

We've all experienced meltdowns with our children. Maybe a friend broke their favorite toy. Perhaps a change in family plans has canceled a trip to the zoo.

We may have had a few meltdowns ourselves. Our hopes, dreams, and preconceived agendas are swept away like a bunch of balloons. We're feeling on top of the world, when suddenly life takes a turn for the worse, and we are left empty-handed. Anxiety, worry, and disappointment replace the hope we once had.

When the balloons of life are snatched from our hand, God is still there. He loves and cares for us. When our hearts are heavy-laden and emotions are melting, He wants us to turn to Him. He will pick us up and carry us. Our spirits will soar once again. Instead of giving in to a meltdown, cast your anxiety upon the Lord.

Dear Lord, help me turn to You in my anxious moments.
Help me remember how much You love and care for me. Amen.

A Mother to Israel

Barak said to her, "If you go with me, I will go;
but if you don't go with me, I won't go."
Judges 4:8 NIV

*I*n the book of Judges, Israel had slipped back into idolatry and had been oppressed for twenty years by an evil Canaanite king. Finally, at the point when Israel cried out to God for relief, Deborah walked onstage, appearing out of the blue, to lead Israel.

Barak, a general, refused to go to war without her, believing Deborah was the mouthpiece of the Lord. In fact, she had to remind Barak to go down from Mount Tabor and advance into battle! Remember, this was a patriarchal society. Warriors didn't usually need to be prodded into battle. But Deborah was a highly respected woman who loved the Lord, and He used her in a mighty way. By nightfall, the Israelites had destroyed that Canaanite king.

Deborah was married, possibly a parent. She certainly felt a maternal love for her people. Was she really so different from us? Or was she just available to God?

If or when God asks, we need to be ready to walk onstage. Are we preparing ourselves by deepening our relationship with God, studying the Word, and modeling integrity to others? God is always in need of ready and willing hearts to lead His people—whether toddlers or teenagers or elderly neighbors across the street. Are we getting ready?

Lord, make me ready! Give me a vision of who You want me to be.
Show me how to serve Your people.

Selfless Living

*"Now that I, your Lord and Teacher, have washed your feet,
you also should wash one another's feet. I have set you an
example that you should do as I have done for you."*
John 13:14–15 NIV

$\mathcal{B}$renda and Joy spend twenty-four hours, seven days a week, serving as moms; however, Brenda has embraced the martyr-mother attitude, whereas Joy has embraced the selfless living attitude. Brenda does everything and whines about doing everything. Joy on the other hand, serves with happiness, knowing she is serving the Lord (Colossians 3:17, 23).

Joy models Jesus' attitude of selfless living. In the example Jesus provides of washing His disciples' feet, we are encouraged as mothers to do likewise. We are inspired that if Jesus, God made flesh (John 1:14), willingly washed His disciples' feet, we need to be able to serve our loved ones in that same manner and attitude. Jesus looked to the interests of others before His own and humbled Himself, obeying the Father's will of dying on the cross for our sins (Philippians 2:4–8). Do we have the mind of Christ? Do we meet the needs of our preschoolers as acts of service that are first done for the Lord in obedience to His call for our lives? Do we glorify the Lord in selfless living? As we model Christ's selfless living, we will be blessed (John 13:17). Our preschoolers will learn by our examples how to live a selfless life.

Thank You, Lord, for providing an example of selfless living. Mold my heart and mind to follow Your example, thereby teaching my preschooler selfless living.

Learn to Be Merry

Is any among you afflicted? let him pray. Is any merry? let him sing psalms.
James 5:13 KJV

God does not promise that the minute we accept Him our lives will be without trial. It is also not His intention that when trials come we mope around or worry. This is where faith and prayer come into play. Is your child prone to illness? Give your concerns to God. Seek His wisdom in how to handle the situation. Is your child's behavior difficult at best? Realize that God has dealt with many hard cases and has a wealth of wisdom to share.

Don't get caught up in the tough circumstances. You are a child of the all-powerful God. Let Him handle the problems. Begin looking for reasons to rejoice. There are many. Find humor in situations. Concentrate on God's blessings and offer praise to Him as you begin to notice them. Soon you will be so filled with His joy that you will not have reason to concentrate on the difficulties. When they do arise, you will be able to join the apostle Paul in rejoicing even during times of affliction.

> *Lord, I'm often tempted to complain. Help me instead
> to turn my trials over to You and to learn to rejoice.*

Contributors

Tina C. Elacqua, PhD, teaches, writes, and publishes in journal articles, books, conference papers/presentations, and technical reports/presentations. She is a mom of two small children and lives with her husband in Tennessee.

Nancy Farrier is the author of twelve books and numerous articles and short stories. She is married and has five children. She lives with her family in Southern California.

Suzanne Woods Fisher's historical novels, *Copper Star* and its sequel, *Copper Fire*, are inspired by true events. Fisher writes for many magazines, is a wife and mother, and a puppy raiser for Guide Dogs for the Blind.

Rhonda Gibson lives in New Mexico with her husband, James. She has two children and one beautiful grandchild. Visit her at www.rhondagibson.com.

Jennifer Hahn is a freelance writer, compiler, and proofreader who lives in Pennsylvania's Amish country. She and her husband, Mark, have two daughters and a son.

Helen Widger Middlebrooke is a homemaker, home educator, and the mother of nine. She is a freelance columnist and the author of *Lessons for a Supermom* (Barbour Publishing, 2002).

Nicole O'Dell, wife and mother of three, is an accomplished writer of books, devotions, and Bible studies. She has been a Bible study leader and teacher for over fifteen years.

Rachael Phillips, an award-winning fiction and humor writer, is also the author of four biographies published by Barbour Publishing. Rachael and her husband live in Indiana. Visit her at www.rachaelwrites.com.

Rachel Quillin and her husband, Eric, and their five children live on a dairy farm in Ohio. She enjoys gardening, writing, and spending time with her family.

Julie Rayburn is a public speaker and an area director for Community Bible Study. She lives in Atlanta with her husband, Scott. They have two grown children and one granddaughter.

Kate E. Schmelzer graduated from Taylor University, Fort Wayne in 2008 with a double major in professional writing and counseling and a minor in Christian education.

Author Index

Phillips, Rachael
3, 12, 17, 27, 51, 60, 69, 72, 104, 112, 129, 136, 154, 171, 173, 185, 190, 197, 206, 219, 227, 238, 244, 259, 268, 273, 276, 283, 291, 309, 320, 328, 350, 359, 360

Quillin, Rachel
2, 9, 13, 23, 35, 55, 65, 74, 87, 105, 113, 121, 139, 148, 160, 167, 172, 182, 199, 212, 224, 235, 242, 253, 266, 270, 285, 295, 306, 317, 327, 329, 340, 357, 365

Rayburn, Julie
19, 25, 40, 58, 64, 75, 89, 94, 110, 127, 135, 147, 152, 162, 178, 187, 192, 203, 210, 221, 230, 240, 247, 257, 265, 272, 286, 293, 303, 310, 325, 334, 344, 358, 362

Schmelzer, Kate E.
11, 22, 29, 38, 50, 59, 63, 71, 83, 95, 103, 118, 130, 141, 150, 157, 170, 179, 189, 201, 208, 218, 225, 243, 249, 262, 267, 282, 298, 308, 323, 333, 343, 348, 355

Scripture Index

Old Testament

New Testament